BATH SPA UNIV.

THE POEMS OF

WILLIAM DRUMMOND.

AMS PRESS INC.
NEW YORK, N.Y. 10003

JOHNSON REPRINT CORP.
NEW YORK, N.Y. 10003

Guilielmus Drummond.

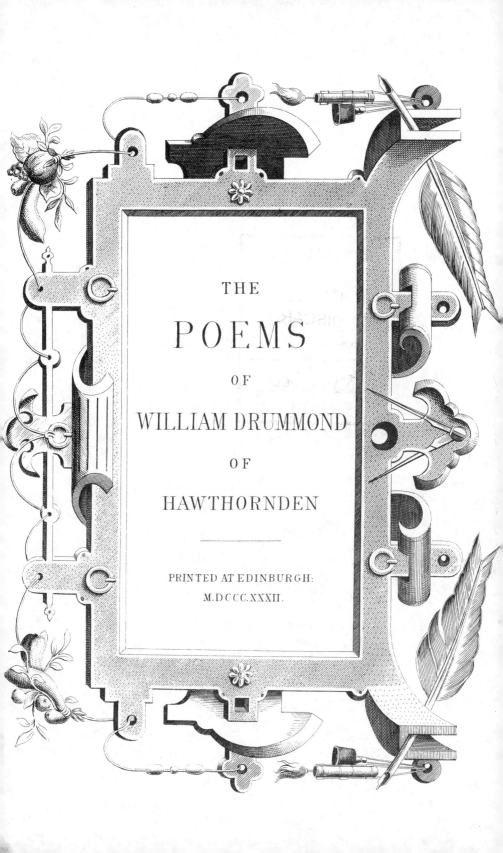

THE
POEMS
OF
WILLIAM DRUMMOND
OF
HAWTHORNDEN

PRINTED AT EDINBURGH:
M.DCCC.XXXII.

Reprinted from the edition of 1832, Edinburgh
First reprint edition published 1971
Manufactured in the United States of America

International Standard Book Number:
Complete Set :0-404-52920-8
Volume 18   :0-404-52956-9
Library of Congress Number :77-144419

AMS PRESS INC.   JOHNSON REPRINT CORP.
NEW YORK, N.Y. 10003   NEW YORK, N.Y. 10003

THE MAITLAND CLUB.

M.DCCC.XXXII.

THE EARL OF GLASGOW,

PRESIDENT.

THE MAITLAND CLUB.

JAMES HILL, ESQ.
LAURENCE HILL, ESQ.
JOHN KERR, ESQ.
R. A. KIDSTON, ESQ.
G. R. KINLOCH, ESQ.
JOHN GIBSON LOCKHART, ESQ. LL. B.
ALEXANDER MACDONALD, ESQ.
WILLIAM MACDOWALL, ESQ.
THE VERY REV. PRINCIPAL MACFARLAN, D.D.
ANDREW MACGEORGE, ESQ.
ALEXANDER MACGRIGOR, ESQ.
DONALD MACINTYRE, ESQ.
JOHN W. MACKENZIE, ESQ.
GEORGE MACINTOSH, ESQ.
ALEXANDER MACNEILL, ESQ.
JAMES MAIDMENT, ESQ.
THOMAS MAITLAND, ESQ.
J. H. MAXWELL, ESQ.
WILLIAM MEIKLEHAM, ESQ.
W. H. MILLER, ESQ.
WILLIAM MOTHERWELL, ESQ.
WILLIAM MURE, ESQ.
ALEXANDER OSWALD, ESQ.
JOHN M. PAGAN, M.D.
WILLIAM PATRICK, ESQ.
EDWARD PIPER, ESQ.
ROBERT PITCAIRN, ESQ.
J. C. PORTERFIELD, ESQ.
HAMILTON PYPER, ESQ.
P. A. RAMSAY, ESQ.
WILLIAM ROBERTSON, ESQ.

THE MAITLAND CLUB.

SIR WALTER SCOTT, BARONET.
JAMES SMITH, ESQ.
JOHN SMITH, ESQ.
JOHN SMITH, ESQ.
WILLIAM SMITH, ESQ.
GEORGE SMYTHE, ESQ.
MOSES STEVEN, ESQ.
DUNCAN STEWART, ESQ.
SYLVESTER DOUGLAS STIRLING, ESQ.
JOHN STRANG, ESQ.
H. R. H. THE DUKE OF SUSSEX.
THOMAS THOMSON, ESQ.
PATRICK FRASER TYTLER, ESQ.
ADAM URQUHART, ESQ.
SIR PATRICK WALKER, KNIGHT.
WILSON D. WILSON, ESQ.
JOHN WYLIE, ESQ.

INTRODUCTION.

T has been stated as an apology for col-
lecting the scattered details of a poet's
life, however uninteresting, that "we are
fond of talking of those who have given us pleasure,
not that we have any thing important to say, but because the subject is pleasing."[1] This feeling is insepa-
rable from any attempt to find materials for biography
in the slight notices which remain of William Drummond of Hawthornden.

This accomplished person was lineally descended
from the family of Perth, which he has traced through
six centuries to a Hungarian origin.[2] Maurice Drummond, a native of Hungary, is said to have accompanied
Edgar Atheling and his two sisters to Scotland in the
year 1068. Malcolm Canmore married Margaret, the

---

[1] Goldsmith's Life of Parnell.   [2] Dedication to the History of Scotland, ed. 1711.

elder of the Saxon princesses; and under her auspices
Drummond is supposed to have acquired large possessions in Scotland, and to have been the founder of the noble family of Perth.

Late in the fourteenth century, William Drummond, a
younger son of this family, and brother to Annabella, the
queen of Robert the Third, married Elizabeth Airth,
daughter and one of the co-heiresses of Sir William Airth
of Airth.   By this marriage he acquired the barony of
Carnock, in the county of Stirling, from which his family
afterwards took their designation.   The elder branch of
the family of Carnock is generally understood to have
terminated in the person of Sir John Drummond, great
grandson of Sir Robert Drummond of Carnock.   Sir John
sold the family estate to Sir Thomas Nicolson, and afterwards fell at the battle of Alford, in 1645, fighting under
the banners of the Marquis of Montrose.

John Drummond, second son of Sir Robert Drummond,
acquired the estate, and founded the family of Hawthornden.   He has been described as a man of " distinguished
worth and honor."[3]   In the year 1590, he was appointed
Gentleman Usher to James the Sixth; and on the acces-
sion of that monarch to the throne of England, he received
the honour of knighthood.[4]   He married Susannah Fowler, daughter of Sir William Fowler, originally a burgess
of Edinburgh, and afterwards Secretary to Queen Anne.
A family of four sons and three daughters was the fruit
of this marriage, of whom the poet of Hawthornden was
the eldest.

[3] Douglas's Baronage of Scotland, p. 572.   [4] 23d July, 1603.

William Drummond was born on the 13th of December, 1585. He received the rudiments of his education at the High School, and afterwards prosecuted his maturer studies in the University of Edinburgh, where he took the degree of Master of Arts on the 27th of July, 1605. Both at school and college he distinguished himself among his contemporaries, and gave early promise of that eminence which he was afterwards destined to attain in various departments of polite literature. Upon leaving the university, his father sent him to study the civil law at Bourges ; and he appears to have resided in France for about three years. During this period he is said to have applied himself to his legal studies " with great diligence and applause ;" and an observation of President Lockhart is recorded, that if he " had followed the practice, he might have made the best figure of any lawyer in his time."[5] The accuracy of this tradition, however, may reasonably be doubted. Drummond has left a record[6] of the books read by him between 1606 and 1614, from which it is apparent that literature occupied a much larger portion of his attention than law. In the detail of his studies, which were in a great measure confined to the most popular poetry and romances of the time, he mentions no other work on law than the Institutes of Justinian.

Drummond returned to Scotland in 1609 ; and upon his father's death, in the following year, he retired to Hawthornden, with the avowed purpose of devoting him-

[5] Bishop Sage's Life of Drummond, p. 2, prefixed to the collection of his Works Edinburgh, 1711, fol.
[6] Extracts from the Hawthornden Manuscripts, printed in the Transactions of the Society of Antiquaries of Scotland, vol. iv. p. 17.

self to his favourite pursuits. In this charming retreat, which his biographer has well described as " a sweet and solitary seat, and very fit and proper for the Muses,"[7] Drummond continued for many years to cultivate the art of poetry with great success.

It is impossible to pass over this period of his life without noticing the celebrated pedestrian pilgrimage of Ben Jonson from London to Hawthornden, for the purpose of visiting the Scottish poet, although more has already been written upon this subject than its importance appears to justify. It is agreed on all hands that the two poets spent some weeks together upon the banks of the Esk, early in 1619; and, perhaps unfortunately for the future fame of both, Drummond preserved notes of their conversations. These notes, although published only in a very imperfect and unauthentic form in the folio edition of Drummond's Works, which issued from the press in 1711, have, on the one hand, been referred to by Malone and others as affording conclusive evidence of Jonson's malignant jealousy of Shakspeare, his great rival in dramatic poetry; while, on the other, Mr Godwin and Mr Gifford have discovered in them a proof that Drummond *inveigled* the English poet to his house for the express purpose of betraying his open and unsuspecting confidence. It required not the acrimonious pen of Mr Gifford to clear the fame of Jonson from imputations which Drummond never meant to cast upon him; and ample justice has been done to the good name of the latter by Sir Walter Scott in his Provincial Antiquities. It seems indisputable that the poets met

[7] Sage's Life of Drummond, p. 2.

and parted on the best terms, and continued ever after to entertain the strongest feelings of mutual respect and attachment. Of this abundant evidence exists in Drummond's correspondence with his *good friend Ben Jonson;* and in the following inscription with which the English poet accompanied the transmission of his beautiful madrigal, " On a lover's dust made sand for an hour-glass," to his Scottish friend:

TO THE HONOURING RESPECT
BORN
TO THE FRIENDSHIP CONTRACTED WITH
THE RIGHT VIRTUOUS AND LEARNED
MR WILLIAM DRUMMOND,
AND THE PERPETUATING THE SAME BY ALL OFFICES OF LOVE HEREAFTER,
I, BENJAMIN JONSON,
WHOM HE HATH HONOURED WITH THE LEAVE TO BE CALLED HIS,
HAVE, WITH MINE OWN HAND, TO SATISFY HIS REQUEST,
WRITTEN THIS IMPERFECT SONG.

It was during his retirement at Hawthornden that Drummond first yielded to the soft influences of love. The object of his attachment was a daughter of Cunningham of Barns, whose beauty has been described, it may be, with somewhat of romantic exaggeration, as

More than painting can express,
Or youthful poets fancy when they love.[8]

In a letter, supposed to have been addressed to her by Drummond, with a volume of his early poems, he says, " Heere you have the poemes, the first fruits your beautye

---

[8] Cibber's Lives of the Poets, vol. i. p. 305.

and many many good parts did bring forth in me.—In them, with your outward beautyes, are the excellent vertues of your rare mind limned, though, I must confess, as painters doe angells and the celestiall world, which represent them no wayes as they are, but in mortall shapes and shadowes." After a season of anxious but successful courtship, a day was appointed for the marriage ceremony; but before that day arrived, the bride was unhappily cut off by a fever, leaving her affianced and disconsolate lover a prey to the most poignant distress. After vainly attempting to alleviate his sorrow, by indulging in the composition of sad and mournful poetry, he resolved to leave his native country for a time, and endeavour to " ease himself of his melancholy thoughts" [9] amidst the varieties of foreign travel. It seems probable that he was on the continent for several years subsequent to 1623. During this period he visited France, Italy, and Germany, contracted acquaintance with many learned men of the foreign universities, and collected a valuable library in all departments of literature, the greater part of which he afterwards presented to the University of Edinburgh, in 1627, 1628, and 1638. [10]

In 1632, Drummond married Elizabeth Logan, who is said to have won his heart by her resemblance to his first love. She has generally been described as grand-daughter to Sir Robert Logan of Restalrig; but of her genealogy, Father Hay, almost a contemporary of Drummond, gives a different account. " Att 45 years of adge," says Hay,

---

[9] Sage's Life of Drummond, p. 3.
[10] A Catalogue of his original donation in 1627, was printed in the same year.

speaking of Drummond, " he married unexpectedly Elizabeth Logan, a minister's daughter of Edliston, which
church is within a quarter of a mile of Darnhill, principall
dwelling-house to Blackbarrony. Her mother was a shepherd's daughter: the family of Hawthornden pretends
that she was daughter of Cottfield, and grandchild to Sir
Robert Logan of Lestalrig, but no sutch matter." [11] The
lady, whether of high or low degree, proved an affectionate wife, and bore five sons and four daughters to Drummond. John, the eldest son, died young. The second
son, William, married first a daughter of Sir John Ach-
moutie of Gosford, and afterwards a daughter of Lord
Clerkington, by both of whom he had issue. He was
knighted in the time of Charles the Second, and survived
till the year 1713.

After the commencement of the great civil war, Drummond resided for some time with his brother-in-law, Sir John
Scot of Scotstarvet. During this period he composed his
History of Scotland from 1423 to 1542; and he also wrote
a variety of tracts, generally on political subjects, and all
in support of the cause of royalty. He died on the 4th of
December 1649, at the age of 64. He had been for some
time much weakened by severe study and acute disease;
but his death has been attributed to " extreme grief and
anguish" [12] for the fate of his Royal Master. He was buried
in the family vault at Lasswade, in the immediate vicinity
of Hawthornden. It appears from his will, dated 1st Sep-

[11] Father Hay's Manuscript Collections, vol. ii, p. 105.
[12] Sage's Life of Drummond, p. 10.

tember, 1643, and registered in the record of the Commis-
sary Court at Edinburgh, 22d July, 1653, that he left considerable property.

No account of Drummond's personal appearance is extant, and the greater proportion of the numerous portraits
bearing his name are certainly apocryphal. There are
three pictures of the poet, in the possession of Sir Francis
Walker Drummond of Hawthornden, Bart. One of these,
a miniature, but conveying no very pleasing idea of our
author's physiognomy, is an undoubted original, and by
the kind permission of Sir Francis, it has been engraved
for the present work. The fac-simile of Drummond's sig-
nature has been taken from an autograph on a set of his
poetical works presented by him to the University of Edinburgh.

Of the editions of Drummond's Poetical Works published during his lifetime, the following is a chronological list,
so far as can now be ascertained with accuracy :

Teares on the Death of Meliades. Edinbvrgh, printed by Andro
    Hart, and are to bee sold at his shop on the north-side of the
    high-streete, a litle beneath the Crosse, 1613, 4to.
The same, second impression.[13]
Teares on the Death of Moeliades. By William Drummond of
    Hawthornden. The third Edition. Edinbvrgh, printed by
    Andro Hart, 1614, 4to.
Poems : Amorous, Funerall, Diuine, Pastorall, in Sonnets, Songs,
    Sextains, Madrigals. By W. D. the Author of the Teares on

---

[13] No copy of this edition has been discovered, from which the imprint can be
given.

the Death of Mœliades. Edinbvrgh, printed by Andro Hart, 1616, 4to.[14]

Poems : by William Drvmmond of Hawthorne-denne. The second Impression. Edinbvrgh, printed by Andro Hart, 1616, 4to.[15]

Forth Feasting. A Panegyricke to the Kings most excellent Majestie. Edinbvrgh, printed by Andro Hart, 1617, 4to.[16]

The same, included in Adamson's collection, entitled, " The Muses Welcome to King James at his Majestie's happie returne to his olde and natiue kingdome of Scotland, after 14 yeeres absence, in 1617. Imprinted at Edinburgh, 1618," fol.

Flowres of Sion. By William Drvmmond of Hawthorne-denne. To which is adjoyned his Cypresse Groue. [Printed at Edinburgh] 1623, 4to.[17]

The same. Eden-bovrgh, printed by Iohn Hart, 1630, 4to.[18]

The Entertainment of the high and mighty monarch Charles, King of Great Britaine, France, and Ireland, into his auncient and royall citie of Edinbvrgh, the fifteenth of Iune, 1633. Printed at Edinbvrgh by Iohn Wreittoun, 1633, 4to.

To the Exequies of the Honovrable Sr Antonye Alexander, Knight, &c. A pastorall Elegie. Edinbvrgh, printed in King James his College, by George Anderson, 1638, 4to.

[14] The only perfect copy of this edition known to exist, sold for L.16, at the sale of the Gordonstoun Library, at London, in the year 1816.

[15] There are copies of this edition on large paper, which are very rare. But whether the volume itself is an actual reprint, or the former edition with a new title, is somewhat uncertain.

[16] Copies of this poem were also printed on large paper.

[17] Of this volume there are fine paper copies, which have an engraved border round the title, marked " P. B." probably the initials of the engraver. This border, which is curious as an early specimen of engraving on copperplate, has been introduced in the general title page of the present volume.

[18] This volume is a republication of the previous edition, with corrections and several additional poems. There are copies on large paper. Some copies have the woodcut border used for the title of the poems printed in 1616 ; and others have a simple printed title, with this imprint, " Printed at Eden-Bourgh, by the Heires of Andro Hart. Anno 1630."

In 1656, seven years after Drummond's death, his poetical works were collected, and published in a small octavo
volume, by Edward Phillips, the nephew of Milton, under
the title of " Poems by that most famous wit, Mr William
Drummond of Hawthornden."[19] Mr Godwin states it as " a
curious point, to ascertain how far Phillips is to be consi-
dered as the first collector, or in any emphatical sense the
preserver of the poetical works of Drummond."[20]   To the
merit of having been the "first collector" of the poems of
Drummond, Phillips is certainly entitled, as before his edition issued from the press they existed only in the separate
publications already enumerated.   But in all other respects
his merits as an editor are inconsiderable.   His book is
remarkable for inaccurate typography, and so far from being "in any emphatical sense the preserver" of the poetical
works of Drummond, his *various* and *prosaic* readings, for
which no authority has ever been discovered, are so numerous, that the poetry almost loses its identity to those who
are familiar with the purer text of the earlier editions.
Bishop Sage states that Sir John Scot suggested the publication of the edition of 1656.[21]   But it has been supposed, with much greater probability, that, in selecting the

[19] Copies of this edition are sometimes found with the date of 1659, and the
following title : " The most elegant and elabourate Poems of that great court-wit,
Mr William Drummond of Hawthornden, whose labours, both in verse and prose,
being heretofore so precious to Prince Henry and to King Charles, shall live and
flourish in all ages, whiles there are men to read them, or art and judgment to
approve them."
[20] Godwin's Lives of Edward and John Phillips, p. 136.
[21] Copies of this edition occasionally occur with a dedication to Sir John Scot,
subscribed T. R., and bearing that " these ingenious poems" had been received
from him.

poetry of Drummond for publication, Phillips may have
been guided by " the taste and partiality of Milton." [22]
Drummond's poems were again published in a collected
shape, in folio, in 1711, under the superintendence of
Bishop Sage, and Thomas Ruddiman, the celebrated gram-
marian. In this edition, the text of Phillips is generally
adopted, and, if the title-page is worthy of credit, some
additional poems are inserted " from the author's original
copies." The whole were most inaccurately reprinted, in
a duodecimo volume, at London, in 1791, and they also
form part of the general collections of Anderson and Chal-
mers.

Of the Polemo-Middinia the separate editions have
been numerous, but the earliest which bears a date, is
that printed at Edinburgh in the year 1684. This celebrated but vulgar *macaronic* effusion, has been generally
attributed to Drummond, and it occurs in all the later
collections of his poems. It was first published with his
name, by Dr Edmund Gibson, at Oxford, in 1691. This
learned person gives no authority for ascribing the poem
to the Scottish poet ; but as Drummond's son was alive at
the time, and as Gibson was himself a native of the north
of England, his information regarding the authorship of
Polemo-Middinia may probably have been accurate. The
poem, it must be admitted, adds little to the fame of its
reputed author.

It is not consistent with the plan or the limits of this
Introduction, to give any detailed account of Drummond's
prose works, which, with the exception of the Cypresse
Grove, a didactic discourse on death, and the vanities of

[22] Godwin's Lives of Edward and John Phillips, p. 133.

human life, were posthumous publications. His History
of Scotland, a work of little authority or value, was first
printed at London in 1680, with an elaborate Prefatory
Introduction by Mr Hall of Gray's Inn, and it has been
several times reprinted. Drummond's other prose works
were published for the first time in the folio collection of
1711. " They are," says Bishop Sage, " generally against
rebellion, and the bad consequences of a civil war, and
they deserve very well to be published, to be a beacon to
warn posterity not to split on so dangerous rocks ; and
also to shew that there has been so considerable a man for
religion, wisdom, learning, and loyalty, in so bad times.[23]

In preparing a new and complete collection of Drummond's Poetical Works, it has been thought expedient to
adopt the text of the original editions which were published in his lifetime, and under his personal superintendence. This volume accordingly commences with a reprint of Andrew Hart's second impression of the *Poems*,
published in 1616; which is followed by a reprint of
the original edition of *Forth Feasting*, published in 1617,
and of the enlarged edition of the *Flowres of Zion*, printed
by John Hart in 1630. To this is subjoined the *Cypresse Grove*, which has been retained in the present
publication as a curious specimen of poetical prose. The
Entertainment of King Charles, to which, with the exception of the Panegyricke by Walter Forbes,[24] Drummond
contributed all the poetry, has been reprinted from the
original and rare edition of 1633.[25] This is followed by

[23] Sage's Life of Drummond, p. 7.
[24] A writer only known as the author of the concluding poem in the Entertainment of King Charles, and of some commendatory verses.

Commendatory Verses, taken from various works to which they were prefixed by Drummond between 1614 and 1635. The *Pastorall Elegie* on the death of Sir Anthonye Alexander, the Earl of Stirling's second son, and Master of the King's Works in Scotland, has been printed from an unique, but unfortunately imperfect copy of the first edition of 1638, collated with the edition of 1656, in which the poem is erroneously given as " A Pastorall Elegie on the Death of Sir W[illiam] A[lexander]." The additional poems in Phillips's edition, not contained in those published during Drummond's lifetime, with the poems which appeared for the first time in the folio edition of 1711, have also been printed; and they are followed by Extracts from the Hawthornden Manuscripts, preserved in the Library of the Society of Antiquaries of Scotland. These Extracts were originally selected and printed in their Transactions, with a valuable memoir and notices by Mr Laing; and they have been reprinted by permission of the Society. The volume concludes with the *Polemo-Middinia,* reprinted from the edition of 1684, collated with those of Gibson and Ruddiman. The *Poems in commendation of the Author* are taken from the edition of 1656. The verses by Phillips and Mary Oxlie have considerable merit.

It must be satisfactory to the Club to know, that Dr Irving, Keeper of the Advocates Library, has contributed his valuable assistance in passing the work through the press.

[25] This work is very inaccurately printed; and various emendations have been adopted from the later edition of 1656.

PUBLIC opinion has, as usual, dealt justly with Drummond, both in the degree of fame with which it has left
him invested, and the degree of neglect into which it
has allowed him to fall. His place certainly is not among
the great poets. Even the partiality of an editor must admit that he has not much passion, or force, or facility. His
charm is that of elegance, ingenuity, and learning. He
has a scholarlike and somewhat fastidious fancy, which
will only wanton with the personages of the classic mytho-
logies, and disports itself "high and disposedly" in a maze
of elaborate expressions, and turns of thought, consider-
ably less natural than ingenious. His great merit, perhaps, consists in the singular melody and exactness of his
versification; a grace of which, with a few brilliant excep-
tions, our language had at that time afforded scarcely any
example. But the truth is that he had not sought for
examples at home; his poetry is essentially exotic. His
model, beyond all doubt, was Petrarch; and it must be
admitted that he did not study it in vain. If he has
copied, and perhaps exaggerated, the strained ingenuity
and hyperbolical conceits of the Italian, he cannot be de-
nied the praise of having also rivalled, in many instances,
the exquisite polish of his diction, and the sweet flow of
his numbers. Some of his sonnets approach nearly to
translations of those of his great master; and are at all
events, even to this day, the happiest and most perfect
imitations of them, both in matter and manner, that our
own or any other language has yet to boast of. Many of his
larger compositions, which, although nowise lyrical in their
structure, he has been pleased to denominate Songs, are

palpable, and scarcely less successful imitations of the *Canzoni* of the same author.

It may seem absurd to place the name of Shakspeare beside that of Drummond; and it would be absurd, if Shakspeare had only written those immortal dramas to which the world will never show a parallel. But the author of Lear and Othello was also the author of Venus and Adonis. The genius which embodied the beautiful conceptions of Ariel and Hamlet, gave also to the world an assortment of elaborate sonnets. If Drummond condescended to study any domestic patterns, we should suspect him of having studied these. There is a striking resemblance in the general style of his sonnets to those of the great dramatist; and there are some which we should not hesitate to call superior to any of Shakspeare's.

The greater and the better part of his poetry is anterior to that of Waller and Denham, who have been commonly reputed the first that gave to our regular rhymed verse a uniform smoothness and symmetrical structure. It is not very likely that Drummond shewed them the way to this improvement; but it seems certain that he had entered on it before them.

It is very remarkable, that although educated in Scotland, and almost exclusively resident in that country after his return from the continent, his poems bear scarcely any traces of his vernacular dialect, and differ little from the best English of his time, except where they are wilfully defaced by vain and scholastic affectation. In some of his devotional pieces there is a greater compass of thought, and a richer volume of melody, than in most of his other poems. His attempts at satire and pleasantry are, on the whole, eminently unhappy; they are generally pedantic, always heavy and laborious, and often coarse and indelicate. His genius wanted not a certain considerate sprightliness, but had nothing in it of natural merriment or playfulness, and, in spite of the Polemo-Middinia, of which the authorship is doubtful, no touch of humour.

After all, perhaps, there can be no happier introduction to the *wilderness of sweets* displayed in the poetry of Drummond, than the address of Edward Phillips to the Ingenious reader,[26] which has by some been ascribed to Milton.

" To say that these poems are the effects of a genius the most polite and verdant that ever the Scottish nation produced, although it be a commendation not to be rejected, (for it is well known that that country hath afforded many rare and admirable wits,) yet it is not the highest that may be given him; for should I affirme that neither Tasso nor Guarini, nor any of the most neat and refined spirits of Italy, nor even the choicest of our English poets can challenge to themselves any advantages above him, it could not be judged any attribute superiour to what he deserves; nor shall I thinke it any arrogance to maintain, that among all the severall fancies that in these times have exercised the most nice and curious judgements, there hath not come forth any thing that deserves to be welcom'd into the world with greater estimation and applause. And though he hath not had the fortune to be so generally fam'd abroad, as many others perhaps of lesse esteeme, yet this is a consideration that cannot at all diminish, but rather advance his credit; for, by breaking forth of obscurity, he

26 Prefixed to the edition of 1656.

will attract the higher admiration, and, like the sun emerging from a cloud, appeare at length with so much the more forcible rayes. Had there been nothing extant of him but his History of Scotland, consider but the language how florid and ornate it is, consider the order and the prudent conduct of his story, and you will ranke him in the number of the best writers, and compare him even with Thuanus himselfe. Neither is he lesse happy in his verse than prose ; for here are all those graces met together that conduce any thing toward the making up of a compleat and perfect poet, a decent and becomming majesty, a brave and admirable height, and a wit so flowing, that Jove himselfe never dranke nectar that sparkled with a more spritly lustre. Should I dwell any longer, ingenuous reader, upon the commendation of this incomparable author, I should injure thee by forestalling the freedome of thy owne judgement, and him by attempting a vain designe, since there is nothing can so well set him forth as his own works ; besides the losse of time, which is but triffled away, so long as thou art detained from perusing the poems themselves."

JANUARY, M.DCCC.XXXII.

d

For the accompanying fac-simile of Drummond's handwriting, the Editor is indebted to the Society of Antiquaries of Scotland.

Damon To ...

Though I haue beene beaten at the oares of Death
and beene ... from these ports light oure minde,
Tys but a rest it is a Palass of breth,
for I by signes find I shall soone retire

Amidst thy greeuen-... ... and earthly Toyles
A Cell wher thou shalt haue ... same
Tell Death yow ... o're my mortall spoyles
and yet I am on ... but a sad name;
If thou ... ... mee deare? by all our ...
By ... soft-discourse ... ...,
I ... thee, and the mayds of ...
To wryte thee sad remembrance on my ...,
The Damon that thyself did sometyme ...
The ... ... Roses
Death ... ...

_____

Madame,

your deserf and good opinion of mee gane by a
gratious bnoleure (if I can be so happye as to
doe you seruice) moue mee to remaine your L.

May
26
1622

Euer to command
W. Drummond.

POEMS IN COMMENDATION OF THE AUTHOR.

[REPRINTED FROM THE EDITION OF M.DC.LVI.]

VPON THE INCOMPARABLE POEMS OF MR WILLIAM DRUMMOND.

To praise these poems well, there doth require
The selfe-same spirit, and that sacred fire
That first inspir'd them ; yet I cannot choose
But pay an admiration to a Muse
That sings such handsome things ; never brake forth,
From climes so neare the Beare, so bright a worth ;
And I beleeve the Caledonian bow'rs
Are full as pleasant, and as rich in flow'rs
As Tempe e're was fam'd, since they have nourish'd
A wit the most sublime that ever flourish'd.
There's nothing cold or frozen here contain'd,
Nothing that's harsh, unpolish'd, or constrain'd,
But such an ardour as creates the spring,
And throws a chearfulnesse on every thing ;
Such a sweet calmnesse runs through every verse,
As shews how he delighted to converse
With silence and his Muse, among those shades
Which care, nor busie tumult, e're invades :
There would he oft the adventures of his loves
Relate unto the fountaines and the groves,
In such a straine as Laura had admir'd
Her Petrarch more, had he been so inspir'd.
Some Phœbus gives a smooth and streaming veine,
A great and happy fancy some attaine,
Others unto a soaring height he lifts ;
But here he hath so crouded all his gifts,
As if he had design'd in one to try
To what a pitch he could bring poetry :

For every grace should he receive a crown,
There were not bays enough in Helicon.
Fame courts his verse, and with immortall wings
Hovers about his monument, and brings
A deathlesse trophy to his memory ;
Who for such honour would not wish to dye ?
Never could any times afford a story
Of one so match'd unto great Sidney's glory,
Or fame so well divided, as between
Penshurst's renowned shades and Hawthornden.

EDWARD PHILLIPS.

JOANNI SCOTO SCOTO-TARVATIO, EQUITI PRÆLUSTRI,
DE LITERATURA OPTIME MERITO.

Tarvati, immensos recolens labores,
Jure queis partes potiore primas
Asseram, haud vanis dubie laborant
            Pectora curis ;

Sive quod divæ cathedra renidens
Ultimæ terras habitantis, annos
Ter quater ternos, veluti sacer fons
            Juris et æqui ;

Sive quod cæcos patriæ recessus
Ut stilo pingat mage qui polito,
Tesqua et incultas salebras recenti
            Inserat Orbi ;

Sive quod vates patriæ minores,
Forte noscendi serius nec ipsis
Civibus, toto celebrentur orbe
            Vindice Scoto.

Blandiores quid memorem Camœnas,
Oris antiqua prope sede pulsas,
Sedibus priscis prope restitutas,
            Auspice Scoto ?

Orphanos sanis quod et instruendos
Artibus curæ tibi censibus, quos
Ambitu pravo repulere Musis
        Gymnasiarchæ.

Sit licet rarum putatis horum
Quodlibet curæ specimen, fatiscunt
Dum frui postliminio recordor
        Te duce fratrem.

Nempe sic olim studio et labore
Torvus Alcides Stygiis ab undis
Reddidit terris domito trifauci
        Thesea monstro.

Sic eat ; clari hæc monumenta vatis
Nesciant ævi imperium severi
Regia, ast spernant Phlegetonta, et Orci
        Jura superbi.
                    D. F.

DE GULIELMO DRUMMONDO.

Quæsivit Latio Buchananus carmine laudem,
   Et patrios dura respuit aure modos ;
Cum possit Latiis Buchananum vincere Musis
   Drummondus, patrio maluit ore loqui :
Major ut est, primas hinc defert Scotia, vates,
   Vix inter Latios ille secundus erat.
              [ARTURUS JONSTONUS.]

TO W. D.

Some will not leave that trust to friend nor heire,
But their own winding-sheet themselves prepare,
Fearing perhaps some courser cloath might shroud
The wormes descended from their noble bloud :
And shalt not thou, that justlier maist suspect
Far courser stuffe, in such a dull neglect
Of all the arts, and dearth of poetry,
Compose before hand thine own elegy ?

Who but thy selfe is capable to write
A verse, or, if they can, to fashion it
Unto thy praises?   None can draw a line
Of thy perfections but a hand divine.
If thou wilt needs impose this task on us,
A greater work than best wits can discusse,
We will but only so far embleme thee,
As in a circle men the Deity.
A wreath of bayes we'll lay upon thy herse,
For that shall speake thee better than our verse :
That art in number of those things, whose end
Nor whose beginning we can comprehend ;
A star which did the other day appeare
T' enlighten up our dark'ned hemispheare ;
Nor can we tell nor how nor whence it came,
Yet feele the heat of thy admired flame.
'Twas thou that thaw'd our north, 'twas thou didst cleare
The eternall mists which had beset us here,
Till by thy golden beames and powerfull ray
Thou chas'd hence darknesse, and brought out the day.
But as the sun, though he bestow all light
On us, yet hinders by the same our sight
To gaze on him ; so thou, though thou dispence
Far more on us by thy bright influence,
Yet such is thy transcendent brightnesse, we
Thereby are dazled, and cannot reach thee :
Then art thou less'ned, should we bound thy praise
T' our narrow dull conceit, which cannot raise
Themselves beyond a vulgar theame, nor flye
A pitch like unto thine in poesie ;
Yet, as the greatest kings have sometimes dain'd
The smallest presents from a poore man's hand,
When pure devotion gave them, it may be
Your genius will accept a mite from me ;
It speaks my love, although it reach not you,
And you are praised when I would so do.
                              JOHN SPOTSWOOD.

TO WILLIAM DRUMMOND OF HAWTHORNDEN.

I NEVER rested on the Muses' bed,
Nor dipt my quill in the Thessalian fountaine ;
My rustick muse was rudely fostered,
And flies too low to reach the double mountaine :
Then do not sparkes with your bright suns compare,
Perfection in a woman's worke is rare ;
From an untroubled mind should verses flow,
My discontents make mine too muddy show,
And hoarse encumbrances of houshold care ;
Where these remaine, the Muses ne're repaire.
    If thou dost extoll her haire,
Or her ivory forehead faire,
Or those stars whose bright reflection
Thrals thy heart in sweet subjection ;
Or when to display thou seeks
The snow-mixt roses on her cheekes,
Or those rubies soft and sweet,
Over those pretty rows that meet ;
The Chian painter as asham'd
Hides his picture so far fam'd ;
And the queen he carv'd it by,
With a blush her face doth dye,
Since those lines do limne a creature
That so far surpast her feature.
When thou shew'st how fairest Flora
Prankt with pride the banks of Ora,
So thy verse her streames doth honour,
Strangers grow enamoured on her :
All the swans that swim in Po,
Would their native brooks forgo,
And, as loathing Phœbus' beames,
Long to bath in cooler streames.
Tree-turn'd Daphne would be seen
In her groves to flourish green,
And her boughs would gladly spare
To frame a garland for thy haire,

That fairest nymphs with finest fingers,
May thee crown the best of singers.
    But when thy Muse dissolv'd in show'rs,
Wailes that peerlesse prince of ours,
Cropt by too untimely fate,
Her mourning doth exasperate
Senselesse things to see thee moane,
Stones do weep, and trees do groane,
Birds in aire, fishes in flood,
Beasts in field forsake their food ;
The nymphs forgoing all their bow'rs
Teare their chaplets deckt with flow'rs ;
Sol himselfe with misty vapour
Hides from earth his glorious tapor,
And, as mov'd to heare thee plaine,
Shews his griefe in show'rs of raine.

MARY OXLIE OF MORPET.

POEMS BY

WILLIAM DRVMMOND

OF HAWTHORNE-DENNE.

REPRINTED

FROM THE EDITION OF

M.DC.XVI.

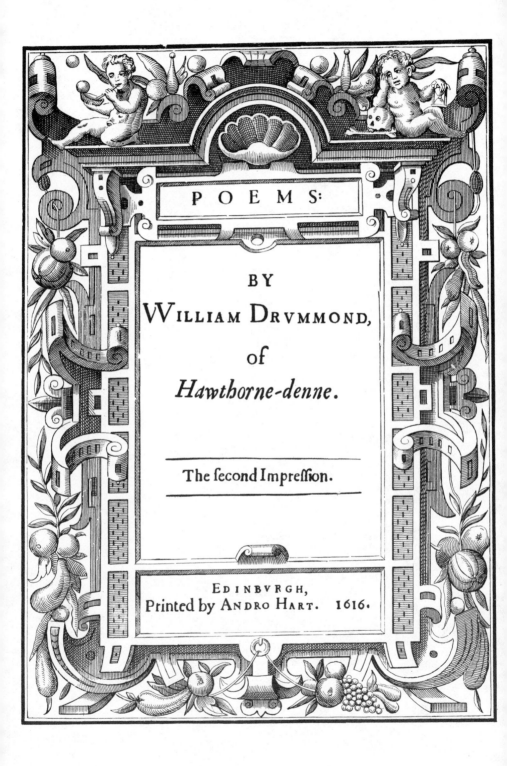

POEMS:

BY

WILLIAM DRVMMOND,

of

Hawthorne-denne.

The second Impreſſion.

EDINBVRGH,
Printed by ANDRO HART. 1616.

TO THE AUTHOR.

W HILE thou dost praise the roses, lillies, gold,
Which in a dangling tresse and face appeare,
Still stands the sunne in skies thy songs to heare,
A silence sweet each whispering wind doth hold ;
Sleepe in Pasithea's lap his eyes doth fold,
The sword falls from the God of the fift spheare,
The heards to feede, the birds to sing, forbeare,
Each plant breathes loue, each flood and fountaine cold ;
And hence it is, that that once Nymphe, now tree,
Who did th' Amphrysian shepheard's sighes disdaine,
And scorn'd his layes, mou'd by a sweeter veine,
Is become pittifull, and followes thee,
    Thee loues, and vanteth that shee hath the grace,
    A garland for thy lockes to enterlace.

PARTHENIVS.

POEMS.

THE FIRST PART.

SONNET.

In my first yeeres, and prime yet not at hight,
When sweet conceits my wits did entertaine,
Ere beautie's force I knew or false delight,
Or to what oare shee did her captiues chaine,
Led by a sacred troupe of Phœbus' traine,
I first beganne to reade, then loue to write,
And so to praise a perfect red and white,
But, God wot, wist not what was in my braine:
Loue smylde to see in what an awfull guise
I turn'd those antiques of the age of gold,
And, that I might moe mysteries behold,
Hee set so faire a volumne to mine eyes,
    That I, (quires clos'd, which dead, dead sighs but breath,)
    Ioye on this liuing booke to read my death.

SONNET.

I KNOW that all beneath the moone decayes,
And what by mortalles in this world is brought,
In Time's great periods shall returne to nought ;
That fairest states haue fatall nights and dayes ;
I know how all the Muse's heauenly layes,
With toyle of spright which are so dearely bought,
As idle sounds, of few or none are sought,
And that nought lighter is than airie praise ;
I know fraile beautie like the purple flowre,
To which one morne oft birth and death affords ;
That loue a iarring is of mindes' accords,
Where sense and will inuassall reason's power :
   Know what I list, this all can not mee moue,
   But that, O mee ! I both must write and loue.

SONNET.

YEE who so curiously doe paint your thoughts,
Enlightning eu'rie line in such a guise,
That they seeme rather to haue fallen from skies,
Than of a humane hand bee mortall draughts ;
In one part Sorrow so tormented lies,
As if his life at eu'ry sigh would parte ;
Loue here blindfolded stands with bow and dart,
There Hope lookes pale, Despaire with rainie eyes :
Of my rude pincell looke not for such arte,
My wit I finde now lessened to deuise
So high conceptions to expresse my smart,
And some thinke loue but fain'd, if too too wise.
   These troubled words and lines confus'd you finde,
   Are like vnto their modell, my sicke minde.

SONNET.

FAIRE is my yoke, though grieuous bee my paines,
Sweet are my wounds, although they deeply smart,
My bit is gold, though shortned bee the raines,
My bondage braue, though I may not depart:
Although I burne, the fire which doth impart
Those flames, so sweet reuiuing force containes,
That, like Arabia's bird, my wasted heart,
Made quicke by death, more liuely still remaines.
I joye, though oft my waking eyes spend teares,
I neuer want delight, euen when I grone,
Best companied when most I am alone;
A heauen of hopes I haue midst hells of feares.
  Thus euery way contentment strange I finde,
  But most in her rare beautie, my rare minde.

SONNET.

How that vaste Heauen intitled First is rold,
If any other worlds beyond it lie,
And people liuing in eternitie,
Or essence pure that doth this all vphold;
What motion haue those fixed sparkes of gold,
The wandring carbuncles which shine from hie,
By sprights, or bodies, contrare-wayes in skie
If they bee turn'd, and mortall things behold;
How sunne postes heauen about, how night's pale queene
With borrowed beames lookes on this hanging round,
What cause faire Iris hath, and monsters seene
In aire's large fields of light, and seas profound,
  Did hold my wandring thoughts, when thy sweet eye
  Bade mee leaue all, and only thinke on thee.

SONNET.

Vaunt not, faire Heauens, of your two glorious lights,
Which, though most bright, yet see not when they shine,
And shining, cannot shew their beames diuine
Both in one place, but parte by dayes and nights;
Earth, vaunt not of those treasures yee enshrine,
Held only deare because hidde from our sights,
Your pure and burnish'd gold, your diamonds fine,
Snow-passing iuorie that the eye delights;
Nor, Seas, of those deare wares, are in you found,
Vaunt not rich pearle, red corrall, which doe stirre
A fond desire in fooles to plunge your ground.
Those all, more faire, are to bee had in her;
    Pearle, iuorie, corrall, diamond, sunnes, gold,
    Teeth, necke, lips, heart, eyes, haire, are to behold.

SONNET.

That learned Græcian, who did so excell
In knowledge passing sense, that hee is nam'd
Of all the after-worlds diuine, doth tell,
That at the time when first our soules are fram'd,
Ere in these mansions blinde they come to dwell,
They liue bright rayes of that eternall light,
And others see, know, loue, in heaven's great hight,
Not toylde with ought to reason doth rebell.
Most true it is, for straight at the first sight
My minde mee told, that in some other place
It elsewhere saw the idea of that face,
And lou'd a loue of heauenly pure delight:
    No wonder now I feele so faire a flame,
    Sith I her lou'd ere on this earth shee came.

SONNET.

Now while the night her sable vaile hath spred,
And silently her restie coach doth rolle,
Rowsing with her from Tethys' azure bed
Those starrie nymphes which dance about the pole;
While Cynthia, in purest cipres cled,
The Latmian shepheard in a trance descries,
And whiles lookes pale from hight of all the skies,
Whiles dyes her beauties in a bashfull red;
While sleepe, in triumph, closed hath all eyes,
And birds and beastes a silence sweet doe keepe,
And Protevs' monstrous people in the deepe,
The winds and waues, husht vp, to rest entise;
I wake, muse, weepe, and who my heart hath slaine
See still before me to augment my paine.

SONNET.

SLEEPE, Silence' child, sweet father of soft rest,
Prince, whose approach peace to all mortalls brings,
Indifferent host to shepheards and to kings,
Sole comforter of minds with griefe opprest;
Loe, by thy charming rod all breathing things
Lie slumbring, with forgetfulnesse possest,
And yet o're me to spred thy drowsie wings
Thou spares, alas! who cannot be thy guest.
Since I am thine, O come, but with that face
To inward light which thou are wont to show,
With fained solace ease a true felt woe;
Or if, deafe God, thou doe denie that grace,
  Come as thou wilt, and what thou wilt bequeath,
  I long to kisse the image of my death.

B

SONNET.

FAIRE Moone, who with thy cold and siluer shine
Makes sweet the horrour of the dreadfull night,
Delighting the weake eye with smiles diuine,
Which Phebvs dazells with his too much light;
Bright Queene of the first Heauen, if in thy shrine,
By turning oft, and Heauen's eternall might,
Thou hast not yet that once sweet fire of thine
Endymion forgot, and louer's plight;
If cause like thine may pitie breede in thee,
And pitie somewhat els to it obtaine,
Since thou hast power of dreames, as well as hee
Who paints strange figures in the slumbring braine,
 Now while she sleepes, in dolefull guise her show
 These teares, and the blacke mappe of all my woe.

SONNET.

LAMPE of Heauen's christall hall that brings the hours,
Eye-dazaler, who makes the vglie night
At thine approach flie to her slumbrie bowrs,
And fills the world with wonder and delight;
Life of all lifes, death-giuer by thy flight
To southerne pole from these sixe signes of ours,
Goldsmith of all the starres, with siluer bright
Who moone enamells, Apelles of the flowrs;
Ah! from those watrie plaines thy golden head
Raise vp, and bring the so long lingring morne;
A graue, nay, hell, I finde become this bed,
This bed so grieuously where I am torne;
 But, woe is me! though thou now brought the day,
 Day shall but serue more sorrowe to display.

It was the time when to our northerne pole
The brightest lampe of Heauen beginnes to rolle;
When earth more wanton in new robes appeareth,
And scorning skies her flowrs in raine-bowes beareth,
On which the aire moist saphires doth bequeath,
Which quake to feele the kissing zephire's breath;
When birds from shadie groues their loue foorth warble,
And sea like Heauen, Heauen lookes like smoothest marble;
When I, in simple course, free from all cares,
Farre from the muddie world's captiuing snares,
By Ora's flowrie bancks alone did wander,
Ora that sports her like to old Meander;
A floud more worthie fame and lasting praise
Than that which Phaeton's fall so high did raise,
Into whose moouing glasse the milk-white lillies
Doe dresse their tresses and the daffadillies.
Where Ora with a wood is crown'd about,
And seemes forget the way how to come out,
A place there is, where a delicious fountaine
Springs from the swelling paps of a proud mountaine,
Whose falling streames the quiet caues doe wound,
And make the ecchoes shrill resound that sound.
The lawrell there the shining channell graces,
The palme her loue with long stretch'd armes embraces,
The poplar spreds her branches to the skie,
And hides from sight that azure cannopie;
The streames the trees, the trees their leaues still nourish,
That place graue winter finds not without flourish.
If liuing eyes Elysian fields could see,
This little Arden might Elysium bee.
Here Diane often vsed to repose her,

And Acidalia's queene with Mars reioyce her ;
The nymphes oft here doe bring their maunds with flowres,
And anadeames weaue for their paramours ;
The Satyres in those shades are heard to languish,
And make the shepheards partners of their anguish,
The shepheards who in barkes of tender trees
Doe graue their loues, disdaines, and ielousies,
Which Phillis, when there by her flockes she feedeth,
With pitie whyles, sometime with laughter reedeth.
    Neare to this place, when sunne in midst of day
In highest top of Heauen his coach did stay,
And, as aduising, on his carier glanced
The way did rest, the space he had aduanced
His panting steeds along those fields of light,
Most princely looking from that gastly hight ;
When most the grashoppers are heard in meadowes,
And loftie pines haue small, or els no shadowes,
It was my hap, O ! wofull hap ! to bide
Where thickest shades me from all rayes did hide,
Into a shut-vp place, some Syluan's chamber,
Whose seeling spred was with the lockes of amber
Of new-bloom'd sicamors, floore wrought with flowres
More sweete and rich than those in princes' bowres.
Here Adon blush't, and Clitia all amazed
Lookt pale, with him who in the fountaine gazed,
The amaranthus smyl'd, and that sweet boy
Which sometime was the God of Delos' joy ;
The braue carnation, speckled pinke here shined,
The violet her fainting head declined
Beneath a drowsie chasbow, all of gold
The marigold her leaues did here vnfold.

Now, while that rauish'd with delight and wonder,
Halfe in a trance I lay those arches vnder,
The season, silence, place, did all entise
Eyes' heauie lids to bring night on their skies,
Which softly hauing stollen themselues together,
Like euening clouds, me plac'd I wote not whether.
As cowards leaue the fort which they should keepe,
My senses one by one gaue place to Sleepe,
Who, followed with a troupe of golden slombers,
Thrust from my quiet braine all base encombers,
And thrise me touching with his rod of gold,
A heauen of visions in my temples roll'd,
To countervaile those pleasures were bereft me ;
Thus in his silent prison clos'd he left me.
    Me thought through all the neighbour woods a noyce
Of quiristers, more sweet than lute or voyce,
(For those harmonious sounds to Ioue are giuen
By the swift touches of the nyne-string'd heauen,
Such are, and nothing else,) did wound mine eare,
No, soule, that then became all eare to heare :
And whilst I listning lay, O gastly wonder !
I saw a pleasant mirtle cleaue asunder,
A mirtle great with birth, from whose rent wombe
Three naked nymphes more white than snow foorth come
For nymphes they seem'd ; about their heauenly faces
In waues of gold did flow their curling tresses ;
About each arme, their armes more white than milke,
Each weare a blushing armelet of silke.
The goddesses such were that by Scamander
Appeared to the Phrygian Alexander ;
Aglaia, and her sisters, such perchance

Be, when about some sacred spring they dance.
But scarce the groue their naked beauties graced,
And on the amorous verdure had not traced,
When to the floud they ran, the floud in robes
Of curling christall to brests' yuorie globes
Who wrapt them all about, yet seem'd take pleasure
To showe warme snowes throughout her liquid azure.

    Looke howe Prometheus' man, when heauenly fire
First gaue him breath, daye's brandon did admire,
And wondred of this world's amphitheater;
So gaz'd I on those new guests of the water.
All three were faire, yet one excell'd as farre
The rest, as Phebus doth the Cyprian starre,
Or diamonds small gemmes, or gemmes doe other,
Or pearles that shining shell is call'd their mother.

    Her haire, more bright than are the morning's beames,
Hang in a golden shower aboue the streames,
And, sweetly tous'd, her forehead sought to couer,
Which seene did straight a skie of milke discouer,
With two faire browes, loue's bowes, which neuer bend
But that a golden arrow foorth they send;
Beneath the which two burning planets glancing,
Flasht flames of loue, for loue there still is dancing.
Her either cheeke resembl'd a blushing morne,
Or roses gueules in field of lillies borne,
Betwixt the which a wall so faire is raised,
That it is but abased euen when praised;
Her lips like rowes of corrall soft did swell,
And th' one like th' other only doth excell:
The Tyrian fish lookes pale, pale looke the roses,
The rubies pale, when mouth's sweet cherrie closes.

Her chinne like siluer Phebe did appeare
Darke in the midst to make the rest more cleare ;
Her necke seem'd fram'd by curious Phidias' master,
Most smooth, most white, a piece of alabaster.
Two foaming billowes flow'd vpon her brest,
Which did their tops with corrall red encrest ;
There all about, as brookes them sport at leasure,
With circling branches veines did swell in azure :
Within those crookes are only found those Isles
Which Fortunate the dreaming old world stiles.
The rest the streames did hide, but as a lillie
Suncke in a christall's faire transparent bellie.
    I, who yet humane weaknesse did not know,
For yet I had not felt that archer's bow,
Ne could I thinke that from the coldest water
The winged youngling burning flames could scatter,
On euery part my vagabounding sight
Did cast, and drowne mine eyes in sweet delight.
What wondrous thing is this that beautie's named,
Said I, I finde I heretofore haue dreamed,
And neuer knowne in all my flying dayes
Good vnto this, that only merites praise.
My pleasures haue beene paines, my comforts crosses,
My treasure pouertie, my gaines but losses.
O precious sight ! which none doth els descrie,
Except the burning sunne, and quiuering I.
And yet, O deare bought sight ! O would for euer
I might enioy you, or had ioy'd you never !
O happie floud ! if so yee might abide,
Yet euer glorie of this moment's pride,
Adjure your rillets all now to beholde her,

And in their christall armes to come and fold her ;
And sith yee may not ay your blisse embrace,
Draw thousand pourtraits of her on your face,
Pourtraits which in my heart be more apparent,
If like to yours my brest but were transparent.
O that I were, while she doth in you play,
A daulphine to transport her to the sea,
To none of all those gods I would her rander,
From Thule to Inde though I should with her wander.
Oh! what is this? the more I fixe mine eye,
Mine eye the more new wonders doth espie ;
The more I spie, the more in vncouth fashion
My soule is ravish'd in a pleasant passion.
   But looke not, eyes: as more I would haue said,
A sound of whirling wheeles me all dismayde,
And with the sound foorth from the timorous bushes,
With storme-like course, a sumptuous chariot rushes,
A chariot all of gold, the wheeles were gold,
The nailes, and axetree gold on which it roll'd ;
The vpmost part a scarlet vaile did couer,
More rich than Danae's lap spred with her louer :
In midst of it, in a triumphing chaire,
A ladie sate, miraculously faire,
Whose pensiue countenance, and lookes of honor,
Doe more allure the mind that thinketh on her,
Than the most wanton face and amorous eyes,
That Amathus or flowrie Paphos sees.
A crue of virgins made a ring about her,
The diamond shee, they seeme the gold without her.
Such Thetis is, when to the billowes' rore
With mermaids nyce shee danceth on the shore :

So in a sable night the sunne's bright sister
Among the lesser twinckling lights doth glister.
Faire yoakes of ermelines, whose colour passe
The whitest snowes on aged Grampius' face,
More swift than Venus' birds this chariot guided
To the astonish'd bancke where as it bided :
But long it did not bide, when poore those streames
Aye me ! it made, transporting those rich gemmes,
And by that burthen lighter, swiftly driued
Till, as me thought, it at a towre arriued.
    Vpon a rocke of christall shining cleare,
Of diamonds this castle did appeare,
Whose rising spires of gold so high them reared,
That, Atlas-like, it seem'd the heauen they beared.
Amidst which hights on arches did arise,
Arches which guilt flames brandish to the skies,
Of sparking topaces, prowde, gorgeous, ample,
Like to a litle heauen, a sacred temple,
Whose walls no windowes haue, nay all the wall
Is but one window ; night there doth not fall
More when the sunne to westerne worlds declineth,
Than in our zenith when at noone he shineth.
Two flaming hills the passage strait defend
Which to this radiant building doth ascend,
Vpon whose arching tops, on a pilastre,
A port stands open, rais'd in loue's disastre ;
For none that narrow bridge and gate can passe,
Who haue their faces seene in Venus' glasse.
If those within but to come foorth doe venter,
That stately place againe they neuer enter.
The precinct strengthened with a ditch appeares,

C

In which doth swell a lake of inkie teares
Of madding louers, who abide there moning,
And thicken euen the aire with piteous groning.
This hold, to braue the skies, the Destines fram'd,
The world the Fort of Chastitie it nam'd.
The Queene of the third Heauen once to appall it
The god of Thrace here brought, who could not thrall it,
For which he vow'd ne're armes more to put on,
And on Riphean hills was heard to grone.
Here Psyche's louer hurles his darts at randon,
Which all for nought him serue as doth his brandon.
    What bitter anguish did inuade my minde,
When in that place my hope I saw confinde,
Where with high-towring thoughts I onely reacht her,
Which did burne vp their wings when they approacht her?
Mee thought I set me by a cypresse shade,
And night and day the hyacinthe there reade;
And that bewailing nightingalles did borrow
Plaints of my plaint, and sorrowes of my sorrow.
My food was wormewood, mine owne teares my drinke,
My rest on death and sad mishaps to thinke.
And for such thoughts to haue my heart enlarged,
And ease mine eyes with brinie tribute charged,
Ouer a brooke, me thought, my pining face
I laid, which then, as grieu'd at my disgrace,
A face me shew'd againe so ouer-clouded,
That at the sight mine eyes afray'd them shrowded.
This is the guerdon, Loue, this is the gaine
In end which to thy seruants doth remaine,
I would haue said, when feare made sleepe to leaue me,
And of those fatall shadowes did bereaue me.

But ah, alas ! in stead to dreame of loue,
And woes, mee made them in effect to proue ;
For what into my troubled braine was painted,
I waking found that time and place presented.

SONNET.

AH ! burning thoughts, now let me take some rest,
And your tumultuous broyles a while appease ;
Is 't not enough, starres, fortune, loue molest
Me all at once, but yee must to displease ?
Let hope, though false, yet lodge within my brest,
My high attempt, though dangerous, yet praise.
What though I trace not right heauen's steppie wayes ?
It doth suffice, my fall shall make me blest.
I doe not doate on dayes, nor feare not death,
So that my life be braue, what though not long ?
Let me renown'd liue from the vulgare throng,
And when ye list, Heauens ! take this borrowed breath.
Men but like visions are, time all doth claime ;
He liues, who dies to winne a lasting name.

MADRIGALL.

A DEDALE of my death,
Now I resemble that subtile worme on earth,
Which, prone to its owne euill, can take no rest ;
For with strange thoughts possest,
I feede on fading leaues
Of hope, which me deceaues,
And thousand webs doth warpe within my brest :
And thus in end vnto my selfe I weaue
A fast-shut prison, no, but euen a graue.

SEXTAIN.

THE Heauen doth not containe so many starres,
So many leaues not prostrate lie in woods,
When autumne's old, and Boreas sounds his warres,
So many waues have not the ocean floods,
As my rent mind hath torments all the night,
And heart spends sighes, when Phebvs brings the light.

Why should I beene a partner of the light,
Who, crost in birth by bad aspects of starres,
Haue neuer since had happie day nor night?
Why was not I a liuer in the woods,
Or citizen of Thetis' christall floods,
Then made a man, for loue and fortune's warres?

I looke each day when death should ende the warres,
Vnciuill warres, 'twixt sense and reason's light;
My paines I count to mountaines, meads, and floods,
And of my sorrow partners make the starres;
All desolate I haunt the fearfull woods,
When I should giue my selfe to rest at night.

With watchfull eyes I ne're beholde the night,
Mother of peace, but ah! to me of warres,
And Cynthia queene-like shining through the woods,
When straight those lamps come in my thought, whose light
My iudgement dazel'd, passing brightest starres,
And then mine eyes en-isle themselues with floods.

Turne to their springs againe first shall the floods,
Cleare shall the sunne the sad and gloomie night,
To dance about the pole cease shall the starres,

The elements renew their ancient warres
Shall first, and bee depriu'd of place and light,
Ere I find rest in citie, fields, or woods.

Ende these my dayes, endwellers of the woods,
Take this my life, yee deep and raging floods;
Sunne, neuer rise to cleare mee with thy light,
Horror and darknesse, keepe a lasting night;
Consume me, care, with thy intestine warres,
And stay your influence o're me, bright starres!

In vaine the starres, endwellers of the woods,
Care, horror, warres, I call, and raging floods,
For all haue sworne no night shall dimme my sight.

SONNET.

O sacred blush, impurpling cheekes' pure skies,
With crimson wings which spred thee like the morne;
O bashfull looke, sent from those shining eyes,
Which, though cast down on earth, couldst Heauen adorne;
O tongue, in which most lushious nectar lies,
That can at once both blesse and make forlorne;
Dear corrall lip, which beautie beautifies,
That trembling stood ere that her words were borne,
And you her words, words, no, but golden chaines,
Which did captiue mine eares, ensnare my soule,
Wise image of her minde, minde that containes
A power, all power of senses to controule;
    Yee all from loue disswade so sweetly mee,
    That I loue more, if more my loue could bee.

SONNET.

Nor Arne, nor Mincius, nor stately Tyber,
Sebethus, nor the floud into whose streames
He fell who burnt the world with borrow'd beames,
Gold-rolling Tagus, Munda, famous Iber,
Sorgue, Rosne, Loire, Garron, nor prowd-banked Seine,
Peneus, Phasis, Xanthus, humble Ladon,
Nor shee whose nymphes excell her who lou'd Adon,
Faire Tamesis, nor Ister large, nor Rheine,
Euphrates, Tigris, Indus, Hermus, Gange,
Pearlie Hydaspes, serpent-like Meander,
The golfe bereft sweet Hero her Leander,
Nile, that farre farre his hidden head doth range,
　　Haue euer had so rare a cause of praise,
　　As Ora, where this northerne Phenix stayes.

SONNET.

To heare my plaints, faire riuer christalline,
Thou in a silent slumber seemes to stay;
Delicious flowrs, lillie and columbine,
Yee bowe your heades when I my woes display;
Forrests, in you the mirtle, palme, and bay,
Haue had compassion listning to my grones;
The winds with sighes haue solemniz'd my mones
'Mong leaues, which whisper'd what they could not say;
The caues, the rockes, the hills the Syluans' thrones,
As if euen pitie did in them appeare,
Haue at my sorrowes rent their ruethlesse stones;
Each thing I finde hath sense except my deare,
　　Who doth not thinke I loue, or will not know
　　My griefe, perchance delighting in my woe.

SONNET.

Sweet brooke, in whose cleare christall I mine eyes
Haue oft seene great in labour of their teares ;
Enamell'd banke, whose shining grauell beares
These sad characters of my miseries ;
High woods, whose mounting tops menace the spheares ;
Wild citizens, Amphions of the trees,
You gloomie groues at hottest noones which freeze,
Elysian shades which Phebus neuer cleares ;
Vaste solitarie mountaines, pleasant plaines,
Embrodred meads that ocean-wayes you reach,
Hills, dales, springs, all that my sad cry constraines
To take part of my plaints, and learne woe's speach,
  Will that remorselesse faire e're pitie show ?
  Of grace now answere if yee ought know.   No.

SONNET.

With flaming hornes the Bull now brings the yeare,
Melt doe the horride mountaines' helmes of snow,
The siluer flouds in pearlie channells flow,
The late-bare woods greene anadeams doe weare ;
The nightingall, forgetting winter's woe,
Calls vp the lazie morne her notes to heare ;
Those flowrs are spred which names of princes beare,
Some red, some azure, white, and golden grow ;
Here lowes a heifer, there bea-wailing strayes
A harmlesse lambe, not farre a stag rebounds,
The sheepe-heards sing to grazing flockes sweet layes,
And all about the ecchoing aire resounds.
  Hills, dales, woods, flouds, and euery thing doth change,
  But shee in rigour, I in loue am strange.

SONNET.

WHEN Nature now had wonderfully wrought
All Avristella's parts, except her eyes,
To make those twinnes two lamps in beautie's skies,
Shee counsell of her starrie senate sought.
Mars and Apollo first did her aduise
In colour blacke to wrappe those comets bright,
That Loue him so might soberly disguise,
And vnperceiued, wound at euery sight.
Chaste Phebe spake for purest azure dyes,
But Ioue and Venvs greene about the light
To frame thought best, as bringing most delight,
That to pin'd hearts hope might for ay arise:
    Nature, all said, a paradise of greene
    There plac'd, to make all loue which haue them seene.

MADRIGALL.

    To the delightfull greene
Of you, faire radiant eine,
Let each blacke yeeld beneath the starrie arche.
Eyes, burnisht heauens of loue,
Sinople lampes of Ioue,
Saue that those hearts which with your flames yee parche
Two burning sunnes you proue,
All other eyes compar'd with you, deare lights,
Bee hells, or if not hells yet dumpish nights.
The heauens, if we their glasse
The sea beleeue, be greene, not perfect blew:
They all make faire what euer faire yet was,
And they bee faire because they looke like you.

SONNET.

IN vaine I haunt the colde and siluer springs,
To quench the feuer burning in my vaines;
In vaine, loue's pilgrime, mountaines, dales, and plaines
I ouer-runne; vain helpe long absence brings:
In vaine, my friends, your counsell me constraines
To flie, and place my thoughts on other things.
Ah! like the bird that fired hath her wings,
The more I moue, the greater are my paines.
Desire, alas! Desire, a Zeuxis new,
From Indies borrowing gold, from westerne skies
Most bright Cynoper, sets before mine eyes
In euery place, her haire, sweet looke, and hew;
   That flie, runne, rest I, all doth proue but vaine,
   My life lies in those lookes which haue me slaine.

SONNET.

ALL other beauties, how so e're they shine
In haires more bright than is the golden ore,
Or cheekes more faire than fairest eglantine,
Or hands like hers who comes the sunne before;
Match'd with that heauenly hue, and shape diuine,
With those deare starres which my weake thoughts adore,
Looke but like shaddowes, or if they bee more,
It is in that, that they are like to thine.
Who sees those eyes, their force and doth not proue,
Who gazeth on the dimple of that chinne,
And findes not Venus' sonne entrench'd therein,
Or hath not sense, or knowes not what is loue.
   To see thee had Narcissus had the grace,
   Hee sure had died with wondring on thy face.

D

SONNET.

My teares may well Numidian lions tame,
And pitie breed into the hardest hart
That euer Pyrrha did to maide impart,
When shee them first of blushing rockes did frame.
Ah! eyes which only serue to waile my smart,
How long will you mine inward woes proclaime?
Let it suffice, you beare a weeping part
All night, at day though yee doe not the same:
Cease, idle sighes, to spend your stormes in vaine,
And these calme secret shades more to molest;
Containe you in the prison of my brest,
You not doe ease but aggrauate my paine;
    Or, if burst foorth you must, that tempest moue
    In sight of her whome I so dearely loue.

SONNET.

Nymphes, sister nymphes, which haunt this christall brooke,
And, happie, in these floting bowrs abide,
Where trembling roofes of trees from sunne you hide,
Which make ideall woods in euery crooke;
Whether yee garlands for your lockes prouide,
Or pearlie letters seeke in sandie booke,
Or count your loues when Thetis was a bride,
Lift vp your golden heads and on mee looke.
Read in mine eyes mine agonizing cares,
And what yee read recount to her againe:
Faire nymphes, say, all these streames are but my teares,
And if shee aske you how they sweet remaine,
    Tell, that the bittrest teares which eyes can powre,
    When shed for her doe cease more to be sowre.

MADRIGALL.

LIKE the Idalian queene,
Her haire about her eyne,
With necke and brest's ripe apples to be seene,
At first glance of the morne,
In Cyprus' gardens gathering those faire flowrs
Which of her bloud were borne,
I saw, but fainting saw, my paramours.
The Graces naked danc'd about the place,
The winds and trees amaz'd
With silence on her gaz'd;
The flowrs did smile, like those vpon her face,
And as their aspine stalkes those fingers band,
That shee might read my case,
A hyacinth I wisht mee in her hand.

SONNET.

THEN is shee gone? O foole and coward I!
O good occasion lost, ne're to be found!
What fatall chaines haue my dull senses bound,
When best they may, that they not fortune trie?
Here is the flowrie bed where shee did lie,
With roses here shee stellified the ground,
Shee fix'd her eyes on this yet smyling pond,
Nor time, nor courteous place, seem'd ought denie.
Too long, too long, respect, I doe embrace
Your counsell, full of threats and sharpe disdaine;
Disdaine in her sweet heart can haue no place,
And though come there, must straight retire againe:
  Hencefoorth, respect, farewell, I oft heare tolde,
  Who liues in loue can neuer be too bolde.

SONNET.

In mind's pure glasse when I my selfe behold,
And viuely see how my best dayes are spent,
What clouds of care aboue my head are roll'd,
What comming harmes which I can not prevent !
My begunne course I, wearied, doe repent,
And would embrace what reason oft hath told,
But scarce thus thinke I, when loue hath control'd
All the best reasons reason could inuent.
Though sure I know my labour's end is griefe,
The more I striue that I the more shall pine,
That only death can be my last reliefe,
Yet when I thinke vpon that face diuine,
    Like one with arrow shot in laughter's place,
    Malgre my heart, I ioye in my disgrace.

SONNET.

Deare quirister, who from those shaddowes sends,
Ere that the blushing dawne dare show her light,
Such sad lamenting straines, that night attends,
Become all eare, starres stay to heare thy plight;
If one whose griefe euen reach of thought transcends,
Who ne're, not in a dreame, did taste delight,
May thee importune who like case pretends,
And seemes to ioy in woe, in woe's despight;
Tell me, (so may thou fortune milder trie,
And long, long sing,) for what thou thus complaines?
Sith, winter gone, the sunne in dapled skie
Now smiles on meadowes, mountaines, woods, and plaines.
    The bird, as if my questions did her moue,
    With trembling wings sobb'd foorth, I loue, I loue.

SONNET.

Trust not, sweet soule, those curled waues of gold,
With gentle tides which on your temples flow,
Nor temples spread with flackes of virgine snow,
Nor snow of cheekes with Tyrian graine enroll'd;
Trust not those shining lights which wrought my woe,
When first I did their burning rayes beholde,
Nor voyce, whose sounds more strange effects doe show
Than of the Thracian harper haue beene tolde.
Looke to this dying lillie, fading rose,
Darke hyacinthe, of late whose blushing beames
Made all the neighbouring herbes and grasse reioyce,
And thinke how litle is 'twixt life's extreames :
    The cruell tyrant that did kill those flowrs,
    Shall once, aye mee ! not spare that spring of yours.

SONNET.

That I so slenderly set foorth my minde,
Writing I wote not what in ragged rimes,
And charg'd with brasse into these golden times,
When others towre so high, am left behinde ;
I craue not Phebus leaue his sacred cell
To binde my browes with fresh Aonian bayes ;
Let them haue that who tuning sweetest layes
By Tempe sit, or Aganippe's well ;
Nor yet to Venus' tree do I aspire,
Sith shee for whome I might affect that praise,
My best attempts with cruell words gainsayes,
And I seeke not that others me admire.
    Of weeping myrrhe the crowne is which I craue,
    With a sad cypresse to adorne my graue.

SONNET.

SOUND hoarse, sad lute, true witnesse of my woe,
And striue no more to ease selfe-chosen paine
With soule-enchanting sounds ; your accents straine
Vnto these teares vncessantly which flow.
Shrill treeble, weepe, and you, dull basses, show
Your master's sorrow in a deadly vaine ;
Let neuer ioyfull hand vpon you goe,
Nor consort keepe but when you doe complaine.
Flie Phœbus' rayes, nay, hate the irkesome light ;
Woods, solitarie shades, for thee are best,
Or the blacke horrours of the blackest night,
When all the world, saue thou and I, doth rest :
   Then sound, sad lute, and beare a mourning part,
   Thou hell may'st mooue, though not a woman's heart.

SONNET.

YOU restlesse seas, appease your roaring waues,
And you who raise hudge mountaines in that plaine,
Aire's trumpeters, your blustring stormes restraine,
And listen to the plaints my griefe doth cause.
Eternall lights, though adamantine lawes
Of destinies to mooue still you ordaine,
Turne hitherward your eyes, your axetree pause,
And wonder at the torments I sustaine.
Earth, if thou bee not dull'd by my disgrace,
And senselesse made, now aske those powers aboue,
Why they so crost a wretch brought on thy face,
Fram'd for mishap, th' anachorite of loue ?
   And bid them, if they would moe Ætnas burne,
   In Rhodopee or Erimanthe mee turne.

SONNET.

WHAT cruell starre into this world mee broughte?
What gloomie day did dawne to giue me light?
What vnkinde hand to nourse mee, orphane, sought,
And would not leaue mee in eternall night?
What thing so deare as I hath essence bought?
The elements, drie, humid, heauie, light,
The smallest liuing things by nature wrought,
Bee freed of woe, if they haue small delight.
Ah! only I, abandon'd to despaire,
Nail'd to my torments, in pale horrour's shade,
Like wand'ring clouds see all my comforts fled,
And euill on euill with hours my life impaire:
    The heauen and fortune which were wont to turne,
    Fix't in one mansion, staye to cause mee mourne.

SONNET.

DEARE eye, which daig'nst on this sad monument
The sable scroule of my mishaps to view,
Though with the mourning Muses' teares besprent,
And darkly drawne, which is not fain'd, but true,
If thou not dazell'd with a heauenly hue,
And comely feature, did'st not yet lament,
But happie liu'st vnto thy self content,
O let not loue thee to his lawes subdue.
Looke on the wofull shipwracke of my youth,
And let my ruines for a Phare thee serue,
To shunne this rocke Capharean of vntrueth,
And serue no god who doth his church-men sterue:
    His kingdome is but plaints, his guerdon teares,
    What hee giues more are iealousies and feares.

SONNET.

IF crost with all mishaps bee my poore life,
If one short day I neuer spent in mirth,
If my spright with itselfe holds lasting strife,
If sorrowe's death is but new sorrowe's birth;
If this vaine world bee but a sable stage
Where slaue-born man playes to the scoffing starres,
If youth bee toss'd with loue, with weaknesse age,
If knowledge serue to holde our thoughts in warres;
If time can close the hundreth mouths of fame,
And make, what long since past, like that to bee,
If vertue only bee an idle name,
If I, when I was borne, was borne to die;
   Why seeke I to prolong these loathsome dayes?
   The fairest rose in shortest time decayes.

SONNET.

LET fortune triumph now, and Iö sing,
Sith I must fall beneath this load of care;
Let her, what most I prize of eu'rie thing,
Now wicked trophees in her temple reare.
Shee, who high palmie empires doth not spare,
And tramples in the dust the prowdest king,
Let her vaunt how my blisse shee did impaire,
To what low ebbe shee now my flow doth bring;
Let her count how, a new Ixion, mee
Shee in her wheele did turne, how high nor low
I neuer stood, but more to tortur'd bee:
Weepe, soule, weepe, plaintfull soule, thy sorrowes know,
   Weepe, of thy teares till a blacke riuer swell,
   Which may Cocytus be to this thy hell.

SONNET.

O cruell beautie, meekenesse inhumaine,
That night and day contend with my desire,
And seeke my hope to kill, not quench my fire,
By death, not baulme, to ease my pleasant paine ;
Though yee my thoughts tread downe which would aspire,
And bound my blisse, doe not, alas ! disdaine
That I your matchlesse worth and grace admire,
And for their cause these torments sharpe sustaine.
Let great Empedocles vaunt of his death,
Found in the midst of those Sicylian flames,
And Phaëton, that heauen him reft of breath,
And Dædal's sonne he nam'd the Samian streames :
    Their haps I enuie not, my praise shall bee,
    The fairest shee that liu'd gaue death to mee.

SONNET.

THE Hyperborean hills, Ceraunus' snow,
Or Arimaspus cruell, first thee bred,
The Caspian tigers with their milke thee fed,
And Faunes did humane bloud on thee bestow ;
Fierce Orithya's louer in thy bed
Thee lull'd asleepe, where he enrag'd doth blow ;
Thou didst not drinke the flouds which here doe flow,
But teares, or those by ycie Tanais' hed.
Sith thou disdaines my loue, neglects my griefe,
Laughs at my grones, and still affects my death,
Of thee, nor heauen, I'll seeke no more reliefe,
Nor longer entertaine this loathsome breath,
    But yeeld vnto my starre, that thou mayst proue
    What losse thou hadst in losing such a loue.

E

SONG.

　　Phoebus, arise,
And paint the sable skies
With azure, white, and red ;
Rowse Memnon's mother from her Tython's bed,
That shee thy cariere may with roses spred ;
The nightingalles thy comming each where sing ;
Make an eternall spring,
Giue life to this darke world which lieth dead ;
Spreade foorth thy golden haire
In larger lockes than thou wast wont before,
And, emperour like, decore
With diademe of pearle thy temples faire :
Chase hence the vglie night,
Which serues but to make deare thy glorious light.
This is that happie morne,
That day, long wished day,
Of all my life so darke,
(If cruell starres haue not my ruine sworne,
And fates not hope betray,)
Which, only white, deserues
A diamond for euer should it marke :
This is the morne should bring vnto this groue
My loue, to heare and recompense my loue.
Faire king, who all preserues,
But show thy blushing beames,
And thou two sweeter eyes
Shalt see, than those which by Peneus' streames
Did once thy heart surprise ;
Nay, sunnes, which shine as cleare
As thou when two thou did to Rome appeare.
Now, Flora, decke thy selfe in fairest guise ;

If that yee, winds, would heare
A voice surpassing farre Amphion's lyre,
Your stormie chiding stay ;
Let zephyre only breath,
And with her tresses play,
Kissing sometimes these purple ports of death.
The windes all silent are,
And Phœbus in his chaire,
Ensaffroning sea and aire,
Makes vanish euery starre :
Night like a drunkard reeles
Beyond the hills to shunne his flaming wheeles ;
The fields with flowrs are deckt in euery hue,
The clouds bespangle with bright gold their blew :
Here. is the pleasant place,
And eu'ry thing, saue her, who all should grace.

SONNET.

Who hath not seene into her saffron bed
The morning's goddesse mildly her repose,
Or her, of whose pure bloud first sprang the rose,
Lull'd in a slumber by a mirtle shade ?
Who hath not seene that sleeping white and red
Makes Phœbe look so pale, which shee did close
In that Ionian hill, to ease her woes,
Which only liues by nectare kisses fed ?
Come but and see my ladie sweetly sleepe,
The sighing rubies of those heauenly lips,
The Cupids which brest's golden apples keepe,
Those eyes which shine in midst of their ecclipse,
   And hee them all shall see, perhaps, and proue
   Shee waking but perswades, now forceth loue.

POEMS.

38

SONNET.

Of Citherea's birds, that milke-white paire,
On yonder leauie mirtle tree which grone,
And waken, with their kisses in the aire,
Enamour'd zephyres murmuring one by one,
If thou but sense hadst like Pigmalion's stone,
Or hadst not seene Medusa's snakie haire,
Loue's lessons thou mightst learne; and learne, sweete faire,
To summer's heat ere that thy spring bee growne.
And if those kissing louers seeme but cold,
Looke how that elme this iuie doth embrace,
And bindes, and claspes with many a wanton fold,
And courting sleepe o'reshadowes all the place;
   Nay, seemes to say, deare tree, we shall not parte,
   In signe whereof, loe! in each a leafe a heart.

SONNET.

The sunne is faire when hee with crimson crowne,
And flaming rubies, leaues his easterne bed;
Faire is Thaumantias in her christall gowne,
When clouds engemm'd hang azure, greene, and red:
To westerne worlds when wearied day goes downe,
And from Heauen's windowes each starre showes her head,
Earth's silent daughter, night, is faire, though browne;
Faire is the moone, though in loue's liuerie cled;
Faire Chloris is when shee doth paint Aprile,
Faire are the meads, the woods, the flouds are faire;
Faire looketh Ceres with her yellow haire,
And apples' queene when rose-cheekt shee doth smile.
   That heauen, and earth, and seas are faire is true,
   Yet true that all not please so much as you.

MADRIGALL.

WHEN as shee smiles I finde
More light before mine eyes,
Nor when the sunne from Inde
Brings to our world a flowrie Paradise :
But when shee gently weepes,
And powres foorth pearlie showres
On cheekes' faire blushing flowres,
A sweet melancholie my senses keepes.
Both feede so my disease,
So much both doe me please,
That oft I doubt, which more my heart doth burne,
Like loue to see her smile, or pitie mourne.

SONNET.

SLIDE soft, faire Forth, and make a christall plaine,
Cut your white lockes, and on your foamie face
Let not a wrinckle bee, when you embrace
The boat that earth's perfections doth containe.
Windes, wonder, and through wondring hold your peace ;
Or if that yee your hearts cannot restraine
From sending sighes, mou'd by a louer's case,
Sigh, and in her faire haire yourselues enchaine ;
Or take these sighes which absence makes arise
From mine oppressed brest, and waue the sailes,
Or some sweet breath new brought from Paradise :
Flouds seeme to smile, loue o're the winds preuailes,
And yet hudge waues arise ; the cause is this,
The ocean striues with Forth the boate to kisse.

SONNET.

Ah! who can see those fruites of Paradise,
Celestial cherries, which so sweetly swell,
That sweetnesse selfe confinde there seemes to dwell,
And all those sweetest parts about despise?
Ah! who can see and feele no flame surprise
His hardened heart? for mee, alas! too well
I know their force, and how they doe excell:
Now burne I through desire, now doe I freeze;
I die, deare life, vnlesse to mee bee giuen
As many kisses as the spring hath flowrs,
Or as the siluer drops of Iris' showrs,
Or as the starres in all-embracing heauen;
   And if, displeas'd, yee of the matche complaine,
   Yee shall haue leaue to take them backe againe.

SONNET.

Is't not enough, aye mee! mee thus to see
Like some heauen-banish'd ghost still wailing goe,
A shadow which your rayes doe only show?
To vexe mee more, vnlesse yee bid mee die,
What could yee worse allotte vnto your foe?
But die will I, so yee will not denie
That grace to mee which mortall foes euen trie,
To chuse what sort of death should ende my woe.
One time I found when as yee did me kisse,
Yee gaue my panting soule so sweet a touch,
That halfe I sown'd in midst of all my blisse;
I doe but craue my death's wound may bee such;
   For though by griefe I die not and annoy,
   Is't not enough to die through too much ioy?

MADRIGALL.

Sweete rose, whence is this hue
Which doth all hues excell?
Whence this most fragrant smell,
And whence this forme and gracing grace in you?
In flowrie Paestum's field perhaps yee grew,
Or Hybla's hills you bred,
Or odoriferous Enna's plaines you fed,
Or Tmolus, or where bore young Adon slew;
Or hath the queene of love you dy'd of new
In that deare bloud, which makes you looke so red?
   No, none of those, but cause more high you blist,
   My ladie's brest you bare, and lips you kist.

SONNET.

Shee whose faire flowrs no autumne makes decay,
Whose hue celestiall, earthly hues doth staine,
Into a pleasant odoriferous plaine
Did walke alone, to braue the pride of Maye;
And whilst through checkred lists shee made her way,
Which smil'd about her sight to entertaine,
Loe, vnawares, where Loue did hid remaine,
Shee spide, and sought to make of him her prey;
For which, of golden lockes a fairest haire,
To binde the boy, she tooke; but hee, afraid
At her approach, sprang swiftly in the aire,
And mounting farre from reach, look'd backe and said,
   Why shouldst thou, sweet, me seeke in chaines to binde,
   Sith in thine eyes I dayly am confinde.

MADRIGALL.

On this colde world of ours,
Flowre of the seasons, season of the flowrs,
Sonne of the sunne, sweet Spring,
Such hote and burning dayes why doest thou bring?
Is this for that those high eternall pow'rs
Flash downe that fire this all enuironing,
Or that now Phœbus keepes his sister's spheare?
Or doth some Phaëton
Enflame the sea and aire?
Or rather is it, vsher of the yeare,
For that, last day, amongst thy flowrs alone,
Vnmask'd thou saw'st my faire?
    And whilst thou on her gaz'd shee did thee burne,
    And in thy brother summer doth thee turne.

SONNET.

Deare wood, and you, sweet solitarie place,
Where from the vulgare I estranged liue,
Contented more with what your shades mee giue,
Than if I had what Thetis doth embrace;
What snakie eye, growne iealous of my peace,
Now from your silent horrours would mee driue,
When sunne, progressing in his glorious race
Beyond the Twinnes, doth neare our pole arriue?
What sweet delight a quiet life affords,
And what it is to bee of bondage free,
Farre from the madding worldling's hoarse discords,
Sweet flowrie place I first did learne of thee:
    Ah! if I were mine owne, your deare resorts
    I would not change with princes' stately courts.

SEXTAIN.

SITH gone is my delight and only pleasure,
The last of all my hopes, the chearfull sunne
That clear'd my life's darke day, nature's sweet treasure,
More deare to mee than all beneath the moone,
What resteth now, but that vpon this mountaine
I weepe, till Heauen transforme me in a fountaine?

Fresh, faire, delicious, christall, pearlie fountaine,
On whose smooth face to looke shee oft took pleasure,
Tell me, (so may thy streames long cheare this mountaine,
So serpent ne're thee staine, nor scorch the sunne,
So may with gentle beames thee kisse the moone,)
Doest thou not mourne to want so faire a treasure?

While shee her glass'd in thee, rich Tagus' treasure
Thou enuie needed not, nor yet the fountaine
In which that hunter saw the naked moone;
Absence hath robb'd thee of thy wealth and pleasure,
And I remaine like marigold of sunne
Depriu'd, that dies by shadow of some mountaine.

Nymphes of the forrests, nymphes who on this mountaine
Are wont to dance, shewing your beautie's treasure
To goate-feete Syluans, and the wondring sunne,
When as you gather flowres about this fountaine,
Bid her farewell who placed here her pleasure,
And sing her praises to the starres and moon.

Among the lesser lights as is the moone,
Blushing through scarfe of clouds on Latmos' mountaine,

F

Or when her siluer lockes shee lookes for pleasure
In Thetis' streames, prowde of so gay a treasure,
Such was my faire when shee sate by this fountaine
With other nymphes, to shunne the amorous sunne.

As is our earthe in absence of the sunne,
Or when of sunne depriued is the moone,
As is without a verdant shade a fountaine,
Or wanting grasse, a mead, a vale, a mountaine,
Such is my state, bereft of my deare treasure,
To know whose only worth was all my pleasure.

Ne're thinke of pleasure, heart; eyes, shunne the sunne,
Teares be your treasure, which the wand'ring moone
Shall see you shed by mountaine, vale, and fountaine.

SONNET.

THOU window, once which serued for a spheare
To that deare planet of my heart, whose light
Made often blush the glorious queene of night,
While shee in thee more beautious did appeare,
What mourning weedes, alas! now do'st thou weare?
How loathsome to mine eyes is thy sad sight?
How poorely look'st thou, with what heauie cheare,
Since that sunne set, which made thee shine so bright?
Vnhappie now thee close, for as of late
To wond'ring eyes thou wast a paradise,
Bereft of her who made thee fortunate,
A gulfe thou art, whence cloudes of sighes arise;
    But vnto none so noysome as to mee,
    Who hourly see my murth'red ioyes in thee.

SONNET.

ARE these the flowrie bankes, is this the mead,
Where she was wont to passe the pleasant hours?
Did here her eyes exhale mine eyes' salt showrs,
When on her lap I laide my wearie head?
Is this the goodly elme did vs o'respread,
Whose tender rine, cut out in curious flowrs
By that white hand, containes those flames of ours?
Is this the rusling spring vs musicke made?
Deflourish'd mead, where is your heauenly hue?
Banke, where that arras did you late adorne,
How look ye, elme, all withered and forlorne?
Onely, sweet spring, nought altered seemes in you;
 But while here chang'd each other thing appeares,
 To sowre your streames take of mine eyes these teares.

SONNET.

ALEXIS, here shee stay'd; among these pines,
Sweet hermitresse, she did alone repaire;
Here did shee spreade the treasure of her haire,
More rich than that brought from the Colchian mines.
She set her by these musket eglantines,
The happie place the print seemes yet to beare;
Her voyce did sweeten here thy sugred lines,
To which winds, trees, beasts, birds, did lend their eare.
Me here shee first perceiu'd, and here a morne
Of bright carnations did o'respreade her face;
Here did shee sigh, here first my hopes were borne,
And I first got a pledge of promis'd grace:
 But, ah! what seru'd it to be happie so?
 Sith passed pleasures double but new woe.

SONNET.

O NIGHT, cleare night, O dark and gloomie day!
O wofull waking! O soule-pleasing sleepe!
O sweet conceits which in my braines did creepe,
Yet sowre conceits which went so soone away!
A sleepe I had more than poore words can say,
For clos'd in armes, mee thought, I did thee keepe;
A sorie wretch plung'd in misfortunes deepe
Am I not wak'd, when light doth lies bewray?
O that that night had euer still bene blacke!
O that that day had neuer yet begunne!
And you, mine eyes, would yee no time saw sunne!
To haue your sunne in such a zodiacke:
    Loe! what is good of life is but a dreame,
    When sorrow is a neuer-ebbing streame.

SONNET.

HAIRE, precious haire which Midas' hand did straine,
Part of the wreathe of gold that crownes those browes
Which winter's whitest white in whitenesse stain,
And lillie, by Eridian's banke that growes;
Haire, fatall present, which first caus'd my woes,
When loose yee hang like Danae's golden raine,
Sweet nettes, which sweetly doe all hearts enchaine,
Strings, deadly strings, with which Loue bends his bowes,
How are yee hither come? tell me, O haire,
Deare armelet, for what thus were yee giuen?
I know a badge of bondage I you weare,
Yet, haire, for you, O that I were a heauen!
    Like Berenice's locke that yee might shine,
    But brighter farre, about this arme of mine.

MADRIGALL.

VNHAPPIE light,
Doe not approach to bring the wofull day,
When I must bid for ay
Farewell to her, and liue in endlesse plight.
Faire moone, with gentle beames
The sight who neuer marres,
Long cleare heauen's sable vault; and you, bright starres,
Your golden lockes long glasse in earth's pure streames,
Let Phœbus neuer rise
To dimme your watchfull eyes:
  Prolong, alas! prolong my short delight,
  And, if ye can, make an eternall night.

SONNET.

WITH griefe in heart, and teares in sowning eyes,
When I to her had giu'n a sad fare-well,
Close sealed with a kisse, and dew which fell
On my else-moystned face from beauties skies,
So strange amazement did my minde surprise,
That at each pace I fainting turn'd againe,
Like one whome a torpedo stupifies,
Not feeling honour's bit, nor reason's raine.
But when fierce starres to parte mee did constraine,
With back-caste lookes I enui'd both and bless'd
The happie walles and place did her containe,
Till that sight's shafts their flying obiect miss'd.
  So wailing parted Ganamede the faire,
  When eagles' talents bare him through the aire.

MADRIGALL.

I FEARE not hencefoorth death,
Sith after this departure yet I breath ;
Let rocks, and seas, and wind,
Their highest treasons show,
Let skie and earth combinde
Striue, if they can, to ende my life and woe ;
Sith griefe can not, mee nothing can o'rethrow,
   Or if that ought can cause my fatall lot,
   It will bee when I heare I am forgot.

SONNET.

How many times night's silent queene her face
Hath hid, how oft with starres in siluer maske
In Heauen's great hall shee hath begunne her taske,
And chear'd the waking eye in lower place !
How oft the sunne hath made by Heauen's swift race
The happie louer to forsake the brest
Of his deare ladie, wishing in the west
His golden coach to runne had larger space !
I euer count, and number, since, alas !
I bade farewell to my heart's dearest guest,
The miles I compasse, and in minde I chase
The flouds and mountaines holde mee from my rest :
   But, woe is mee ! long count and count may I,
   Ere I see her whose absence makes mee die.

SONNET.

So grieuous is my paine, so painefull life,
That oft I finde mee in the armes of death,
But, breath halfe-gone, that tyrant called Death
Who others killes, restoreth mee to life:
For while I thinke how woe shall ende with life,
And that I quiet peace shall ioye by death,
That thought euen doth o'repowre the paines of death,
And call mee home againe to lothed life.
Thus doth mine euill transcend both life and death,
While no death is so bad as is my life,
Nor no life such which doth not ende by death,
And Protean changes turne my death and life.
  O happie those who in their birthe finde death,
  Sith but to languish Heauen affordeth life.

SONNET.

Fame, who with golden pennes abroad dost range
Where Phœbus leaues the night, and brings the day;
Fame, in one place who, restlesse, dost not stay
Till thou hast flowne from Atlas vnto Gange;
Fame, enemie to time that still doth change,
And in his changing course would make decay
What here below he findeth in his way,
Euen making vertue to her selfe looke strange;
Daughter of heauen, now all thy trumpets sound,
Raise vp thy head vnto the highest skie,
With wonder blaze the gifts in her are found;
And when she from this mortall globe shall flie,
  In thy wide mouth keepe long, long keepe her name,
  So thou by her, shee by thee liue shall, Fame.

MADRIGALL.

THE iuorie, corrall, gold,
Of brest, of lips, of haire,
So liuely sleepe doth show to inward sight,
That wake I thinke I hold
No shadow, but my faire:
My selfe so to deceaue,
With long-shut eyes I shunne the irkesome light.
Such pleasure thus I haue,
Delighting in false gleames,
If death sleepe's brother be,
    And soules relieu'd of sense haue so sweete dreames,
    That I would wish mee thus to dreame and die.

SONNET.

I CURSE the night, yet doth from day mee hide,
The Pandionian birds I tyre with mones,
The ecchoes euen are weari'd with my grones,
Since absense did mee from my blisse diuide.
Each dreame, each toy my reason doth affright,
And when remembrance reades the curious scroule
Of pass'd contentments caused by her sight,
Then bitter anguish doth inuade my soule.
While thus I liue ecclipsed of her light,
O mee! what better am I than the mole,
Or those whose zenith is the only pole,
Whose hemisphere is hid with so long night,
    Saue that in earthe he rests, they hope for sunne,
    I pine, and finde mine endlesse night begunne?

SONNET.

OF death some tell, some of the cruell paine
Which that bad crafts-man in his worke did trie,
When (a new monster) flames once did constraine
A humane corps to yeeld a brutish crie.
Some tell of those in burning beds who lie,
For that they durst in the Phlegræan plaine
The mightie rulers of the skie defie,
And siege those christall towres which all containe.
An other countes of Phlegethon's hote floods
The soules which drinke, Ixion's endlesse smart,
And his to whom a vulture eates the heart,
One telles of specters in enchanted woods.
    Of all those paines he who the worst would proue,
    Let him bee absent, and but pine in loue.

MADRIGALL.

TRITONS, which bounding diue
Through Neptune's liquide plaine,
When as ye shall arriue
With tilting tides where siluer Ora playes,
And to your king his watrie tribute payes,
    Tell how I dying liue,
    And burne in midst of all the coldest maine.

G

SONNET.

PLACE mee where angry Titan burnes the more,
And thirstie Africke firie monsters brings,
Or where the new-borne phœnix spreades her wings,
And troupes of wond'ring birds her flight adore ;
Place mee by Gange, or Inde's empampred shore,
Where smyling heauens on earth cause double springs ;
Place mee where Neptune's quire of syrens sings,
Or where, made hoarse through cold, hee leaues to roare ;
Me place where Fortune doth her darlings crowne,
A wonder or a sparke in Enuie's eye,
Or late outragious fates vpon mee frowne,
And pittie wailing see disast'red mee,
    Affection's print my minde so deepe doth proue,
    I may forget my selfe, but not my loue.

POEMS.

THE SECOND PART.

Of mortall glorie, O soone darkned raye!
O posting ioyes of man, more swift than winde!
O fond desires! which wing'd with fancies straye,
O traitrous hopes! which doe our iudgements blinde;
Loe! in a flash that light is gone away,
Which dazell did each eye, delight each minde,
And with that sunne, from whence it came, combinde,
Now makes more radiant heauen's eternall day.
Let beautie now be blubbred cheekes with teares,
Let widow'd musicke only roare and plaine;
Poor vertue, get thee wings, and mount the spheares,
And let thine only name on earth remaine.
  Death hath thy temple raz'd, loue's empire foylde,
  The world of honour, worth, and sweetnesse spoylde.

THOSE eyes, those sparkling saphires of delight,
Which thousand thousand hearts did set on fire,
Which made that eye, of heauen that brings the light,
Oft jealous, staye amaz'd them to admire ;
That liuing snow, those crimson roses bright,
Those pearles, those rubies, which did breede desire,
Those lockes of gold, that purple faire of Tyre,
Are wrapt, aye mee! vp in eternall night.
What hast thou more to vaunt of, wretched world,
Sith shee, who cursed thee made blest, is gone ?
Thine euer-burning lamps, rounds euer whorld,
Can vnto thee not modell such a one :
    For if they would such beautie bring on earth
    They should be forc'd againe to make her breath.

SONNET.

O FATE ! conspir'd to powre your worst on mee,
O rigorous rigour, which doth all confound !
With cruell hands yee haue cut down the tree,
And fruit and flowre dispersed on the ground.
A litle space of earth my loue doth bound ;
That beautie which did raise it to the skie,
Turn'd in neglected dust, now low doth lie,
Deafe to my plaints, and senslesse of my wound.
Ah ! did I liue for this, ah ! did I loue ?
For this and was it shee did so excell ?
That ere shee well life's sweet-sowre ioyes did proue,
Shee should, too deare a guest, with horrour dwell ?
    Weake influence of Heauen ! what faire yee frame,
    Falles in the prime, and passeth like a dreame.

SONNET.

O WOEFULL life! life, no, but liuing death,
Fraile boat of christall in a rockie sea,
A sport expos'd to Fortune's stormie breath,
Which, kept with paine, with terrour doth decay :
The false delights, true woes thou dost bequeath,
Mine all-appalled minde doe so affraye,
That I those enuie who are laid in earth,
And pittie them that runne thy dreadfull waye.
When did mine eyes behold one chearefull morne ?
When had my tossed soule one night of rest ?
When did not hatefull starres my projects scorne ?
O ! now I finde for mortalls what is best ;
  Euen, sith our voyage shamefull is, and short,
  Soone to strike saile, and perish in the port.

SONNET.

MINE eyes, dissolue your globes in brinie streames,
And with a cloud of sorrow dimme your sight ;
The sunne's bright sunne is set, of late whose beames
Gaue luster to your day, day to your night.
My voyce, now deafen earth with anatheames,
Roare foorth a challenge in the world's despight,
Tell that disguised griefe is her delight,
That life a slumber is of fearfull dreames.
And, woefull minde, abhorre to thinke of ioy,
My senses all now comfortlesse you hide,
Accept no object but of black annoy,
Teares, plaints, sighs, mourning weeds, graues gaping wide.
  I haue nought left to wish, my hopes are dead,
  And all with her beneath a marble laide.

SONNET.

SWEET soule, which in the Aprill of thy yeares
So to enrich the heauen mad'st poore this round,
And now with golden rayes of glorie crown'd
Most blest abid'st aboue the spheare of spheares ;
If heauenly lawès, alas ! haue not thee bound
From looking to this globe that all vpbeares,
If rueth and pittie there aboue bee found,
O daigne to lend a looke vnto those teares.
Doe not disdaine, deare ghost, this sacrifice,
And though I raise not pillars to thy praise,
Mine offerings take ; let this for mee suffice,
My heart a liuing piramide I raise ;
    And whilst kings' tombes with lawrels flourish greene,
    Thine shall with mirtles and these flowrs bee seene.

MADRIGALL.

THIS life, which seemes so faire,
Is like a bubble blowen vp in the aire,
By sporting children's breath,
Who chase it euery where,
And striue who can most motion it bequeath :
And though it sometime seeme of its owne might,
Like to an eye of gold, to be fix'd there,
And firme to houer in that emptie hight,
That only is because it is so light,
But in that pompe it doth not long appeare ;
    For euen when most admir'd, it in a thought,
    As swell'd from nothing, doth dissolue in nought.

SONNET.

O ! it is not to mee bright lampe of day,
That in the east thou shew'st thy rosie face ;
O ! it is not to mee thou leau'st that sea,
And in these azure lists begin'st thy race.
Thou shin'st not to the dead in any place,
And I, dead, from this world am gone away,
Or if I seeme, a shadow, yet to stay,
It is a while but to bemone my case.
My mirth is lost, my comforts are dismay'd,
And vnto sad mis-haps their place doe yeeld ;
My knowledge doth resemble a bloudie field,
When I my hopes and helps see prostrate lay'd.
 So painefull is life's course which I haue runne,
 That I doe wish it neuer had begunne.

SONG.

SAD Damon being come
To that for-euer lamentable tombe,
Which those eternall powers that all controule,
Vnto his liuing soule
A melancholie prison had prescriu'd ;
Of hue, of heate, of motion quite depriu'd,
In armes wake, trembling, cold,
A marble, hee the marble did infold ;
And hauing made it warme with many a showre,
Which dimmed eyes did powre,
When griefe had giuen him leaue, and sighes them stay'd
Thus with a sad alas at last he said :
 Who would haue thought to mee
The place where thou didst lie could grieuous bee ?

And that, deare body, long thee hauing sought,
O mee! who would have thought
Thee once to finde it should my soule confound,
And giue my heart than death a deeper wound?
Thou didst disdaine my teares,
But grieue not that this ruethfull stone them beares;
Mine eyes serue only now for thee to weepe,
And let their course them keepe;
Although thou neuer wouldst them comfort show,
Doe not repine, they haue part of thy woe.
　　Ah, wretch! too late I finde.
How vertue's glorious titles proue but winde;
For if shee any could release from death,
Thou yet enioy'd hadst breath;
For if shee ere appear'd to mortall eine,
It was in thy faire shape that shee was seene.
But, O! if I was made
For thee, with thee why too am I not dead?
Why doe outragious fates, which dimm'd thy sight,
Let mee see hatefull light?
They without mee made death thee to surprise,
Tyrants, perhaps, that they might kill me twise.
　　O griefe! and could one day
Haue force such excellence to take away?
Could a swift-flying moment, ah! deface
Those matchlesse gifts, that grace
Which art and nature had in thee combinde,
To make thy body paragone thy minde?
Haue all past like a cloud,
And doth eternall silence now them shroud?
Is what so much admir'd was nought but dust,
Of which a stone hath trust?

O change! O cruell change! thou to our sight
Shewes destine's rigour equall doth their might.
   When thou from earth didst passe,
Sweet nymph, perfection's mirrour broken was,
And this of late so glorious world of ours,
Like meadow without flowrs,
Or ring of a rich gemme made blind, appear'd,
Or night, by starre nor Cynthia neither clear'd.
Loue when he saw thee die,
Entomb'd him in the lidde of either eye,
And left his torch within thy sacred vrne,
There for a lampe to burne:
Worth, honour, pleasure, with thy life expir'd,
Death since, growne sweet, beginnes to be desir'd.
   Whilst thou to vs wast giuen,
The earth her Venus had as well as Heauen,
Nay, and her sunne, which burnt as many hearts,
As hee doth easterne parts;
Bright sunne, which, forc'd to leaue these hemispheares,
Benighted set into a sea of teares.
Ah, death, who shall thee flie,
Sith the most worthie bee o'rethrowne by thee?
Thou spar'st the rauens, and nightingalles dost kill,
And triumphes at thy will;
But giue thou canst not such an other blow,
Because like her earth can none other show.
   O bitter sweets of loue!
How better is 't at all you not to proue,
Than when wee doe your pleasure most possesse,
To find them then made lesse?
O! that the cause which doth consume our ioy,
Remembrance of it too, would too destroy!

What doth this life bestow
But flowrs on thornes which grow,
Which though they sometime blandishing delighte,
Yet afterwards vs smite?
And if the rising sunne them faire doth see,
That planet, setting, too beholdes them die.
   This world is made a hell,
Depriu'd of all that in it did excell.
O Pan, Pan, winter is fallen in our May,
Turn'd is in night our day;
Forsake thy pipe, a sceptre take to thee,
Thy lockes dis-garland, thou blacke Ioue shalt be.
The flockes doe leave the meads,
And loathing three-leaf'd grasse, hold up their heads,
The streames not glide now with a gentle rore,
Nor birds sing as before,
Hilles stand with clouds, like mourners, vail'd in blacke,
And owles on caban roofes foretell our wracke.
   That zephyre euerie yeere
So soone was heard to sigh in forrests heere,
It was for her: that wrapt in gownes of greene,
Meads were so earelie seene,
That in the saddest months oft sung the mearles,
It was for her; for her trees dropt foorth pearles.
That prowde and statelie courts
Did enuie those our shades, and calme resorts,
It was for her: and she is gone, O woe!
Woods cut againe doe grow,
Budde doth the rose and dazie, winter done,
But wee, once dead, no more doe see the sunne.
   Whose name shall now make ring
The ecchoes? of whom shall the nymphettes sing?

Whose heauenlie voyce, whose soule-inuading straines,
Shall fill with ioy the plaines ?
What haire, what eyes, can make the morne in east
Weepe, that a fairer riseth in the west ?
Faire sunne, poste still away,
No musicke heere is found thy course to stay.
Sweet Hybla swarmes, with wormwood fill your bowrs,
Gone is the flowre of flowrs ;
Blush no more, rose, nor, lillie, pale remaine,
Dead is that beautie which yours late did staine.
   Aye mee ! to waile my plight
Why haue not I as many eyes as night,
Or as that shepheard which Ioue's loue did keepe,
That I still still may weepe ?
But though I had, my teares vnto my crosse
Were not yet equall, nor grief to my losse :
Yet of your brinie showrs,
Which I heere powre, may spring as many flowrs,
As came of those which fell from Helen's eyes ;
And when yee doe arise,
May euerie leafe in sable letters beare
The dolefull cause for which yee spring vp heere.

MADRIGALL.

DEARE night, the ease of care,
Vntroubled seate of peace,
Time's eldest childe, which oft the blinde doe see,
On this our hemispheare
What makes thee now so sadly darke to bee ?
Comm'st thou in funerall pompe her graue to grace ?
Or doe those starres which should thy horrour cleare,
In Ioue's high hall aduise,
In what part of the skies,
With them, or Cynthia, shee shall appeare ?
Or, ah, alas ! because those matchlesse eyes
Which shone so faire, below thou dost not finde,
　　Striu'st thou to make all other eyes looke blinde ?

SONNET.

MY lute, bee as thou wast when thou didst grow
With thy greene mother in some shadie groue,
When immelodious windes but made thee moue,
And birds on thee their ramage did bestow.
Sith that deare voyce which did thy sounds approue,
Which vs'd in such harmonious straines to flow,
Is reft from earth to tune those spheares aboue,
What art thou but a harbenger of woe ?
Thy pleasing notes be pleasing notes no more,
But orphane wailings to the fainting eare,
Each stoppe a sigh, each sound drawes foorth a teare :
Bee therefore silent as in woods before,
　　Or if that any hand to touch thee daigne,
　　Like widow'd turtle, still her losse complaine.

SONNET.

SWEET spring, thou turn'st with all thy goodlie traine,
Thy head with flames, thy mantle bright with flowrs.
The zephyres curle the greene lockes of the plaine,
The cloudes for ioy in pearles weepe downe their showrs.
Thou turn'st, sweet youth, but, ah ! my pleasant howres
And happie dayes with thee come not againe ;
The sad memorialls only of my paine
Doe with thee turne, which turne my sweets in sowres.
Thou art the same which still thou wast before,
Delicious, wanton, amiable, faire ;
But shee, whose breath embaulm'd thy wholesome aire,
Is gone ; nor gold, nor gemmes her can restore.
 Neglected vertue, seasons goe and come,
 While thine forgot lie closed in a tombe.

SONNET.

WHAT doth it serue to see sunne's burning face,
And skies enamell'd with both the Indies' gold,
Or moone at night in jettie charriot roll'd,
And all the glorie of that starrie place ?
What doth it serue earth's beautie to behold,
The mountaines' pride, the meadowes' flowrie grace,
The statelie comelinesse of forrests old,
The sport of flouds, which would themselues embrace ?
What doth it serue to heare the Syluans' songs,
The wanton mearle, the nightingalle's sad straines,
Which in darke shades seeme to deplore my wrongs ?
For what doth serue all that this world containes,
 Sith shee for whome those once to me were deare,
 No part of them can haue now with me here ?

MADRIGALL.

The beautie, and the life
Of life's and beautie's fairest paragon,
O teares ! O griefe ! hang at a feeble thread,
To which pale Atropos had set her knife ;
The soule with many a grone
Had left each outward part,
And now did take his last leaue of the heart,
Nought else did want, saue death, euen to be dead,
When the afflicted band about her bed,
    Seeing so faire him come in lips, cheekes, eyes,
    Cried, ah ! and can death enter paradise ?

SONNET.

Ah ! napkin, ominous present of my deare,
Gift miserable, which doth now remaine
The only guerdon of my helpelesse paine,
When I thee got thou shew'd my state too cleare :
I neuer since haue ceas d to complaine,
Since I the badge of griefe did euer weare,
Ioy on my face durst neuer since appeare,
Care was the food which did me entertaine.
Now, since made mine, deare napkin, doe not grieue
That I this tribute pay thee from mine eine,
And that, these posting houres I am to live,
I laundre thy faire figures in this brine :
    No, I must yet euen begge of thee the grace,
    That thou wouldst daigne in graue to shrowde my face.

MADRIGALL.

Poore turtle, thou bemones
The losse of thy deare loue,
And I for mine send foorth those smoking grones,
Vnhappie widow'd doue,
While all about doe sing,
I at the roote, thou on the branche aboue,
Even wearie with our mones the gaudie spring.
  Yet these our plaints wee doe not spend in vaine,
  Sith sighing zephyres answere vs againe.

SONNET.

As in a duskie and tempestuous night,
A starre is wont to spreade her lockes of gold,
And while her pleasant rayes abroad are roll'd,
Some spitefull cloude doth rob vs of her sight ;
Faire soule, in this blacke age so shin'd thou bright,
And made all eyes with wonder thee beholde,
Till vglie Death, depriuing vs of light,
In his grimme mistie armes thee did enfolde.
Who more shall vaunt true beautie heere to see ?
What hope doth more in any heart remaine,
That such perfections shall his reason raine,
If beautie, with thee borne, too died with thee ?
  World, plaine no more of Love, nor count his harmes ;
  With his pale trophees Death hath hung his armes,

SONNET.

SITH it hath pleas'd that First and onlie Faire
To take that beautie to himselfe againe,
Which in this world of sense not to remaine,
But to amaze, was sent, and home repaire,
The loue which to that beautie I did beare,
(Made pure of mortall spots which did it staine,
And endlesse, which euen death cannot impaire,)
I place on him who will it not disdaine.
No shining eyes, no lockes of curling gold,
No blushing roses on a virgine face,
No outward show, no, nor no inward grace,
Shall force hereafter haue my thoughts to hold :
    Loue here on earth hudge stormes of care doe tosse,
    But, plac'd aboue, exempted is from losse.

MADRIGALL.

MY thoughts hold mortall strife,
I doe detest my life,
And with lamenting cries,
Peace to my soule to bring,
Oft calles that prince which here doth monarchise ;
But hee, grimme-grinning king,
Who catiues scornes, and doth the blest surprise,
    Late hauing deckt with beautie's rose his tombe,
    Disdaines to croppe a weede, and will not come.

IT autumne was, and on our hemispheare
Faire Ericyne began bright to appeare ;
Night westward did her gemmie world decline,
And hide her lights, that greater light might shine ;
The crested bird had giuen alarum twise
To lazie mortalls, to vnlocke their eyes,
The owle had left to plaine, and from each thorne
The wing'd musicians did salute the morne,
Who, while shee glass'd her lockes in Ganges' streames,
Set open wide the christall port of dreames ;
When I, whose eyes no drowsie night could close,
In sleepe's soft armes did quietly repose,
And, for that heauens to die mee did denie,
Death's image kissed, and as dead did lie.
I lay as dead, but scarce charm'd were my cares,
And slaked scarce my sighes, scarce dried my teares,
Sleepe scarce the vglie figures of the day
Had with his sable pincell put away,
And left mee in a still and calmie mood,
When by my bed me thought a virgine stood,
A virgine in the blooming of her prime,
If such rare beautie measur'd bee by time.
Her head a garland ware of opalls bright,
About her flow'd a gowne as pure as light,
Deare amber lockes gaue vmbrage to her face,
Where modestie high majestie did grace ;
Her eyes such beames sent foorth, that but with paine
Here weaker sights their sparckling could sustaine.
No deitie faign'd which haunts the silent woods
Is like to her, nor syrene of the floods :

I

Such is the golden planet of the yeare,
When blushing in the east hee doth appeare.
Her grace did beautie, voyce yet grace did passe,
Which thus through pearles and rubies broken was.
  How long wilt thou, said shee, estrang'd from ioy,
Paint shadowes to thy selfe of false annoy?
How long thy minde with horride shapes affrighte,
And in imaginarie euills delighte,
Esteeme that losse which, well when view'd, is gaine,
Or if a losse, yet not a losse to plaine?
O leaue thy tyred soule more to molest,
And thinke that woe when shortest then is best.
If shee for whom thou deafnest thus the skie
Bee dead, what then? was shee not borne to die?
Was she not mortall borne? If thou dost grieue
That times should bee in which shee should not liue,
Ere e're shee was weepe that daye's wheele was roll'd,
Weepe that shee liu'd not in the age of gold;
For that shee was not then, thou may'st deplore
As duely as that now shee is no more.
If onely shee had died, thou sure hadst cause
To blame the destines and heauen's yrone lawes;
But looke how many millions her aduance,
What numbers with her enter in this dance,
With those which are to come: shall heauens them stay,
And all's faire order breake, thee to obaye?
Euen as thy birth, death, which thee doth apall,
A piece is of the life of this great all.
Strong cities die, die doe high palmie raignes,
And, weakling, thou thus to bee handled plaines.
  If shee bee dead, then shee of lothsome dayes
Hath past the line, whose length but losse bewrayes;

Then shee hath left this filthie stage of care,
Where pleasure seldome, woe doth still repaire ;
For all the pleasures which it doth containe,
Not conteruaile the smallest minute's paine.
And tell mee, thou who dost so much admire
This litle vapour, smoake, this sparke, or fire,
Which life is call'd, what doth it thee bequeath
But some few yeeres which birth drawes out to death ?
Which if thou paragone with lusters runne,
And them whose carriere is but now begunne,
In daye's great vaste they shall farre lesse appeare,
Than with the sea when matched is a teare.
But why wouldst thou her longer wish to bee ?
One yeere doth serue all nature's pompe to see,
Nay, even one day and night : this moone, that sunne,
Those lesser fires about this round which runne,
Bee but the same which, vnder Saturne's raigne,
Did the serpenting seasons enterchaine.
How oft doth life grow lesse by liuing long ?
And what excelleth but what dieth yong ?
For age which all abhorre, yet would embrace,
Whiles makes the minde as wrinckled as the face ;
And when that destinies conspire with worth,
That yeeres not glorie wrong, life soone goes forth.
Leaue then laments, and thinke thou didst not liue,
Lawes to that first eternall cause to giue,
But to obey those lawes which hee hath giuen,
And bow vnto the just decrees of heauen,
Which can not erre, what euer foggie mists
Doe blinde men in these sublunarie lists.
    But what if shee for whom thou spend'st those grones,
And wastest life's deare torch in ruethfull mones,

Shee for whose sake thou hat'st the joyfull light,
Court'st solitarie shades, and irkesome night,
Doth liue ? O ! if thou canst, through teares a space
Lift thy dimm'd lights, and looke vpon this face,
Looke if those eyes which, foole, thou didst adore,
Shine not more bright than they were wont before ;
Looke if those roses death could ought impaire,
Those roses to thee once which seem'd so faire ;
And if these lockes haue lost ought of that gold,
Which earst they had when thou them didst behold.
I liue, and happie liue, but thou art dead,
And still shalt bee, till thou be like mee made.
Alas ! whilst wee are wrapt in gownes of earth,
And blinde, heere sucke the aire of woe beneath,
Each thing in sense's ballances wee wie,
And but with toyle and paine the trueth descrie.
   Aboue this vaste and admirable frame,
This temple visible, which world wee name,
Within whose walles so many lamps doe burne,
So many arches opposite doe turne,
Where elementall brethren nurse their strife,
And by intestine warres maintaine their life,
There is a world, a world of perfect blisse,
Pure, immateriall, bright, more farre from this
Than that high circle, which the rest enspheares,
Is from this dull ignoble vale of teares ;
A world, where all is found, that heere is found,
But further discrepant than heauen and ground.
It hath an earth, as hath this world of your's,
With creatures peopled, stor'd with trees and flowrs ;
It hath a sea, like saphire girdle cast,
Which decketh of harmonious shores the waste ;

It hath pure fire, it hath delicious aire,
Moone, sunne, and starres, heauens wonderfully faire:
But there flowrs doe not fade, trees grow not olde,
The creatures doe not die through heat nor colde ;
Sea there not tossed is, nor aire made blacke,
Fire doth not nurse itselfe on others' wracke ;
There heauens bee not constrain'd about to range,
For this world hath no neede of any change ;
The minutes grow not houres, houres rise not dayes,
Dayes make no months but euer-blooming Mayes.
    Heere I remaine, and hitherward doe tend
All who their spanne of dayes in vertue spend :
What euer pleasure this low place containes,
It is a glance but of what high remaines.
Those who, perchance, thinke there can nothing bee
Without this wide expansion which they see,
And that nought else mounts starres' circumference,
For that nought else is subject to their sense,
Feele such a case, as one whom some abisme
Of the deepe ocean kept had all his time ;
Who borne and nourish'd there, can scarcely dreame
That ought can liue without that brinie streame,
Cannot beleeue that there be temples, towres,
Which goe beyond his caues and dampish bowres,
Or there bee other people, manners, lawes,
Than them hee finds within the roaring waues ;
That sweeter flowrs doe spring than grow on rockes,
Or beasts bee which excell the skalie flockes,
That other elements bee to bee found,
Than is the water, and this ball of ground.
But thinke that man from those abismes were brought,
And saw what curious nature here hath wrought,

Did see the meads, the tall and shadie woods,
The hilles did see, the clear and ambling floods,
The diuerse shapes of beasts which kinds foorth bring,
The feathred troupes, that flie and sweetly sing;
Did see the palaces, the cities faire,
The forme of humane life, the fire, the aire,
The brightnesse of the sunne that dimmes his sight,
The moone, the gastly splendors of the night:
What vncouth rapture would his minde surprise?
How would hee his late-deare resort despise?
How would hee muse how foolish hee had beene
To thinke nought bee, but what hee there had seene?
Why did wee get this high and vaste desire,
Vnto immortall things still to aspire?
Why doth our minde extend it beyond time,
And to that highest happinesse euen clime,
If wee be nought but what to sense wee seeme,
And dust, as most of worldlings vs esteeme?
Wee bee not made for earth, though here wee come,
More than the embryon for the mother's wombe;
It weepes to bee made free, and wee complaine
To leaue this loathsome iayle of care and paine.
  But thou who vulgare foot-steps dost not trace,
Learne to raise vp thy minde vnto this place,
And what earth-creeping mortalles most affect,
If not at all to scorne, yet to neglect:
O chase not shadowes vaine, which, when obtain'd,
Were better lost, than with such trauell gain'd.
Thinke that on earth which humanes greatnesse call,
Is but a glorious title to liue thrall;
That scepters, diadems, and chaires of state,
Not in themselues, but to small mindes are great;

How those who loftiest mount, doe hardest light,
And deepest falls bee from the highest hight;
How fame an eccho is, how all renowne
Like to a blasted rose, ere night falles downe;
And though it something were, thinke how this round
Is but a litle point, which doth it bound.
O leaue that loue which reacheth but to dust,
And in that loue eternall only trust,
And beautie, which, when once it is possest,
Can only fill the soule, and make it blest.
Pale enuie, jealous emulations, feares,
Sighs, plaints, remorse, here haue no place, nor teares,
False ioyes, vaine hopes, here bee not hate nor wrath;
What ends all loue, here most augments it, death.
If such force had the dimme glance of an eye,
Which some few dayes thereafter was to die,
That it could make thee leaue all other things,
And like the taper-flie there burne thy wings;
And if a voyce, of late which could but waile,
Such power had, as through eares thy soule to steale;
If once thou on that only faire couldst gaze,
What flames of loue would hee within thee raise?
In what a mazing maze would it thee bring,
To heare but once that quire celestiall sing?
The fairest shapes on which thy loue did sease,
Which earst did breede delight, then would displease,
Then discords hoarse were earth's entising sounds,
All musicke but a noyse which sense confounds.
This great and burning glasse that cleares all eyes,
And musters with such glorie in the skies,
That siluer starre which with its sober light
Makes day oft enuie the eye-pleasing night,

Those golden letters which so brightly shine
In heauen's great volume gorgeously diuine,
The wonders all in sea, in earth, in aire,
Bee but darke pictures of that soueraigne Faire ;
Bee tongues, which still thus crie into your eare,
Could yee amidst worlds' cataracts them heare,
From fading things, fond wights, lift your desire,
And in our beautie, his, vs made, admire :
If wee seeme faire, O thinke how faire is hee
Of whose faire fairnesse shadowes, steps, we bee.
No shadow can compare it with the face,
No step with that deare foot which did it trace ;
Your soules immortall are, then place them hence,
And doe not drowne them in the must of sense :
Doe not, O doe not, by false pleasures' might
Depriue them of that true and sole delight.
That happinesse yee seeke is not below,
Earth's sweetest ioy is but disguised woe.
    Heere did shee pause, and with a milde aspect
Did towards mee those lamping twinnes direct ;
The wonted rayes I knew, and thrice essay'd
To answere make, thrice faultring tongue it stay'd ;
And while vpon that face I fed my sight,
Mee thought shee vanish'd vp in Titan's light,
Who guilding with his rayes each hill and plaine,
Seem'd to have brought the gold-smith's world againe.

TO THE AUTHOR OF

TEARES ON THE DEATH OF

MŒLIADES.

In waues of woe thy sighes my soule doe tosse,
And doe burst vp the conduits of my teares,
Whose ranckling wound no smoothing baulme long beares,
But freshly bleedes when ought vpbraides my losse.
Then thou so sweetly sorrow makes to sing,
And troubled passions dost so well accord,
That more delight thine anguish doth afford,
Than others' ioyes can satisfaction bring.
What sacred wits, when rauish'd, doe affect,
To force affections, metamorphose mindes,
Whilst numbrous power the soule in secret bindes,
Thou hast perform'd, transforming in effect:
　For neuer plaints did greater pittie moue,
　The best applause that can such notes approue.

SIR W. ALEXANDER.

K

TEARES ON THE DEATH

OF MŒLIADES.

O HEAUENS ! then is it true that thou art gone,
And left this woefull ile her losse to mone,
Mœliades,* bright day starre of the west,
A comet, blazing terrour to the east ;
And neither that thy spright so heauenly wise,
Nor bodie, though of earth, more pure than skies,
Nor royall stemme, nor thy sweet tender age,
Of adamantine Fates could quench the rage ?
O fading hopes ! O short-while-lasting ioy
Of earth-borne man, which one houre can destroy !
Then euen of vertue's spoyles death trophees reares,
As if hee gloried most in many teares.
Forc'd by grimme Destines, Heauens neglect our cryes,
Starres seeme set only to acte tragœdies :
And let them doe their worst, since thou art gone,
Raise whom they list to thrones, enthron'd dethrone,
Staine princely bowres with blood, and euen to Gange,
In cypresse sad, glad Hymen's torches change.
Ah ! thou hast left to liue, and in the time
When scarce thou blossom'd in thy pleasant prime :
So falles by northerne blast a virgine rose,
At halfe that doth her bashfull bosome close ;

* The name which in these verses is giuen Prince Henrie, is that which he himself, in the challenges of his martial sports and mascarads, was wont to vse, MŒLIADES, PRINCE OF THE ISLES, which, in anagramme, maketh MILES A DEO.

So a sweet flourish languishing decayes,
That late did blush when kist by Phœbus' rayes ;
So Phœbus mounting the meridian's hight,
Choack'd by pale Phœbe, faints vnto our sight ;
Astonish'd nature sullen stands to see
The life of all this all so chang'd to bee ;
In gloomie gownes the starres about deplore,
The sea with murmuring mountaines beates the shore,
Blacke darknesse reeles or'e all, in thousand showres
The weeping aire on earth her sorrow powres,
That, in a palsey, quakes to finde so soone
Her louer set, and night burst foorth ere noone.
　　If heauen, alas ! ordain'd thee young to die,
Why was it not where thou thy might did'st trie,
And to the hopefull world at least set forth
Some little sparke of thine expected worth ?
Mœliades, O that by Ister's streames,
Amongst shrill-sounding trumpets, flaming gleames
Of warme encrimson'd swords, and cannons' roare,
Balls thicke as raine pour'd by the Caspian shore,
Amongst crush'd lances, ringing helmes, and shields,
Dismembred bodies rauishing the fields,
In Turkish blood made red like Marses starre,
Thou ended hadst thy life, and Christian warre ;
Or as braue Burbon thou hadst made old Rome,
Queene of the world, thy triumph's place and tombe !
So heauen's faire face, to the vnborne which reades,
A booke had beene of thine illustrous deedes ;
So to their nephewes aged syres had told
The high exploits perform'd by thee of old,
Townes raz'd, and rais'd, victorious, vanquish'd bands,
Fierce tyrants flying, foyl'd, kill'd by thy hands.

And in deare arras, virgines faire had wrought
The bayes and trophees to thy countrey brought;
While some new Homer, imping pennes to fame,
Deafe Nilus' dwellers had made heare thy name.
That thou didst not attaine those honours' spheares,
It was not want of worth, O no, but yeares.
A youth more braue pale Troy with trembling walles
Did neuer see, nor shee whose name apalles
Both Titan's golden bowres, for bloody fights
Mustring on Marses field such Marse-like knights.
The heauens had brought thee to the highest hight
Of wit, and courage, shewing all their might
When they thee fram'd: ay mee! that what is braue
On earth, they as their owne so soone should craue!
Mœliades sweet courtly nymphes deplore,
From Thuly to Hydaspes' pearlie shore.
    When Forth thy nurse, Forth where thou first didst passe
Thy tender dayes, (who smyl'd oft on her glasse
To see thee gaze,) meandring with her streames,
Heard thou hadst left this round, from Phœbus' beames
She sought to flie, but forced to returne
By neighbour brookes, shee gaue her selfe to mourne;
And as shee rush'd her Cyclades among,
Shee seem'd to plaine that heauen had done her wrong.
With a hoarse plaint, Cleyd down her steepie rockes,
And Tweed through her greene mountaines cled with flockes,
Did wound the ocean, murmuring thy death;
The ocean that roar'd about the earth,
And it to Mauritanian Atlas told,
Who shrunke through griefe, and downe his white haires roll'd
Hudge streames of teares, that changed were in floods,
With which hee drown'd the neighbour plaines and woods.

The lesser brookes, as they did bubbling goe,
Did keepe a consort vnto publike woe:
The shepheards left their flockes with downe-cast eyes,
Disdaining to looke vp to angrie skies;
Some broke their pipes, and some in sweet-sad layes
Made senslesse things amazed at thy praise.
His reed Alexis hung vpon a tree,
And with his teares made Doven great to bee.
Mœliades sweet courtly nymphes deplore,
From Thuly to Hydaspes' pearlie shore.

    Chaste maides which haunt faire Aganippe well,
And you in Tempe's sacred shade who dwell,
Let fall your harpes, cease tunes of ioy to sing,
Discheueled make all Parnassus ring
With antheames sad; thy musicke Phœbus turne
In dolefull plaints, whilst ioy it selfe doth mourne:
Dead is thy darling, who decor'd thy bayes,
Who oft was wont to cherish thy sweet layes,
And to a trumpet raise thine amorous stile,
That floting Delos enuie might this ile.
You Acidalian archers breake your bowes,
Your brandons quench, with teares blot beautie's snowes,
And bid your weeping mother yet againe
A second Adon's death, nay, Marses plaine.
His eyes once were your darts, nay, euen his name,
Where euer heard, did euery heart inflame:
Tagus did court his loue with golden streames,
Rhein with his townes, faire Seine with all shee claimes.
But ah! poore louers, death did them betrey,
And, not suspected, made their hopes his prey.
Tagus bewailes his losse with golden streames,
Rhein with his townes, faire Seine with all shee claimes.

Mœliades sweet courtly nymphes deplore,
From Thuly to Hydaspes' pearly shore.
  Delicious meads, whose checkred plaine foorth brings
White, golden, azure flowres, which once were kings,
In mourning blacke their shining colours dye,
Bow downe their heads, whilst sighing zephyres flye.
Queene of the fields, whose blush makes blushe the morne,
Sweet rose, a prince's death in purple mourne.
O hyacinthes, for ay your AI keepe still,
Nay, with moe markes of woe your leaues now fill;
And you, O flowre of Helen's teares first borne,
Into those liquide pearles againe you turne.
Your greene lockes, forrests, cut, in weeping myrrhes,
The deadly cypresse, and inke-dropping firres,
Your palmes and mirtles change; from shadowes darke
Wing'd syrens waile; and you, sad ecchoes, marke
The lamentable accents of their mone,
And plaine that braue Mœliades is gone.
Stay, skie, thy turning course, and now become
A stately arche, vnto the earth his tombe;
Ouer which ay the watrie Iris keepe,
And sad Electra's sisters which still weepe.
Mœliades sweet courtly nymphes deplore,
From Thuly to Hydaspes' pearlie shore.
  Deare ghost, forgiue these our vntimely teares,
By which our louing minde, though weake, appeares;
Our losse, not thine, when wee complaine, wee weepe;
For thee the glistring walles of heauen doe keepe
Beyond the planets' wheeles, aboue that source
Of spheares, that turnes the lower in its course,
Where sunne doth neuer set, nor vgly night
Euer appeares in mourning garments dight;

Where Boreas' stormie trumpet doth not sound,
Nor cloudes, in lightnings bursting, minds astound.
From care's cold climates farre, and hote desire,
Where time is banish'd, ages ne're expire;
Amongst pure sprights enuironed with beames,
Thou think'st all things below to bee but dreames,
And joy'st to looke downe to the azur'd barres
Of heauen, indented all with streaming starres;
And in their turning temples to behold,
In siluer robe the moone, the sunne in gold,
Like young eye-speaking louers in a dance,
With majestie by turnes retire, aduance.
Thou wondrest earth to see hang like a ball,
Clos'd in the gastly cloyster of this all;
And that poore men should proue so madly fond,
To tosse themselues for a small foot of ground,
Nay, that they euen dare braue the powers aboue,
From this base stage of change that cannot moue.
All worldly pompe and pride thou seest arise
Like smoake, that scattreth in the emptie skies.
Other hilles and forrests, other sumptuous towres,
Amaz'd thou find'st, excelling our poore bowres;
Courts voyde of flatterie, of malice mindes,
Pleasure which lasts, not such as reason blindes:
Farre sweeter songs thou hear'st and carrolings,
Whilst heauens doe dance, and quire of angells sings,
Than moldie mindes could faine: euen our annoy,
If it approach that place, is chang'd in ioy.
    Rest blessed spright, rest saciate with the sight
Of him whose beames both dazell and delight,
Life of all liues, cause of each other cause,
The spheare and center where the minde doth pause;

Narcissus of himselfe, himselfe the well,
Louer, and beautie, that doth all excell.
Rest, happie ghost, and wonder in that glasse
Where seene is all that shall be, is, or was,
While shall be, is, or was doe passe away,
And nought remaine but an eternall day :
For euer rest ; thy praise fame may enroule
In golden annalles, whilst about the pole
The slow Boötes turnes, or sunne doth rise
With skarlet scarfe, to cheare the mourning skies :
The virgines to thy tombe may garlands beare
Of flowres, and on each flowre let fall a teare.
Mœliades sweet courtly nymphes deplore,
From Thuly to Hydaspes' pearlie shore.

SONNET.

A passing glance, a lightning long the skies,
That, vsh'ring thunder, dies straight to our sight ;
A sparke, of contraries which doth arise,
Then drownes in the huge depthes of day and night ;
Is this small small call'd life, held in such price
Of blinded wights, who nothing judge aright ?
Of Parthian shaft so swift is not the flight
As life, that wastes it selfe, and liuing dies.
O ! what is humane greatnesse, valour, wit,
What fading beautie, riches, honour, praise ?
To what doth serue in golden thrones to sit,
Thrall earth's vaste round, triumphall arches raise ?
    All is a dreame, learne in this prince's fall,
    In whome, saue death, nought mortall was at all.

EPITAPH.

[FROM THE THIRD EDITION OF TEARES ON THE DEATH OF MŒLIADES,

EDINBVRG, M.DC.XIV.]

STAY, passenger, see where enclosed lyes
The paragon of princes, fairest frame
Time, nature, place, could show to mortal eyes,
In worth, wit, vertue, miracle to fame :
At lest that part the earth of him could clame
This marble holds, hard like the Destinies ;
For as to his braue spirit and glorious name,
The one the world, the other fills the skies.
Th' immortall amaranthus, princely rose,
Sad violet, and that sweet flowre that beares
In sangvine spots the tenor of our woes,
Spred on this stone, and wash it with thy teares :
    Then go and tell, from Gades vnto Inde,
    Thou saw where earth's perfections were confinde.

L

OF IET,

OR PORPHYRIE,

OR THAT WHITE STONE

PAROS AFFORDES ALONE,

OR THOSE IN AZURE DYE,

WHICH SEEME TO SCORNE THE SKIE;

HERE MEMPHIS' WONDERS DOE NOT SET,

NOR ARTEMISIA'S HUDGE FRAME,

THAT KEEPES SO LONG HER LOVER'S NAME:

MAKE NO GREAT MARBLE ATLAS TREMBLE WITH GOLD,

TO PLEASE A VULGARE EYE THAT DOTH BEHOLD:

THE MUSES, PHŒBUS, LOVE, HAUE RAISED OF THEIR TEARES

A CHRYSTALL TOMBE TO HIM, THROUGH WHICH HIS WORTH APPEARES.

VRANIA, OR SPIRITUALL POEMS.

TRIUMPHING chariots, statues, crownes of bayes,
Skie-threatning arches, the rewards of worth,
Workes heauenly wise in sweet harmonious layes,
Which sprights diuine vnto the world set forth ;
States, which ambitious mindes with blood doe raise,
From frozen Tanais to sunne-gilded Gange,
Giganticke frames, held wonders rarely strange,
Like spiders' webbes, are made the sport of dayes.
All only constant is in constant change,
What done is, is vndone, and when vndone,
Into some other fashion doth it range :
Thus goes the floting world beneath the moone,
 Where for, my minde, aboue time, motion, place,
 Thee raise, and steps vnknowne to nature trace.

Too long I follow'd haue my fond desire,
And too long painted on the ocean streames,
Too long refreshment sought amidst the fire,
And hunted ioyes, which to my soule were blames.
Ah ! when I had what most I did admire,
And seene of life's delights the last extreames,
I found all but a rose hedg'd with a bryer,
A nought, a thought, a show of mocking dreames.
Hencefoorth on thee mine only good I'll thinke,
For only thou canst grant what I doe craue ;
Thy naile my penne shall bee, thy blood mine inke,
Thy winding-sheet my paper, studie, graue.
 And till that soule forth of this bodie flie,
 No hope I'll haue but only onelie thee.

To spreade the azure canopie of heauen,
And make it twinckle all with spanges of gold,
To place this pondrous globe of earth so euen,
That it should all, and nought should it vphold ;
To giue strange motions to the planets seuen,
And Ioue to make so meeke, and Mars so bold ;
To temper what is moist, drie, hote, and cold,
Of all their iarres that sweet accords are giuen,
Lord, to thy wit is nought, nought to thy might :
But that thou shouldst, thy glorie laid aside,
Come basely in mortalitie to bide,
And die for them deseru'd eternall plight,
 A wonder is so farre aboue our wit,
 That angells stand amaz'd to thinke on it.

COME forth, come forth, yee blest triumphing bands,
Faire citizens of that immortall towne,
Come see that king, who all this all commands,
Now, ouercharg'd with loue, die for his owne :
Looke on those nailes which pierce his feete and hands,
What a strange diademe his browes doth crowne !
Beholde his pallide face, his eyes which sowne,
And what a throng of thieues him mocking stands :
Come forth, yee empyrean troupes, come forth,
Preserue this sacred blood, which earth adornes ;
Gather those liquide roses from his thornes,
O ! to bee lost they bee of too much worth ;
 For streames, iuice, baulme, they are, which quench; killes, charme
 Of God, death, hell, the wrath, the life, the harmes.

SOULE, which to hell wast thrall,
Hee, hee for thine offence
Did suffer death, who could not die at all :
O soueraigne excellence,
O life of all that liues,
Eternall bountie, which all goodnesse giues,
How could death mount so hie ?
No wit this point can reach ;
Faith onely doth vs teach,
For vs hee died, at all who could not die.

IF with such passing beautie, choise delights,
The architect of this great round did frame
This pallace visible, which world we name,
Yet sillie mansion but of mortall wights ;
How many wonders, what amazing lights,
Must that triumphing seate of glorie claime,
Which doth transcend all this great all's high hights,
Of whose bright sunne ours heere is but a beame ?
O blest abode ! O happie dwelling place,
Where visiblie th' Inuisible doth raigne !
Blest people, who doe see true beautie's face,
With whose darke shadowes hee but earth doth daigne,
    All ioy is but annoy, all concord strife,
    Match'd with your endlesse blisse and happie life.

LOUE which is heere a care,
That wit and will doth marre,
Vncertaine truce, and a most certaine warre,
A shrill tempestuous winde,
Which doth disturbe the minde,
And, like wilde waues, our dessignes all commoue ;
Among those sprights aboue
Which see their Maker's face,
It a contentment is, a quiet peace,
  A pleasure voide of griefe, a constant rest,
  Eternall ioy which nothing can molest.

WHAT haplesse hap had I now to bee borne
In these vnhappie times, and dying dayes,
Of this else-doating world, when good decayes,
Loue is quench'd forth, and vertue held a scorne ;
When such are onely priz'd, by wretched wayes
Who with a golden fleece them can adorne,
When auarice and lust are counted praise,
And noble mindes liue orphane-like forlorne ?
Why was not I into that golden age,
When gold yet was not knowne, and those blacke artes,
By which base mortalles vildely play their parts,
And staine with horride actes earth's stately stage ?
  Then to haue beene, heauen ! it had beene my blisse ;
  But blesse mee now, and take mee soone from this.

THRISE happie hee, who by some shadie groue,
Farre from the clamarous world doth liue his owne,
Though solitare, yet who is not alone,
But doth conuerse with that eternall loue.
O how more sweet is birds' harmonious mone,
Or the soft sobbings of the widow'd doue,
Than those smoothe whisp'rings neare a prince's throne,
Which good make doubtfull, doe the euill approue ?
O how more sweet is zephyre's wholesome breath,
And sighs perfum'd, which doe the flowres vnfold,
Than that applause vaine honour doth bequeath ?
How sweete are streames to poyson drunke in gold ?
 The world is full of horrours, falshoods, slights ;
 Woods' silent shades have only true delights.

WHY, worldlings, doe ye trust fraile honour's dreames,
And leane to guilded glories which decay ;
Why doe yee toyle to registrate your names
In ycie columnes, which soone melt away ?
True honour is not here ; that place it claimes,
Where blacke-brow'd night doth not exile the day,
Nor no farre-shining lampe diues in the sea,
But an eternall sunne spreades lasting beames.
There it attendeth you, where spotlesse bands
Of sprights stand gazing on their soueraigne blisse,
Where yeeres not hold it in their cankring hands,
But who once noble euer noble is :
 Looke home, lest he your weakned wit make thrall,
 Who Eden's foolish gard'ner earst made fall.

ASTREA in this time
Now doth not liue, but is fled vp to heauen;
Or if shee liue, it is not without crime
That shee doth vse her power,
And shee is no more virgine, but a whoure,
Whoure prostitute for gold :
For shee doth neuer holde her ballance euen,
And when her sword is roll'd,
    The bad, injurious, false shee not o'rethrowes,
    But on the innocent lets fall her blowes.

WHAT serues it to bee good ? Goodnesse, by thee
The holy-wise is thought a foole to bee;
For thee the man to temperance inclin'de,
Is held but of a base and abject minde ;
The continent is thought for thee but cold ;
Who yet was good, that euer died old ?
The pittifull who others feares to kill,
Is kill'd himselfe, and goodnesse doth him ill :
The meeke and humble man who cannot braue,
By thee is to some giant's brood made slaue.
Poore goodnesse, thine thou to such wrongs sett'st forth,
That O ! I feare mee, thou art nothing worth :
    And when I looke to earth, and not to heauen,
    Ere I were turned doue, I would bee rauen.

GREAT God, whom wee with humble thoughts adore,
Eternall, infinite, almightie king,
Whose pallace heauen transcends, whose throne before
Archangells serue, and seraphins doe sing;
Of nought who wrought all that with wondring eyes
Wee doe behold within this spacious round,
Who mak'st the rockes to rocke, and stand the skies,
At whose command the horride thunders sound;
Ah! spare vs wormes, weigh not how wee, alas!
Euill to our selues, against thy lawes rebell;
Wash off those spots, which still in conscience' glasse,
Though wee bee loth to looke, wee see too well;
Deseru'd reuenge O doe not, doe not take:
If thou reuenge, what shall abide thy blow?
Passe shall this world, this world which thou didst make,
Which should not perish till thy trumpet blow.
For who is hee whom parents' sinne not staines,
Or with his owne offence is not defil'd?
Though iustice ruine threaten, iustice' raines
Let mercie hold, and bee both just and milde.
Lesse are our faults farre farre than is thy loue;
O! what can better seeme thy pow'r diuine,
Than those who euill deserue thy goodnesse proue,
And where thou thunder shouldst there faire to shine?
Then looke, and pittie, pittying forgiue
Vs guiltie slaues, or seruants, at thy will;
Slaues, if, alas! thou look'st how wee doe liue,
Or doing nought at all, or doing ill,

M

Of an vngratefull minde a foule effect.
But if thy gifts, which largely heretofore
Thou hast vpon vs pow'rd, thou doest respect,
Wee bee thy seruants, nay, than seruants more,
Thy children, yes, and children dearly bought ;
But what strange chance vs of this lot bereaues ?
Vile rebells, O ! how basely are wee brought,
Whom grace made children, sinne hath now made slaues ;
Sinne slaues hath made, but let thy grace sinne thrall,
That in our wrongs thy mercie may appeare :
Thy wisdome not so weake is, pow'r so small,
But thousand wayes they can make men thee feare.
    O wisdome boundlesse ! admirable grace !
Grace, wisdome, which doe dazell reason's eye,
And could heauen's king bring from his placelesse place,
On this infamous stage of woe to die,
To die our death, and with the sacred streame
Of bloud and water gushing from his side,
To expiate that sinne and deadly blame,
Contriued first by our first parents' pride ?
Thus thy great loue and pittie, heauenly king,
Loue, pittie, which so well our losse preuents,
Could euen of euill it selfe all goodnesse bring,
And sad beginnings cheare with glad euents.
O loue and pittie ! ill knowne of these times,
O loue and pittie ! carefull of our blisse,
O goodnesse ! with the hainous actes and crimes
Of this blacke age that almost vanquish'd is,

Make this excessiue ardour of thy loue
So warme our coldnesse, so our liues renew,
That wee from sinne, sinne may from vs remoue,
Wit may our will, faith may our wit subdue.
Let thy pure loue burne vp all mortall lust,
That band of ills which thralles our better part,
And fondly makes vs worship fleshly dust,
In stead of thee, in temple of our heart.
    Grant, when at last the spright shall leaue this tombe,
This loathsome shop of sinne, and mansion blinde,
And call'd before thy royall seat doth come,
It may a sauiour, not a iudge, thee finde.

TO THE AUTHOR.

THE sister nymphes who haunt the Thespian springs,
Ne're did their gifts more liberally bequeath
To them who on their hills suck'd sacred breath,
Than vnto thee, by which thou sweetly sings.
Ne're did Apollo raise on Pegase' wings
A muse more neare himselfe, more farre from earth,
Than thine, if shee doe weepe thy ladie's death,
Or sing those sweet-sowre panges which passion brings.
To write our thoughts in verse doth merite praise,
But those our verse to gild in fiction's ore,
Bright, rich, delightfull, doth deserue much more,
As thou hast done these thy delicious layes:
   Thy muse's morning, doubtlesse, doth bewray
   The neare approach of a more glistring day.

D. MURRAY.

MADRIGALLS

AND EPIGRAMMES.

OF that Medvsa strange,
Who those that did her see in rockes did change,
None image caru'd is this ;
Medusa's selfe it is,
For whilst at heat of day,
To quench her thirst, shee by this spring did stay,
Her curling snakes beholding in this glasse,
Life did her leaue, and thus transform'd shee was.

THE TROJANE HORSE.

A HORSE I am, whom bit,
Raine, rod, nor spurre, not feare ;
When I my riders beare,
Within my wombe, not on my backe they sit :
No streames I drinke, nor care for grasse, nor corne ;
Arte mee a monster wrought,
All nature's workes to scorne :
A mother, I was without mother borne ;
In end all arm'd my father I forth brought :
What thousand ships, and champions of renowne
Could not doe free, I captiue raz'd a towne.

A LOUER'S HEAUEN.

THOSE starres, nay, sunnes, which turne
So stately in their spheares,
And daz'ling doe not burne;
The beautie of the morne
Which on those cheekes appeares,
The harmonie which to that voyce is giuen,
Make mee thinke yee are heauen :
If heauen yee bee, O that by pow'rfull charmes
I Atlas were, to holde you in mine armes !

DEEPE IMPRESSION OF LOUE.

WHOM raging dog doth bite,
Hee doth in water still
That Cerberus' image see :
Loue mad, perhaps, when he my heart did smite,
More to dissemble ill,
Transform'd himselfe in thee,
For euer since thou present art to mee :
No spring there is, no floud, nor other place,
Where I, alas ! not see thy heauenly face.

THE POURTRAIT OF MARS AND VENVS.

FAIRE Paphos' wanton queene,
Not drawne in white and red,
Is truely heere, as when in Vvlcan's bed
She was of all heauen's laughing senate seene.
Gaze on her haire and eine,
Her browes, the bowes of loue,
Her backe with lillies spred :
And yee should see her turne, and sweetly moue,
But that shee neither so will doe, nor darre,
For feare to wake the angrie god of warre.

IÖLAS' EPITAPH.

HERE deare Iölas lies,
Who whilst hee liu'd, in beautie did surpasse
That boy whose heauenly eyes
Brought Cypris from aboue,
Or him till death who look'd in watrie glasse,
Euen iudge the god of loue :
And if the nymphe once held of him so deare,
Dorine the faire, would heere but shed one teare,
Thou shouldst, in nature's scorne,
A purple flowre see of this marble borne.

VPON THE DEATH OF A LINNET.

IF cruell death had eares,
Or could bee pleas'd by songs,
This wing'd musician liu'd had many yeares,
And Chloris mine had neuer wept these wrongs :
For when it first tooke breath,
The heauens their notes did vnto it bequeath ;
And, if that Samian's sentence bee found true,
Amphion in this body liu'd of new :
But death, for that hee nothing spares, nought heares,
As hee doth kings, it kill'd, O griefe ! O teares !

ALCON'S KISSE.

WHAT others at their eare,
Two pearles Camilla at her nose did weare ;
Which Alcon, who nought saw,
(For loue is blinde,) robb'd with a prettie kisse ;
But hauing knowne his misse,
And felt what ore hee from that mine did draw,
When shee to charge againe him did desire,
Hee fled, and said, foule water quenched fire.

ICARVS.

Whilst with audacious wings
I sprang those airie wayes,
And fill'd, a monster new, with dread and feares,
The feathred people, and their eagle kings;
Dazel'd with Phœbus' rayes,
And charmed with the musicke of the spheares,
When pennes could moue no more, and force did faile,
I measur'd by a fall these loftie bounds :
Yet doth renowne my losses counteruaile,
For still the shore my braue attempt resounds,
A sea, an element doth beare my name;
Who hath so vaste a tombe in place or fame ?

CHERRIES.

My wanton, weepe no more
The losing of your cherries;
Those, and farre sweeter berries,
Your sister, in good store,
Hath spred on lips and face :
Be glad, kisse but with me, and hold your peace.

OF THAVMANTIA, BEHOLDING HER SELFE IN A MARBLE.

World, wonder not that I
Engraue thus in my brest
This angell face, which mee bereaues of rest;
Since things euen wanting sense cannot denie
To lodge so deare a guest,
And this hard marble stone
Receiues the same, and loues, but cannot grone.

LOUE SUFFERETH NO PARASOL.

THOSE eyes, deare eyes, bee spheares,
Where two bright sunnes are roll'd ;
That faire hand to behold,
Of whitest snowe appeares :
Then while yee coylie stand,
To hide from mee those eyes,
Sweet, I would you aduise
To choose some other fanne than that white hand ;
For if yee doe, for trueth most true this know,
That sunnes ere long must needes consume warme snow.

SLEEPING BEAUTIE.

O SIGHT too dearely bought !
Shee sleepes, and though those eyes,
Which lighten Cupid's skies,
Bee clos'd, yet such a grace
Enuironeth that place,
That I through wonder to grow faint am brought :
Sunnes, if ecclips'd yee haue such power diuine,
O ! how can I endure you when yee shine ?

THE QUALITIE OF A KISSE.

THE kisse with so much strife
Which I late got, sweet heart,
Was it a signe of death, or was it life ?
Of life it could not bee,
For I by it did sigh my soule in thee ;
Nor was it death, death doth no ioy impart.
Thou silent stand'st, ah ! what thou didst bequeath,
To mee a dying life was, liuing death.

N

OF PHILLIS.

In peticote of greene,
Her haire about her eine,
Phillis beneath an oake
Sate milking her faire flocke :
Among that strained moysture, rare delight !
Her hand seem'd milke in milke, it was so white.

KISSES DESIRED.

Though I with strange desire
To kisse those rosie lips am set on fire,
Yet will I cease to craue
Sweet touches in such store,
As hee who long before
From Lesbia them in thousands did receaue.
Heart mine, but once mee kisse,
And I by that sweet blisse
Euen sweare to cease you to importune more :
Poore one no number is ;
Another word of mee yee shall not heare
After one kisse, but still one kisse, my deare.

OF DAMETAS.

Dametas dream'd he saw his wife at sport,
And found that sight was through the hornie port.

THE CANON.

When first the canon from her gaping throte,
Against the heauen her roaring sulphure shote,
Ioue wak'ned with the noyce, and ask'd with wonder,
What mortall wight had stollen from him his thunder :
His christall towres hee fear'd ; but fire and aire
So deepe did stay the ball from mounting there.

APELLES ENAMOUR'D OF CAMPASPE, ALEXANDER'S MISTRESSE.

POORE painter, whilst I sought
To counterfaite by arte
The fairest frame that nature euer wrought,
And hauing limm'd each part,
Except her matchlesse eyes,
Scarce on those twinnes I gaz'd,
As lightning falles from skies,
When straight my hand benumm'd was, mind amaz'd;
And ere that pincell halfe them had exprest,
Loue all had drawne, no, grauen within my brest.

CAMPASPE.

ON starres shall I exclame,
Which thus my fortune change ?
Or shall I else reuenge
Vpon my selfe this shame,
Vnconstant monarch, or shall I thee blame,
Who let'st Apelles proue
The sweet delights of Alexander's loue ?
No, starres, my selfe, and thee, I all forgiue,
And joye that thus I liue:
Kings know not beautie, hence mine was despis'd ;
The painter did, and mee hee dearly priz'd.

VNPLEASANT MUSICKE.

IN fields Ribaldo stray'd
Maye's tapestrie to see,
And hearing on a tree
A cuckooe sing, hee sigh'd, and softly said,
Loe how, alas ! euen birds sit mocking mee.

A IEST.

IN a most holy church a holy man
Vnto a holy saint, with visage wan,
And eyes like fountaines, mumbled forth a prayer,
And with strange words and sighes made blacke the air
And hauing long so stay'd, and long long pray'd,
A thousand crosses on himselfe hee lay'd,
Then with some sacred beads hung on his arme,
His eyes, his mouth, brest, temples did hee charme.
Thus not content, (strange worship hath none end,)
To kisse the earth at last hee did pretend,
And bowing downe, besought with humble grace
An aged woman neare to giue some place :
　　Shee turn'd, and turning vp her pole beneath,
　　Said, sir, kisse heere, for it is all but earth.

NARCISSVS.

FLOUDS cannot quench my flames ; ah ! in this well
I burne, not drowne, for what I cannot tell.

TO THAVMANTIA SINGING.

Is it not too too much
Thou late didst to mee proue
A basiliske of loue,
And didst my wits bewitch ;
Vnlesse, to cause more harme,
Made Syrene too, thou with thy voyce mee charme ?
Ah ! though thou so my reason didst controule,
That to thy lookes I could not proue a mole,
Yet doe mee not that wrong,
As not to let mee turne aspe to thy song.

OF HER DOG.

WHEN her deare bosome clips
That litle curre, which faunes to touch her lips,
Or when it is his hap
To lie lapp'd in her lap,
O! it growes noone with mee ;
With hotter-pointed beames
My burning planet streames,
What rayes were earst, in lightnings changed bee.
When oft I muse, how I to those extreames
Am brought, I finde no cause, except that shee
In loue's bright zodiacke hauing trac'd each roome,
To fatall Syrius now at last is come.

A KISSE.

HARKE, happie louers, harke,
This first and last of ioyes,
This sweetner of annoyes,
This nectare of the gods
Yee call a kisse, is with it selfe at ods ;
And halfe so sweet is not
In equall measure got
At light of sunne, as it is in the darke :
Harke, happie louers, harke.

CORNUCOPIA.

IF for one only horne
Which nature to him gaue,
So famous is the noble vnicorne,
What praise should that man haue,
Whose head a ladie braue
Doth with a goodlie paire at once adorne ?

OF AMINTAS.

Over a christall source
Amintas layde his face,
Of popling streames to see the restlesse course,
But scarce hee had o'reshadowed the place.
When (spying in the ground a childe arise,
Like to himselfe in stature, face, and eyes)
Hee rose o'rejoy'd, and cried,
Deare mates, approch, see whom I haue descried ;
The boy of whom strange stories shepheards tell,
Oft-called Hylas, dwelleth in this well.

PAMPHILVS.

Some ladies wed, some loue, and some adore them,
I like their wanton sport, then care not for them.

VPON A GLASSE.

If thou wouldst see threedes purer than the gold,
Where loue his wealth doth show,
But take this glasse, and thy faire haire behold :
If whitenesse thou wouldst see more white than snow,
And reade on wonder's booke,
Take but this glasse, and on thy forehead looke.
Wouldst thou in winter see a crimsin rose,
Whose thornes doe hurt each heart,
Looke but in glasse how thy sweet lips doe close :
Wouldst thou see planets which all good impart,
Or meteores diuine,
But take this glasse, and gaze vpon thine eine :
No, planets, rose, snow, gold, cannot compare
With you, deare eyes, lips, browes, and amber haire.

OF A BEE.

As an audacious knight,
Come with some foe to fight,
His sword doth brandish, makes his armour ring,
So this prowde bee, at home perhaps a king,
Did buzzing flie about,
And, tyrant, after thy faire lip did sting:
O champion strange as stout!
Who hast by nature found
Sharpe armes, and trumpet shrill, to sound, and wound.

OF THAT SAME.

O! DOE not kill that bee
That thus hath wounded thee;
Sweet, it was no despight,
But hue did him deceaue,
For when thy lips did close,
Hee deemed them a rose:
What wouldst thou further craue?
Hee wanting wit, and blinded with delight,
Would faine haue kiss'd, but mad with ioy did bite.

OF A KISSE.

AH! of that cruell bee
Thy lips haue suckt too much,
For when they mine did touch,
I found that both they hurt, and sweetned mee:
This by the sting they haue,
And that they of the honey doe receaue;
Deare kisse, else by what arte
Couldst thou at once both please and wound my heart?

IDMON TO VENVS.

IF, Acidalia's queene,
Thou quench in mee thy torch,
And with the same Thaumantia's heart shalt scorch,
Each yeere a mirtle tree
Heere I doe vow to consecrate to thee;
And when the meads grow greene,
I will of sweetest flowrs
Weaue thousand garlands to adorne thy bowrs.

A LOUER'S PLAINT.

IN midst of silent night,
When men, birds, beasts, doe rest,
With loue and feare possest,
To heauen and Flore I count my heauie plight.
Againe with roseate wings
When morne peepes forth, and Philomela sings,
Then voyde of all reliefe,
Doe I renew my griefe :
Day followes night, night day, whilst still I proue
That heauen is deafe, Flore carelesse of my loue.

HIS FIREBRAND.

LEAUE, page, that slender torch,
And in this gloomie night
Let only shine the light
Of loue's hote brandon, which my heart doth scorch :
A sigh, or blast of wind,
My teares, or droppes of raine,
May that at once make blinde,
Whilst this, like Ætna, burning shall remaine.

DAPHNIS' VOW.

WHEN sunne doth bring the day
From the Hesperian sea,
Or moone her coach doth rolle
Aboue the northerne pole,
When serpents can not hisse,
And louers shall not kisse;
Then may it be, but in no time till then,
That Daphnis can forget his Orienne.

OF NISA.

NISA Palemon's wife him weeping told,
Hee kept not grammer rules, now beeing old:
For why, quoth shee, position false make yee,
Putting a short thing where a long should bee?

BEAUTIE'S IDEA.

WHO would perfection's faire idea see,
Let him come looke on Chloris sweet with mee:
White is her haire, her teeth white, white her skinne,
Blacke bee her eyes, her eye-browes Cupid's inne;
Her lockes, her body, hands doe long appeare,
But teeth short, bellie short, short either eare;
The space twixt shoulders, eyes, is wide, browes wide,
Straite waste, the mouth straite, and her virgine pride;
Thicke are her lips, thighs, with banckes swelling there,
Her nose is small, small fingers; and her haire,
Her sugred mouth, her cheekes, her nailes bee red;
Litle her foot, pap litle, and her hed.
 Such Venus was, such was the flame of Troy,
 Such Chloris is, my hope, and only ioy.

o

CRATON'S DEATH.

AMIDST the waues profound,
Farre farre from all reliefe,
The honest fisher, Craton, ah! is drownd
Into his litle skife ;
The boords of which did serue him for a beare,
So that to the blacke world when hee came neare,
Of him no waftage greedie Charon got,
For hee in his owne boat
Did passe that floud by which the gods doe sweare.

ARMELIN'S EPITAPH.

NEARE to this eglantine
Enclosed lies the milke-white Armeline,
Once Chloris' onlie ioye,
Now onlie her annoy,
Who enuied was of the most happie swaines,
That keepe their flocks in mountaines, dales, or plaines ;
For oft shee bare the wanton in her arme,
And oft her bed and bosome did he warme :
Now when vnkindlie Fates did him destroy,
Blest dog, he had the grace,
With teares for him that Chloris wet her face.

THE STATUE OF VENVS SLEEPING.

BREAKE not my sweet repose,
Thou, whom free will or chance brings to this place ;
Let lids these comets close,
O doe not seeke to see their shining grace ;
For when mine eyes thou seest, they thine will blinde,
And thou shalt parte, but leaue thy heart behinde.

LILLA'S PRAYER.

Loue, if thou wilt once more
That I to thee returne,
Sweete God, make me not burne
For quiuering age that doth spent dayes deplore;
Nor doe not wound my hart
For some vnconstant boy,
Who ioyes to loue, yet makes of loue a toy:
But, ah! if I must prooue thy golden dart,
Of grace, O let mee finde
A sweet young louer with an aged mind.
Thus Lilla pray'd, and Idas did replie
Who heard, Deare, haue thy wish, for such am I.

THE VNKINDESSE OF RORA.

Whilst sighing forth his wrongs,
In sweet, though dolefull songs,
Alexis seekes to charme his Rora's eares,
The hills are heard to mone,
To sigh each spring appeares;
Trees, euen hard trees, through rine distill their teares,
And soft growes euery stone,
But teares, sighes, songs can not faire Rora moue;
Prowde of his plaints, shee glories in his loue.

ANTHEA'S GIFT.

This virgine locke of haire
To Idmon Anthea giues,
Idmon for whom shee liues,
Though oft shee mixe his hopes with cold despaire:
This now, but absent if hee constant proue,
With gift more deare shee vowes to meet his loue.

TO THAVMANTIA.

COME, let vs liue, and loue,
And kisse, Thaumantia mine ;
I shall the elme bee, bee to mee the vine,
Come let vs teach new billing to the doue ;
Nay, to augment our blisse,
Let soules euen other kisse ;
Let loue a worke-man bee,
Vndoe, distemper, and his cunning proue,
Of kisses three make one, of one make three :
Though moone, sunne, starres bee bodies farre more bright,
Let them not vaunt they match vs in delight.

EPITAPH.

THIS deare, though not respected earth doth hold
One, for his worth, whose tombe should bee of gold.

OF LIDA.

SVCH Lida is, that who her sees,
Through enuie, or through loue, straight dies.

A WISH.

To forge to mightie Ioue
The thunder-bolts aboue,
Nor on this round below
Rich Midas' skill to know,
And make all gold I touch,
I doe not craue, nor other cunning such :
For all those artes bee vnderneath the skie,
I wish but Phillis' lapidare to bee.

A LOUER'S DAY AND NIGHT.

BRIGHT meteore of day,
For mee in Thetis' bowres for euer staye :
Night, to this flowrie globe
Ne're show for mee thy starre-embrodred robe ;
My night, my day doe not proceede from you,
But hang on Mira's browe ;
For when shee lowres, and hides from mee her eyes,
Midst clearest day I finde blacke night arise,
When, smyling, shee againe those twinnes doth turne,
In midst of night I finde noone's torch to burne.

THE STATUE OF ADONIS.

WHEN Venus longst that plaine
This Parian Adon saw,
Shee sigh'd, and said, What power breakes Destine's law,
World-mourned boy, and makes thee liue againe ?
Then with stretcht armes shee ran him to enfold ;
But when shee did behold
The bore whose snowie tuskes did threaten death,
Feare closed vp her breath :
Who can but grant then that these stones doe liue,
Sith this bred loue, and that a wound did giue ?

CLORVS TO A GROUE.

OLD oake, and you thicke groue,
I euer shall you loue,
With these sweet-smelling briers ;
For, briers, oake, groue, yee crowned my desires,
When vnderneath your shade
I left my woe, and Flore her maidenhead.

A COUPLET ENCOMIASTICKE.

L$\overset{1}{\text{O}}$UE, Cy$\overset{2}{\text{p}}$ris, Ph$\overset{3}{\text{œ}}$bus, will f$\overset{1}{\text{e}}$ede, d$\overset{2}{\text{e}}$cke, and cr$\overset{3}{\text{o}}$wne
Thy h$\overset{1}{\text{e}}$art, br$\overset{2}{\text{o}}$wes, v$\overset{3}{\text{e}}$rse, with fl$\overset{1}{\text{a}}$mes, with fl$\overset{2}{\text{o}}$wrs, ren$\overset{3}{\text{o}}$wne.

AN OTHER.

THY muse not-able, full, il-lustred rimes,
Make thee the poet⌄aster of our times.

THE ROSE.

FLOWRE, which of Adon's blood
Sprang, when of that cleare flood
Which Venus wept an other white was borne,
The sweet Cynarean youth thou right dost show:
But this sharpe-pointed thorne,
Which doth so prowde about thy crimsin grow,
What doth it represent?
Boare's tuskes, perhaps, his snowie flancke which rent:
O show of showes! of vnesteemed worth,
Which both what kill'd, and what was kill'd sett'st forth.

TO A RIUER.

SITH shee will not that I
Show to the world my ioy,
Thou who oft mine annoy
Hast heard, deare flood, tell Thetis' nymphettes bright,
That not a happier wight
Doth breath beneath the skie;
More sweet, more white, more faire,
Lips, hands, and amber haire,
Tell none did euer touch;
A smaller, daintier waste,
Tell neuer was embrac't:
But peace, sith shee forbids thou tell'st too much.

THAÏS' METAMORPHOSE.

In Briareus hudge
Thaïs wish'd shee might change
Her man, and pray'd him herefore not to grudge,
Nor fondly thinke it strange :
For if, said shee, I might the parts dispose,
I wish you not an hundreth armes nor hands,
But hundreth things like those
With which Priapus in our garden stands.

VPON A BAYE TREE, NOT LONG SINCE GROWING IN THE RUINES OF VIRGIL'S TOMBE.

Those stones which once had trust
Of Maro's sacred dust,
Which now of their first beautie spoylde are seene,
That they due praise not want,
Inglorious and remaine,
A Delian tree, faire nature's only plant,
Now courtes, and shadowes with her tresses greene :
Sing Iö Pæan, yee of Phœbus' traine,
Though enuie, auarice, time your tombes throw downe,
With maiden lawrells nature will them crowne.

EPITAPH.

Then death thee hath beguild,
Alecto's first borne child ;
Thou who didst thrall all lawes,
Then against wormes canst not maintaine thy cause ;
Yet wormes, more iust than thou, now doe no wrong,
Sith all doe wonder they thee spar'd so long,
For though from life but lately thou didst passe,
Ten springs are gone since thou corrupted was.

FLORA'S FLOWRE.

VENUS doth loue the rose ;
Apollo those deare flowrs
Which were his paramours ;
The queene of sable skies
The subtile lunaries ;
But Flore likes none of those,
For faire to her no flowre seemes saue the lillie :
And why ? because one letter turnes it P.

MELAMPVS' EPITAPH.

ALL that a dog could haue,
The good Melampus had ;
Nay, hee had more than what in beasts wee craue,
For hee could playe the braue,
And often like a Thraso sterne goe mad ;
And if yee had not seene, but heard him barke,
Yee would haue sworne hee was your parish clarke.

KALA'S COMPLAINT.

KALA, old Mopsus' wife,
Kala with fairest face,
For whom the neighbour swaines oft were at strife,
As shee to milke her milke-white flocke did tend,
Sigh'd with a heauie grace,
And said, what wretch like mee doth leade her life ?
I see not how my taske can haue an end ;
All day I draw these streaming dugs in fold,
All night mine emptie husband's soft and cold.

THE HAPPINESSE OF A FLEA.

How happier is that flea
Which in thy brest doth playe,
Than that pied butterflie
Which courtes the flame, and in the same doth die ?
That hath a light delight,
Poore foole, contented only with a sight,
When this doth sporte, and swell with dearest food,
And if hee die, hee knight-like dies in blood.

OF THAT SAME.

Poore flea, then thou didst die,
Yet by so faire a hand,
That thus to die was Destine to command :
Thou die didst, yet didst trie
A louer's last delight,
To vault on virgine plaines, her kisse, and bite :
Thou diedst, yet hast thy tombe
Between those pappes, O deare and stately roome !
Flea, happier farre, more blest
Than Phœnix burning in his spicie nest.

LINA'S VIRGINITIE.

Who Lina weddeth, shall most happie bee,
For hee a maide shall finde,
Though maiden none bee shee,
A girle, or boy, beneath her waste confinde ;
And though bright Ceres' lockes bee neuer shorne,
Hee shall be sure this yeere to lacke no corne.

P

LOVE NAKED.

AND would yee, louers, know
Why Loue doth naked goe ?
Fond, waggish, changeling lad,
Late whilst Thaumantia's voyce
Hee wondring heard, it made him so rejoyce,
That hee o'rejoy'd ran mad,
And in a franticke fit threw cloathes away,
And since from lip and lap hers can not straye.

NIOBE.

WRETCHED Niobe I am,
Let wretches reade my case,
Not such who with a teare ne're wet their face.
Seuen daughters of mee came,
And sonnes as many, which one fatall day
(Orb'd mother !) tooke away :
Thus reft by heauens vnjust,
Griefe turn'd mee stone, stone too mee doth entombe,
Which if thou dost mistrust,
Of this hard rocke but ope the flintie wombe,
And heere thou shalt finde marble, and no dust.

CHANGE OF LOUE.

ONCE did I weepe, and grone,
Drinke teares, draw loathed breath,
And all for loue of one
Who did affect my death :
But now, thankes to disdaine,
I liue relieu'd of paine ;
For sighs, I singing goe,
I burne not as before, no, no, no, no.

WILDE BEAUTIE.

If all but yce thou bee,
How dost thou thus mee burne,
Or how at fire which thou dost raise in mee,
Sith yce, thy selfe in streames dost thou not turne,
But rather, plaintfull case !
Of yce art marble made to my disgrace ?
O miracle of loue, not heard till now !
Cold yce doth burne, and hard by fire doth grow.

CONSTANT LOUE.

Time makes great states decay,
Time doth Maye's pompe disgrace,
Time drawes deepe furrowes in the fairest face,
Time wisdome, force, renowne doth take away,
Time doth consume the yeeres,
Time changes workes in heauen's eternall spheares :
Yet this fierce tyrant, which doth all deuoure,
To lessen loue in mee shall haue no power.

TO CHLORIS.

See, Chloris, how the cloudes
Tilte in the azure lists,
And how with Stygian mists
Each horned hill his giant forehead shroudes ;
Ioue thundreth in the aire,
The aire, growne great with raine,
Now seemes to bring Deucalion's dayes againe :
I see thee quake ; come, let vs home repaire,
Come hide thee in mine armes,
If not for loue, yet to shunne greater harmes.

VPON A POVRTRAIT.

THE goddesse that in Amathus doth raigne,
With siluer tramells, and saphire-colour'd eyes,
When naked from her mother's christall plaine
She first appear'd vnto the wondring skies,
Or when, the golden apple to obtaine,
Her blushing snowes amazed Ida's trees,
Did neuer looke in halfe so faire a guise
As shee heere drawne, all other ages staine.
O God, what beauties to inflame the soule,
And hold the wildest hearts in chaines of gold !
Faire lockes, sweet face, loue's stately capitole,
Deare necke, which dost that heauenly frame vp-hold :
　　If vertue would to mortall eyes appeare
　　To rauish sense, shee would your beautie weare.

VPON THAT SAME.

IF heauen, the starres, and nature did her grace
With all perfections found the moone aboue,
And what excelleth in this lower place
Did place in her, to breede a world of loue ;
If angells' gleames shine on her fairest face,
Which make heauen's ioy on earth the gazer proue,
And her bright eyes, the orbs which beautie moue,
Doe glance like Phœbus in his glorious race,
What pincell paint, what colour to the sight
So sweet a shape can show ? The blushing morne
The red must lend, the milkie-way the white,
And night the starres which her rich crowne adorne,
　　To draw her right : but then that all agree,
　　The heauen, the table, Zeuxis Ioue must bee.

VPON THAT SAME, DRAWNE WITH A PANSIE.

WHEN with braue arte the curious painter drew
This heauenly shape, the hand why made hee beare
With golden veines that flowre of purple hue,
Which followes on the planet of the yeare ?
Was it to show how in our hemispheare
Like him shee shines ; nay, that effects more true
Of power, and wonder, doe in her appeare,
Whilst hee but flowres, shee doth braue minds subdue ?
Or would hee else to vertue's glorious light
Her constant course make knowne ; or is it hee
Doth paralell her blisse with Clytia's plight ?
Right so ; and thus, hee reading in her eye
    Some woefull louer's end, to grace his graue,
    For cypresse tree this mourning flowre her gaue.

VPON THAT SAME.

IF sight bee not beguilde,
And eyes right playe their part,
This flowre is not of arte,
But is faire nature's child :
And though when Phœbus from vs is exilde,
Shee doth not locke her leaues, his losse to mone,
No wonder earth hath now moe sunnes than one.

THIRSIS IN DISPRAISE OF BEAUTIE.

THAT which so much the doating world doth prise,
Fond ladies' only care and sole delight,
Soone-fading beautie, which of hues doth rise,
Is but an abject let of nature's might:
Most woefull wretch, whom shining haire and eyes
Leade to loue's dungeon, traitor'd by a sight
　　Most woefull; for hee might with greater ease
　　Hell's portalls enter, and pale death appease.

As in delicious meads beneath the flowres,
And the most wholsome herbes that May can show,
In christall curles the speckled serpent lowres;
As in the apple, which most faire doth grow,
The rotten worme is clos'd, which it deuoures;
As in gilt cups with Gnossian wine which flow,
Oft poyson pompously doth hide its sowres;
　　So lewdnesse, falshood, mischiefe them aduance,
　　Clad with the pleasant rayes of beautie's glance.

Good thence is chas'd, where beautie doth appeare,
Milde lowlinesse with pittie from it flie;
Where beautie raignes as in their proper spheare,
Ingratitude, disdaine, pride, all descrie
The flowre and fruit which vertue's tree should beare,
With her bad shadowe beautie maketh die:
　　Beautie a monster is, a monster hurld
　　From angrie heauen, to scourge this lower world.

As fruits which are vnripe, and sowre of taste,
To bee confect'd more fit than sweet wee proue,
For sweet in spight of care themselues will waste,
When they, long kept, the appetite doe moue;

So in the sweetnesse of his nectare, loue
The foule confects, and seasons for his feaste :
   Sowre is farre better which wee sweet may make,
   Than sweet which sweeter sweetnesse will not take.

Foule may my ladie bee, and may her nose,
A Tanarife, giue vmbrage to her chinne ;
May her gay mouth, which shee no time may close,
So wide be, that the moone may turne therein ;
May eyes and teeth bee made conforme to those,
Eyes set by chance, and white, teeth blacke and thinne :
   May all what seene is, and is hidde from sight,
   Like vnto these rare parts bee framed right.

I shall not feare thus though shee straye alone,
That others her pursue, entice, admire,
And though shee sometime counterfaite a grone,
I shall not thinke her heart feeles vncouth fire,
I shall not stile her ruethlesse to my mone,
Nor prowde, disdainfull, wayward to desire :
   Her thoughts with mine will hold an equall line,
   I shall bee hers, and shee shall all bee mine.

EVRYMEDON'S PRAISE OF MIRA.

GEMME of the mountaines, glorie of our plaines,
Rare miracle of nature and of loue,
Sweet Atlas, who all beautie's heauens sustaines,
No, beautie's heauen, where all her wonders moue,
   The sunne from east to west who all doth see,
   On this low globe sees nothing like to thee.

One Phœnix only liu'd ere thou wast borne,
And earth but did one queene of loue admire,

Three Graces only did the world adorne,
But thrise three Muses sung to Phœbus' lyre:
    Two Phœnixes bee now, loue's queenes are two,
    Foure Graces, Muses ten, all made by you.

For those perfections which the bounteous heauen
To diuerse worlds in diuerse times assign'd,
With thousands more to thee at once were giuen,
Thy body faire, more faire they made thy mind;
    And that thy like no age should more behold,
    When thou wast fram'd they after brake the mold.

Sweet are the blushes on thy face which shine,
Sweet are the flames which sparkle from thine eyes,
Sweet are his torments who for thee doth pine,
Most sweet his death, for thee who sweetly dies,
    For if hee die, hee dies not by annoy,
    But too much sweetnesse and abundant ioy.

What are my slender layes to show thy worth?
How can base words a thing so high make knowne?
So wooden globes bright starres to vs set forth;
So in a christall is sunne's beautie showne:
    More of thy praises if my muse should write,
    More loue and pittie must the same indite.

THAVMANTIA AT THE DEPARTURE OF IDMON.

    FAIRE Diane, from the hight
Of heauen's first orbe who chear'st this lower place,
Hide now from mee thy light,
And pittying my case,
Spread with a skarfe of clouds thy blushing face.

Come with your dolefull songs,
Night's sable birds, which plaine when others sleepe,
Come, solemnize my wrongs,
And consort to mee keepe,
Sith heauen, earth, hell, are set to cause mee weepe.

This griefe yet I could beare,
If now by absence I were only pinde,
But, ah ! worse euill I feare,
Men absent proue vnkinde,
And change, vnconstant like the moone, their minde.

If thought had so much power
Of thy departure, that it could mee slaye,
How will that vgly houre
My feeble sense dismaye,
Farewell, sweet heart, when I shall heare thee say ?

Deare life, sith thou must goe,
Take all my ioy and comfort hence with thee,
And leaue with mee thy woe,
Which vntill I thee see,
Nor time, nor place, nor change shall take from mee.

ERYCINE AT THE DEPARTURE OF ALEXIS.

AND wilt thou then, Alexis mine, depart,
And leaue these flowrie meads, and christall streames,
These hills as greene as great with gold and gemmes,
Which courte thee with rich treasure in each part ?
Shall nothing hold thee, not my loyall heart,
That burstes to lose the comfort of thy beames,
Nor yet this pipe which wildest Satyres tames,

Q

Nor lambkins' wayling, nor old Dorus' smart ?
O ruethlesse shepheard, forrests strange among
What canst thou else but fearfull dangers finde ?
But, ah ! not thou, but honour doth mee wrong ;
O cruell honour, tyrant of the mind !
    This said sad Erycine, and all the flowres
    Empearled, as shee went, with eyes' salt showres.

ALEXIS TO DAMON.

THE loue Alexis did to Damon beare,
Shall witness'd bee to all the woods and plaines
As singulare, renown'd by neighbouring swaines,
That to our relicts time may trophees reare :
Those madrigals wee sung amidst our flockes,
With garlands guarded from Apollo's beames,
On Ochells whiles, whiles neare Bodotria's streames,
Are registrate by ecchoes in the rockes.
Of forraine shepheards bent to trie the states,
Though I, world's guest, a vagabond doe straye,
Thou mayst that store which I esteeme suruaye,
As best acquainted with my soule's conceits :
    What euer fate heauens haue for mee design'd,
    I trust thee with the treasure of my mind.

FORTH FEASTING.

REPRINTED

FROM THE EDITION OF

M.DC.XVII.

FORTH

FEASTING.

A

PANEGYRICKE

TO THE KINGS

MOST EXCELLENT

MAJESTIE.

Flumina ſenſerunt ipſa.

EDINBVRGH,
Printed by ANDRO HART, 1617.

TO HIS SACRED MAJESTIE.

[From the Muses Welcome to King James.

EDINBURGH, M.DC.XVIII.]

If in this storme of joy, and pompous throng,
This nymphe, great King, come euer thee so neare
That thy harmonious eares her accents heare,
Giue pardon to her hoarse and lowly song :
Faine would shee trophees to thy vertues reare,
But for this statlie task shee is not strong,
And her defects her high attempts doe wrong,
Yet as shee could shee makes thy worth appeare.
So in a mappe is showen this flowrie place,
So wrought in arras by a virgine's hand,
With heauen and blazing starres doth Atlas stand,
So drawen by chare-coale is Narcissus' face.
   Shee maye Aurora be to some bright sunne,
   Which maye perfect the day by her begunne.

FORTH FEASTING.

WHAT blustring noise now interrupts my sleepe,
What echoing shouts thus cleaue my chrystal deep,
And call mee hence from out my watrie court?
What melodie, what sounds of ioye and sport,
Bee these heere hurl'd from eu'rie neighbour spring?
With what lowd rumours doe the mountaines ring,
Which in vnusuall pompe on tip-toes stand,
And, full of wonder, ouer-looke the land?
Whence come these glittring throngs, these meteors bright,
This golden people set vnto my sight?
Whence doth this praise, applause, and loue arise?
What load-starre east-ward draweth thus all eyes?
And doe I wake, or haue some dreames conspir'd
To mocke my sense with shadowes much desir'd?
Stare I that liuing face, see I those lookes,
Which with delight wont to amaze my brookes?
Doe I beholde that worth, that man diuine,
This age's glorie, by these bankes of mine?
Then is it true, what long I wish'd in vaine,
That my much-louing prince is come againe?

So vnto them whose zenith is the pole,
When sixe blacke months are past, the sunne doth rolle :
So after tempest to sea-tossed wights
Faire Helen's brothers show their chearing lights :
So comes Arabia's meruaile from her woods,
And farre farre off is seene by Memphis' floods ;
The feather'd syluans clowd-like by her flie,
And with applauding clangors beate the skie ;
Nyle wonders, Serap's priests entranced raue,
And in Mygdonian stone her shape ingraue,
In golden leaues write downe the joyfull time
In which Apollo's bird came to their clime.
    Let mother earth now deckt with flowrs bee seene,
And sweet-breath'd zephyres curle the medowes greene,
Let heauens weepe rubies in a crimsin showre,
Such as on Indies shores they vse to powre,
Or with that golden storme the fields adorne,
Which Ioue rain'd when his blew-eyed maide was borne.
May neuer houres the webbe of day out-weaue,
May neuer night rise from her sable caue.
Swell prowd, my billowes, faint not to declare
Your ioyes as ample as their causes are ;
For murmures hoarse sound like Arion's harpe,
Now delicatelie flat, now sweetlie sharpe.
And you, my nymphes, rise from your moyst repaire,
Strow all your springs and grotts with lillies faire :
Some swiftest-footed get her hence and pray
Our floods and lakes come keepe this holie-day ;
What e're beneath Albania's hills doe runne,
Which see the rising or the setting sunne,

Which drinke sterne Grampius' mists, or Ochelles' snows ;
Stone-rowling Taye, Tine tortoyse-like that flows,
The pearlie Done, the Deas, the fertile Spay,
Wild Neuerne which doth see our longest day,
Nesse smoaking sulphure, Leaue with mountaines crown'd,
Strange Loumond for his floting isles renown'd,
The Irish Rian, Ken, the siluer Aire,
The snakie Dun, the Ore with rushie haire,
The chrystall-streaming Nid, lowd-bellowing Clyd,
Tweed, which no more our kingdomes shall diuide,
Rancke-swelling Annan, Lid with curled streames,
The Eskes, the Solway where they loose their names :
To eu'rie one proclaime our ioyes and feasts,
Our triumphes, bid all come, and bee our guests ;
And as they meet in Neptune's azure hall,
Bid them bid sea-gods keepe this festiuall.
This day shall by our currents bee renown'd,
Our hills about shall still this day resound :
Nay, that our loue more to this day appeare,
Let vs with it hencefoorth begin our yeare.
    To virgins flowrs, to sun-burnt earth the raine,
To mariners faire winds amidst the maine,
Coole shades to pilgrimes, which hote glances burne,
Please not so much, to vs as thy returne.
That day, deare Prince, which reft vs of thy sight,
Day, no, but darknesse, and a clowdie night,
Did fraight our brests with sighs, our eyes with teares,
Turn'd minutes in sad months, sad months in yeares ;
Trees left to flowrish, meadows to beare flowrs,
Brookes hid their heads within their sedgie bowrs ;
Faire Ceres curst our fields with barren frost,
As if againe shee had her daughter lost ;

R

The Muses left our groues, and for sweete songs
Sate sadlie silent, or did weepe their wrongs :
Yee know it, meads, yee, murmuring woods, it know,
Hilles, dales, and caues, copartners of their woe ;
And yee it know, my streames, which from their eine
Oft on your glasse recieu'd their pearled brine.
O Naïds deare, saide they, Napæas faire,
O nymphes of trees, nymphes which on hills repaire,
Gone are those maiden glories, gone that state,
Which made all eyes admire our hap of late.
As lookes the heauen when neuer starre appeares,
But slow and wearie shroude them in their spheares,
While Tithon's wife embosom'd by him lies,
And world doth languish in a drearie guise ;
As lookes a garden of its beautie spoil'd ;
As wood in winter by rough Boreas foil'd ;
As pourtraicts raz'd of colours vse to bee ;
So lookt these abject bounds depriu'd of thee.
    While as my rills enjoy'd thy royall gleames,
They did not enuie Tyber's haughtie streames,
Nor wealthie Tagus with his golden ore,
Nor cleare Hydaspes, which on pearles doth roare,
Empampred Gange, that sees the sunne new borne,
Nor Acheloüs with his flowrie horne,
Nor floods which neare Elysian fields doe fall ;
For why ? thy sight did serue to them for all.
No place there is so desert, so alone,
Euen from the frozen to the torrid zone,
From flaming Hecla to great Quincy's Lake,
Which thine abode could not most happie make.
All those perfections, which by bounteous heauen
To diuerse worlds in diuerse times were giuen,

FORTH FEASTING. 133

The starrie senate powr'd at once on thee,
That thou examplare mightst to others bee.
  Thy life was kept till the three sisters spunne
Their threedes of gold, and then it was begunne.
With curled clowds when skies doe looke most faire,
And no disordred blasts disturbe the aire ;
When lillies doe them decke in azure gownes,
And new-borne roses blushe with golden crownes ;
To bode how calme wee vnder thee should liue,
What halcyonean dayes thy reigne should giue,
And to two flowrie diadems thy right,
The heauens thee made a partner of the light.
Scarce wast thou borne, when, joyn'd in friendlie bands,
Two mortall foes with other clasped hands,
With vertue fortune stroue, which most should grace
Thy place for thee, thee for so high a place ;
One vow'd thy sacred brest not to forsake,
The other on thee not to turne her backe,
And that thou more her loue's effects mightst feele,
For thee shee rent her saile, and broke her wheele.
  When yeeres thee vigour gaue, O then how cleare
Did smother'd sparkles in bright flames appeare!
Amongst the woods to force a flying hart,
To pearce the mountaine wolfe with feath'red dart,
See faulcons climbe the clowds, the foxe ensnare,
Out-runne the winde-out-running dædale hare,
To loose a trampling steede alongst a plaine,
And in meandring gyres him bring againe,
The preasse thee making place, were vulgare things;
In admiration's aire, on glorie's wings,
O ! thou farre from the common pitch didst rise,
With thy designes to dazell enuie's eyes :

Thou soughtst to know this all's eternall source,
Of euer-turning heauens the restlesse course,
Their fixed eyes, their lights which wand'ring runne,
Whence moone her siluer hath, his gold the sunne,
If destine bee or no, if planets can
By fierce aspects force the free-will of man :
The light and spyring fire, the liquid aire,
The flaming dragons, comets with red haire,
Heauen's tilting launces, artillerie, and bow,
Lowd-sounding trumpets, darts of haile and snow,
The roaring element with people dombe,
The earth, with what conceiu'd is in her wombe,
What on her moues, were set vnto thy sight,
Till thou didst find their causes, essence, might :
But vnto nought thou so thy mind didst straine,
As to bee read in man, and learne to raigne,
To know the weight and Atlas of a crowne,
To spare the humble, prowdlings pester downe.
When from those pearcing cares which thrones inuest,
As thornes the rose, thou weari'd wouldst thee rest,
With lute in hand, full of cœlestiall fire,
To the Pierian groues thou didst retire :
There, garlanded with all Vrania's flowrs,
In sweeter layes than builded Thæbès towrs,
Or them which charm'd the dolphines in the maine,
Or which did call Euridice againe,
Thou sungst away the houres, till from their spheare
Starres seem'd to shoote, thy melodie to heare.
The god with golden haire, the sister maids,
Left nymphall Helicon, their Tempe's shades,
To see thine isle, heere lost their natiue tongue,
And in thy world-diuided language sung.

Who of thine after-age can count the deedes,
With all that fame in time's hudge annales reedes,
How by example more than anie law,
This people fierce thou didst to goodnesse draw,
How while the neighbour worlds, tows'd by the Fates,
So manie Phaëtons had in their states,
Which turn'd in heedlesse flames their burnish'd thrones,
Thou, as ensphear'd, keep'dst temperate thy zones ;
In Africke shores the sands that ebbe and flow,
The speckled flowrs in vnshorne meads that grow,
Hee sure may count, with all the waues that meet
To wash the Mauritanian Atlas' feet.
Though thou were not a crowned king by birth,
Thy worth deserues the richest crowne on earth.
Search this halfe-spheare and the opposite ground,
Where is such wit and bountie to bee found ?
As into silent night, when neare the beare
The virgine huntresse shines at full most cleare,
And striues to match her brother's golden light,
The hoast of starrs doth vanish in her sight,
Arcturus dies, cool'd is the lyon's ire,
Po burnes no more with Phaëtontall fire,
Orion faints to see his armes grow blacke,
And that his blazing sword hee now doth lacke:
So Europe's lights, all bright in their degree,
Loose all their lustre paragon'd with thee.
By just discent thou from moe kings dost shine,
Than manie can name men in all their line:
What most they toyle to finde, and finding hold,
Thou scornest, orient gemmes and flatt'ring gold ;
Esteeming treasure surer in men's brests,
Than when immur'd with marble, clos'd in chests.

No stormie passions doe disturbe thy mind,
No mists of greatnesse euer could thee blind :
Who yet hath beene so meeke ? Thou life didst giue
To them who did repine to see thee liue.
What prince by goodnesse hath such kingdoms gain'd ?
Who hath so long his people's peace maintain'd ?
Their swords are turn'd in sythes, in culters speares,
Some giant post their anticke armour beares :
Now, where the wounded knight his life did bleed,
The wanton swaine sits piping on a reed,
And where the canon did Ioue's thunder scorne,
The gawdie hunts-man windes his shrill-tun'd horne ;
Her greene lockes Ceres without feare doth die,
The pilgrime safelie in the shade doth lie,
Both Pan and Pales carelesse keepe their flockes,
Seas haue no dangers saue the windes and rockes :
Thou art this isle's palladium, neither can,
While thou art kept, it bee o're-throwne by man.
　　Let others boast of blood and spoyles of foes,
Fierce rapines, murders, Iliads of woes,
Of hated pompe, and trophæes reared faire,
Gore-spangled ensignes streaming in the aire,
Count how they make the Scythian them adore,
The Gaditan, the souldier of Aurore ;
Unhappie vauntrie ! to enlarge their bounds,
Which charge themselues with cares, their friends with wounds,
Which haue no law to their ambitious will,
But, man-plagues, borne are humane blood to spill :
Thou a true victor art, sent from aboue,
What others straine by force to gaine by loue ;
World-wand'ring fame this praise to thee imparts,
To bee the onlie monarch of all hearts.

They manie feare who are of manie fear'd,
And kingdomes got by wrongs by wrongs are tear'd,
Such thrones as blood doth raise, blood throweth downe;
No guard so sure as loue vnto a crowne.
  Eye of our westerne world, Mars-daunting King,
With whose renowne the earth's seuen climats ring,
Thy deeds not only claime these diademes,
To which Thame, Liffy, Taye, subject their streames,
But to thy vertues rare, and gifts, is due
All that the planet of the yeare doth view.
Sure if the world aboue did want a prince,
The world aboue to it would take thee hence.
  That murder, rapine, lust, are fled to hell,
And in their roomes with vs the Graces dwell,
That honour more than riches men respect,
That worthinesse than gold doth more effect,
That pietie vnmasked showes her face,
That innocencie keepes with power her place,
That long-exil'd Astrea leaues the heauen,
And vseth right her sword, her weights holds euen,
That the Saturnian world is come againe,
Are wish'd effects of thy most happie raigne.
That daylie peace, loue, truth, delights encrease,
And discord, hate, fraude, with incombers cease,
That men vse strength not to shed others' blood,
But vse their strength now to doe other good,
That furie is enchain'd, disarmed wrath,
That, saue by nature's hand, there is no death,
That late grimme foes like brothers other loue,
That vultures prey not on the harmlesse doue,
That wolues with lambs doe friendship entertaine,
Are wish'd effects of thy most happie raigne.

That towns encrease, that ruin'd temples rise,
And their wind-mouing vanes plante in the skies,
That ignorance and sloth hence runne away,
That buri'd arts now rowse them to the day,
That Hyperion farre beyond his bed
Doth see our lyons rampe, our roses spred,
That Iber courts vs, Tyber not vs charmes,
That Rhein with hence-brought beams his bosome warmes,
That euill vs feare, and good vs doe maintaine,
Are wish'd effects of thy most happie raigne.
    O vertue's patterne, glorie of our times,
Sent of past dayes to expiate the crimes,
Great King, but better farre than thou art great,
Whom state not honours, but who honours state,
By wonder borne, by wonder first enstall'd,
By wonder after to new kingdomes call'd,
Young, kept by wonder, neare home-bred alarmes,
Old, sau'd by wonder, from pale traitours' harmes,
To bee for this thy raigne which wonders brings,
A king of wonder, wonder vnto kings!
If Pict, Dane, Norman, thy smooth yoke had seene,
Pict, Dane, and Norman, had thy subjects beene:
If Brutus knew the blisse thy rule doth giue,
Euen Brutus joye would vnder thee to liue;
For thou thy people dost so dearlie loue,
That they a father, more than prince, thee proue.
    O dayes to bee desir'd, age happie thrice,
If yee your heauen-sent good could duelie prize!
But yee, halfe-palsey-sicke, thinke neuer right
Of what yee hold, till it bee from your sight,
Prize onlie summer's sweet and musked breath,
When armed winters threaten you with death,

In pallid sicknesse doe esteeme of health,
And by sad pouertie discerne of wealth.
I see an age when after manie yeares,
And reuolutions of the slow-pac'd spheares,
These dayes shall bee to other farre esteem'd,
And like Augustus' palmie raigne bee deem'd.
The names of Arthure fabulous palladines,
Grau'n in time's surlie browes in wrinckled lines,
Of Henries, Edwards, famous for their fights,
Their neighbour conquests, orders new of knights,
Shall by this prince's name bee past as farre
As meteors are by the Idalian starre.
If gray-hair'd Proteüs' songs the truth not misse,
And gray-hair'd Proteüs oft a prophet is,
There is a land hence distant manie miles,
Out-reaching fiction and Atlanticke isles,
Which, homelings, from this little world wee name,
That shall imblazon with strange rites his fame,
Shall raise him statues all of purest gold,
Such as men gaue vnto the gods of old,
Name by him fanes, prowd pallaces, and townes,
With some great flood, which most their fields renownes.
This is that king who should make right each wrong,
Of whom the bards and mysticke Sybilles song,
The man long promis'd, by whose glorious raigne
This isle should yet her ancient name regaine,
And more of Fortunate deserue the stile,
Than those where heauens with double summers smile.
Runne on, great Prince, thy course in glorie's way,
The end the life, the euening crownes the day;
Heape worth on worth, and stronglie soare aboue
Those heights which made the world thee first to loue;

s

Surmount thy selfe, and make thine actions past
Bee but as gleames or lightnings of thy last,
Let them exceed them of thy younger time,
As farre as autumne doth the flowrie prime.
Through this thy empire range, like world's bright eye,
That once each yeare suruayes all earth and skie,
Now glaunces on the slow and restie beares,
Then turnes to drie the weeping Auster's teares,
Iust vnto both the poles, and moueth euen
In the infigur'd circle of the heauen.
O! long long haunt these bounds, which by thy sight
Haue now regain'd their former heate and light.
Heere grow greene woods, heere siluer brookes doe glide,
Heere meadowes stretch them out with painted pride,
Embrod'ring all the banks ; heere hills aspire
To crowne their heads with the ætheriall fire ;
Hills, bullwarkes of our freedome, giant walls,
Which neuer fremdling's slight nor sword made thralls ;
Each circling flood to Thetis tribute payes,
Men heere, in health, out-liue old Nestor's dayes ;
Grimme Saturne yet amongst our rockes remaines,
Bound in our caues with manie mettal'd chaines ;
Bulls haunt our shades like Leda's louer white,
Which yet might breede Pasiphae delight ;
Our flocks faire fleeces beare, with which for sport
Endemion of old the moone did court,
High-palmed harts amidst our forrests runne,
And, not impall'd, the deepe-mouth'd hounds doe shunne ;
The rough-foote hare him in our bushes shrowds,
And long-wing'd haulks doe pearch amidst our clowds.
The wanton wood-nymphes of the verdant spring,
Blew, golden, purple flowers shall to thee bring,

Pomona's fruits the paniskes, Thetis' gyrles
Thy Thuly's amber, with the ocean pearles ;
The Tritons, heards-men of the glassie field,
Shall giue thee what farre-distant shores can yeeld,
The Serean fleeces, Erythrean gemmes,
Vaste Plata's siluer, gold of Peru streames,
Antarticke parrots, Æthiopian plumes,
Sabæan odours, myrrhe, and sweet perfumes.
And I my selfe, wrapt in a watchet gowne,
Of reeds and lillies on my heade a crowne,
Shall incense to thee burne, greene altars raise,
And yearlie sing due pæans to thy praise.
    Ah ! why should Isis onlie see thee shine ?
Is not thy Forth as well as Isis thine ?
Though Isis vaunt she hath more wealth in store,
Let it suffice thy Forth doth loue thee more :
Though shee for beautie may compare with Seine,
For swannes and sea-nymphes with imperiall Rhene,
Yet in the title may bee claim'd in thee,
Nor shee, nor all the world, can match with mee.
Now when, by honour drawne, thou shalt away
To her alreadie jelous of thy stay,
When in her amourous armes shee doth thee fold,
And dries thy dewie haires with hers of gold,
Much questioning of thy fare, much of thy sport,
Much of thine absence, long, how e're so short,
And chides perhaps thy comming to the north,
Lothe not to thinke on thy much-louing Forth.
O ! loue these bounds, whereof thy royall stemme
More than an hundreth wore a diademe.
So euer gold and bayes thy browes adorne,
So neuer time may see thy race out-worne,

So of thine owne still mayst hou bee desir'd,
Of strangers fear'd, redoubted, and admir'd ;
So memorie thee praise, so pretious houres
May character thy name in starrie flowres ;
So may thy high exployts at last make euen
With earth thy empire, glorie with the heauen.

FLOWRES OF SION.

BY WILLIAM DRVMMOND

OF HAWTHORNE-DENNE.

REPRINTED

FROM THE EDITION OF

M.DC.XXX.

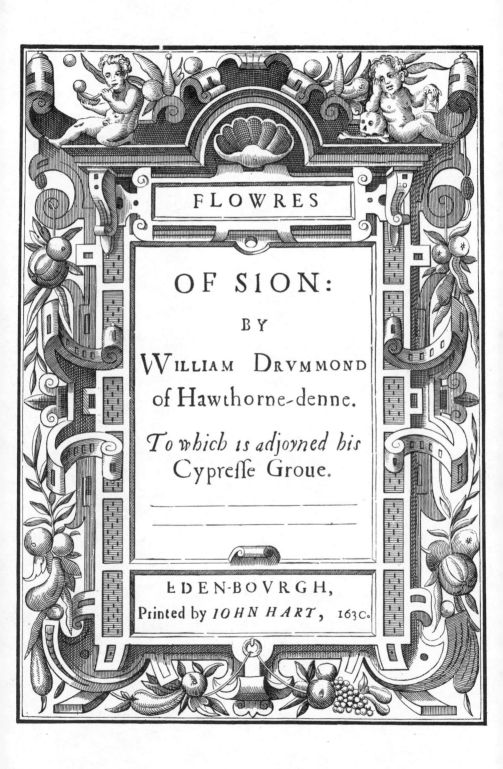

FLOWRES

OF SION:

BY

WILLIAM DRVMMOND
of Hawthorne-denne.

To which is adjoyned his
Cypreſſe Groue.

EDEN-BOVRGH,
Printed by IOHN HART, 1630.

FLOWRES OF SION;

OR SPIRITVALL POEMES.

THE INSTABILITIE OF MORTALL GLORIE.

TRIUMPHANT arches, statues crown'd with bayes,
Proud obeliskes, tombes of the vastest frame,
Colosses, brazen Atlases of fame,
Phanes vainelie builded to vaine idoles' praise ;
States, which vnsatiate mindes in blood doe raise,
From the crosse-starres vnto the articke teame,
Alas ! and what wee write to keepe our name,
Like spiders' caules, are made the sport of dayes :
All onely constant is in constant change,
What done is, is vndone, and, when vndone,
Into some other figure doeth it range ;
Thus moues the restlesse world beneath the moone :
  Wherefore, my minde, aboue time, motion, place,
   Thee raise, and steppes not reach'd by nature trace.

HUMANE FRAILTIE.

A GOOD that neuer satisfies the minde,
A beautie fading like the Aprile flowres,
A sweete with floodes of gall that runnes combin'd,
A pleasure passing ere in thought made ours,
A honour that more fickle is than winde,
A glorie at opinion's frowne that lowres,
A treasurie which bankrout time deuoures,
A knowledge than graue ignorance more blind,
A vaine delight our equalles to command,
A stile of greatnesse, in effect a dreame,
A fabulous thought of holding sea and land,
A seruile lot, deckt with a pompous name,
   Are the strange endes wee toyle for heere below,
   Till wisest death make vs our errores know.

THE PERMANENCIE OF LIFE.

LIFE a right shadow is,
For if it long appeare,
Then is it spent, and deathe's long night drawes neare :
Shadowes are mouing, light,
And is there ought so mouing as is this ?
When it is most in sight,
It steales away, and none can tell how, where,
So neere our cradles to our coffines are.

NO TRUST IN TYME.

Looke how the flowre which lingringlie doth fade,
The morning's darling late, the summer's queene,
Spoyl'd of that iuice which kept it fresh and greene,
As high as it did raise, bowes low the head :
Right so my life, contentments beeing dead,
Or in their contraries but onelie seene,
With swifter speede declines than earst it spred,
And, blasted, scarce now showes what it hath beene.
As doth the pilgrime therefore whom the night
By darknesse would imprison on his way,
Thinke on thy home, my soule, and thinke aright
Of what yet restes thee of life's wasting day :
    Thy sunne postes westward, passed is thy morne,
    And twice it is not giuen thee to bee borne.

WORLDE'S IOYES ARE TOYES.

The wearie mariner so fast not flies
An howling tempest, harbour to attaine,
Nor sheepheard hastes, when frayes of wolues arise,
So fast to fold to saue his bleeting traine,
As I, wing'd with contempt and just disdaine,
Now flie the world and what it most doth prize,
And sanctuarie seeke, free to remaine
From wounds of abject times, and enuie's eyes.
Once did this world to mee seeme sweete and faire,
While senses light minde's prospectiue keept blind,
Now like imagin'd landskip in the aire,
And weeping raine-bowes, her best ioyes I finde ;
    Or if ought heere is had that praise should haue,
    It is a life obscure, and silent graue.

T

NATURE MUST YEELDE TO GRACE.*

Too long I followed haue on fond desire,
And too long painted on deluding streames,
Too long refreshment sought in burning fire,
Runne after ioyes which to my soule were blames.
Ah ! when I had what most I did admire,
And prou'd of life's delightes the last extreames,
I found all but a rose hedg'd with a bryer,
A nought, a thought, a show of golden dreames.
Hence-foorth on thee, mine onelie good, I thinke,
For onelie thou canst grant what I doe craue,
Thy nailes my pennes shall bee, thy blood mine inke,
Thy winding-sheete my paper, studie graue ;
   And till that soule from bodie parted bee,
   No hope I haue, but onelie onelie thee.

THE BOOKE OF THE WORLD.

OF this faire volumne which wee world doe name,
If wee the sheetes and leaues could turne with care,
Of him who it correctes, and did it frame,
Wee cleare might read the art and wisedome rare,
Finde out his power, which wildest pow'rs doth tame,
His prouidence extending euerie-where,
His iustice which proud rebels doeth not spare,
In euerie page, no, period of the same :
But sillie wee, like foolish children, rest
Well pleas'd with colour'd velame, leaues of gold,
Faire dangling ribbones, leauing what is best,
On the great writer's sense ne'er taking hold ;
   Or if by chance our mindes doe muse on ought,
   It is some picture on the margine wrought.

---

* This sonnet, with a few of the subsequent poems in the *Flowres of Sion*, will likewise be
found in that part of the volume which bears the title of *Vrania*. As the variety of reading is
considerable, the Editor has thought it advisable to retain them in both forms.

THE MISERABLE ESTATE OF THE WORLD BEFORE THE INCARNATION OF GOD.

THE griefe was common, common were the cryes,
Teares, sobbes, and groanes of that afflicted traine,
Which of God's chosen did the summe containe,
And earth rebounded with them, pierc'd were skies;
All good had left the world, each vice did raigne
In the most hideous shapes hell could deuise,
And all degrees and each estate did staine,
Nor further had to goe, whom to surprise;
The world beneath the Prince of Darknesse lay,
In eurie phane who had himselfe install'd,
Was sacrifiz'd vnto, by prayers call'd,
Responses gaue, which, fooles, they did obey;
    When, pittying man, God of a virgine's wombe
    Was borne, and those false deities strooke dombe.

THE ANGELS FOR THE NATIUITIE OF OUR LORD.

RVNNE, sheepheards, run where Bethleme blest appeares,
Wee bring the best of newes, bee not dismay'd,
A Sauiour there is borne, more olde than yeares,
Amidst heauen's rolling hights this earth who stay'd:
In a poore cotage inn'd, a virgine maide
A weakling did him beare, who all vpbeares;
There is hee poorelie swadl'd in manger laid,
To whom too narrow swadlings are our spheares:
Runne, sheepheards, runne, and solemnize his birth,
This is that night, no, day, growne great with blisse,
In which the power of Sathan broken is;
In heauen bee glorie, peace vnto the earth.
    Thus singing through the aire the angels swame,
    And cope of starres re-echoed the same.

FOR THE NATIUITIE OF OUR LORD.

O THAN the fairest day, thrice fairer night !
Night to best dayes in which a sunne doth rise,
Of which that golden eye, which cleares the skies,
Is but a sparkling ray, a shadow light :
And blessed yee, in sillie pastors' sight,
Milde creatures, in whose warme cribe now lyes
That heauen-sent yongling, holie-maide-borne wight,
Midst, end, beginning of our prophesies :
Blest cotage that hath flowres in winter spred,
Though withered, blessed grasse, that hath the grace
To decke and bee a carpet to that place.
Thus sang, vnto the soundes of oaten reed,
Before the babe, the sheepheards bow'd on knees,
And springs ranne nectar, honey dropt from trees.

AMAZEMENT AT THE INCARNATION OF GOD.

To spread the azure canopie of heauen,
And make it twinkle with those spangs of gold,
To stay this weightie masse of earth so euen,
That it should all, and nought should it vp-hold ;
To giue strange motions to the planets seuen,
Or Ioue to make so meeke, or Mars so bold,
To temper what is moist, drie, hote, and cold,
Of all their iarres that sweete accords are giuen,
Lord, to thy wisedome nought is, nor thy might ;
But that thou shouldst, thy glorie laid aside,
Come meanelie in mortalitie to bide,
And die for those deseru'd eternalle plight,
    A wonder is so farre aboue our wit,
    That angels stand amaz'd to muse on it.

FOR THE BAPTISTE.

THE last and greatest herauld of heauen's king,
Girt with rough skinnes, hyes to the desarts wilde,
Among that sauage brood the woods foorth bring,
Which hee than man more harmlesse found and milde :
His food was blossomes, and what yong doth spring,
With honey that from virgine hiues distil'd ;
Parcht bodie, hollow eyes, some vncouth thing
Made him appeare, long since from earth exilde.
There burst hee foorth : All yee, whose hopes relye
On God, with mee amidst these desarts mourne,
Repent, repent, and from olde errours turne.
Who list'ned to his voyce, obey'd his crye ?
Onelie the ecchoes, which hee made relent,
Rung from their marble caues, Repent, repent.

FOR THE MAGDALENE.

THESE eyes, deare Lord, once brandons of desire,
Fraile scoutes betraying what they had to keepe,
Which their owne heart, then others set on fire,
Their traitrous blacke before thee heere out-weepe :
These lockes, of blushing deedes the faire attire,
Smooth-frizled waues, sad shelfes which shadow deepe,
Soule-stinging serpents in gilt curles which creepe,
To touch thy sacred feete doe now aspire.
In seas of care behold a sinking barke,
By windes of sharpe remorse vnto thee driuen,
O ! let mee not expos'd be ruine's marke ;
My faults confest, Lord, say they are forgiuen.
  Thus sigh'd to Iesvs the Bethanian faire,
  His teare-wet feete still drying with her haire.

FOR THE PRODIGALL.

I COUNTRIES chang'd, new pleasures out to finde,
But, ah ! for pleasure new I found new paine ;
Enchanting pleasure so did reason blind,
That father's loue and wordes I scorn'd as vaine :
For tables rich, for bed, for frequent traine
Of carefull seruants to obserue my minde,
These heardes I keepe my fellowes are assign'd,
My bed a rocke is, hearbes my life sustaine.
Now while I famine feele, feare worser harmes,
Father and Lord, I turne ; thy love, yet great,
My faults will pardon, pitty mine estate.
This, where an aged oake had spread its armes,
Thought the lost child, while as the heardes hee led,
Not farre off on the ackornes wilde them fed.

FOR THE PASSION.

IF that the world doth in a maze remaine,
To heare in what a sad deploring mood
The pelican powres from her brest her blood,
To bring to life her younglinges backe againe,
How should wee wonder of that soueraigne good,
Who from that serpent's sting, that had vs slaine,
To saue our liues, shed his life's purple flood,
And turn'd in endlesse ioy our endlesse paine ?
Vngratefull soule, that charm'd with false delight,
Hast long long wandr'd in sinne's flowrie path,
And didst not thinke at all, or thoughtst not right
On this thy pelicane's great loue and death,
   Heere pause, and let, though earth it scorne, heauen see
   Thee powre forth teares to him powr'd blood for thee.

AN HYMNE OF THE PASSION.

If, when farre in the east yee doe behold
    Foorth from his christall bed the sunne to rise,
    With rosie robes and crowne of flaming gold;
If gazing on that empresse of the skies,
    That takes so many formes, and those faire brands
    Which blaze in heauen's high vault, night's watchfull eyes;
If seeing how the sea's tumultuous bands
    Of bellowing billowes haue their course confin'd,
    How, vnsustain'd, the earth still steadfast stands;
Poore mortall wights, yee e're found in your minde
    A thought that some great king did sit aboue,
    Who had such lawes and rites to them assign'd;
A king who fix'd the poles, made spheares to moue,
    All wisedome, purenesse, excellence, and might,
    All goodnesse, greatnesse, iustice, beauty, loue;
With feare and wonder hither turne your sight,
    See, see, alas! him now, not in that state
    Thought could fore-cast him into reason's light.
Now eyes with teares, now hearts with griefe make great,
    Bemoane this cruell death and dreary case,
    If euer plaints iust woe could aggrauate.
From sinne and hell to saue vs, humaine race,
    See this great King naill'd to an abiect tree,
    An obiect of reproach and sad disgrace.
O vnheard pitty, loue in strange degree!
    Hee his owne life doth giue, his blood doth shed,
    For wormelings base such excellence to see.
Poore wightes, behold his visage pale as lead,
    His head bow'd to his brest, lockes sadlie rent,
    Like a cropt rose that languishing doth fade.

Weake nature, weepe, astonish'd world, lament,
　　Lament, yee windes, you heauen that all containes,
　　And thou, my soule, let nought thy griefe relent.
Those hands, those sacred hands, which hold the raines
　　Of this great all, and kept from mutuall warres
　　The elements, beare rent for thee their veines :
Those feete which once must tread on golden starres,
　　For thee with nailes would bee pierc'd through and torne,
　　For thee heauen's king from heauen himselfe debarres.
This great heart-quaking dolour waile and mourne,
　　Yee that long since him saw by might of faith,
　　Yee now that are, and yee yet to bee borne.
Not to behold his great Creator's death,
　　The sunne from sinfull eyes hath vail'd his light,
　　And faintly iourneyes vp heauen's saphire path ;
And, cutting from her browes her tresses bright,
　　The moone doth keepe her lord's sad obsequies,
　　Impearling with her teares this robe of night.
All staggering and lazie lowre the skies,
　　The earth and elemental stages quake,
　　The long since dead from bursted graues arise.
And can things wanting sense yet sorrow take,
　　And beare a part with him who all them wrought,
　　And man, though borne with cries, shall pitty lacke ?
Thinke what had beene your state, had hee not brought
　　To these sharpe pangs himselfe, and priz'd so hie
　　Your soules, that with his life them life hee bought.
What woes doe you attend, if still yee lie
　　Plung'd in your wonted ordures, wretched brood ?
　　Shall for your sake againe God euer die ?
O leaue deluding shewes, embrace true good,
　　Hee on you calles, forgoe sinne's shamefull trade,
　　With prayers now seeke heauen, and not with blood.

Let not the lambes more from their dames bee had,
  Nor altars blush for sinne ; liue euery thing,
  That long time long'd-for sacrifice is made.
All that is from you crau'd by this great king
  Is to beleeue, a pure heart incense is ;
  What gift, alas ! can wee him meaner bring ?
Haste, sinne-sicke soules, this season doe not misse,
  Now while remorselesse time doth grant you space,
  And God inuites you to your only blisse.
He who you calles will not denie you grace,
  But low-deepe burie faults, so yee repent ;
  His armes, loe, stretched are you to embrace.
When dayes are done, and life's small sparke is spent,
  So yee accept what freely here is giuen,
  Like brood of angels, deathlesse, all-content,
Yee shall for euer liue with him in heauen.

TO THE ANGELS FOR THE PASSION.

COME forth, come forth, yee blest triumphing bands,
Faire citizens of that immortall towne,
Come see that king which all this all commands,
Now, ouercharg'd with loue, die for his owne ;
Looke on those nailes which pierce his feete and hands,
What a sharpe diademe his browes doth crowne !
Behold his pallid face, his eyes which sowne,
And what a throng of theeues him mocking stands :
Come forth, yee empyrean troupes, come forth,
Preserue this sacred blood, that earth adornes,
Those liquid roses gather off his thornes,
O ! to bee lost they bee of too much worth ;
  For streames, iuice, balm, they are, which quench, kils, charms,
  Of God, death, hel, the wrath, the life, the harmes.

U

FAITH ABOUE REASON.

SOULE, which to hell wast thrall,
Hee, hee for thine offence
Did suffer death, who could not die at all :
O soueraigne excellence,
O life of all that liues,
Eternall bounty, which each good thing giues,
How could death mount so hie?
No wit this hight can reach ;
Faith only doth vs teach,
For vs hee died, at all who could not dye.

VPON THE SEPULCHER OF OUR LORD.

LIFE to giue life depriued is of life,
And death displai'd hath ensigne against death ;
So violent the rigour was of death,
That nought could daunt it but the life of life :
No power had pow'r to thrall life's pow'r to death,
But willingly life hath abandon'd life,
Loue gaue the wound which wrought this work of death,
His bow and shafts were of the tree of life.
Now quakes the author of eternall death,
To finde that they whom earst he reft of life,
Shall fill his roome aboue the listes of death ;
Now all reioyce in death who hope for life.
  Dead Iesvs lies, who death hath kill'd by death,
  His tombe no tombe is, but new source of life.

AN HYMNE OF THE RESURRECTION.

Rise from those fragrant climes thee now embrace,
Vnto this world of ours O haste thy race,
Faire sunne, and though contrary-wayes all yeare
Thou hold thy course, now with the highest spheare
Ioyne thy swift wheeles, to hasten time that lowres,
And lazie minutes turne in perfect houres ;
The night and death too long a league haue made,
To stow the world in horror's vgly shade.
Shake from thy lockes a day with saffron rayes,
So faire, that it out-shine all other dayes ;
And yet doe not presume, great eye of light,
To be that which this day shall make so bright :
See, an eternall sunne hastes to arise,
Not from the easterne blushing seas or skies,
Or any stranger worlds heauen's concaues haue,
But from the darknesse of an hollow graue ;
And this is that all-powerfull sunne aboue,
That crown'd thy browes with rayes, first made thee moue.
Light's trumpetters, yee neede not from your bowres
Proclaime this day, this the angelike powres
Haue done for you ; but now an opall hew
Bepaintes heauen's christall, to the longing view
Earth's late-hid colours glance, light doth adorne
The world, and, weeping ioy, foorth comes the morne ;
And with her, as from a lethargicke transe,
Breath, com'd againe, that bodie doth aduance,
Which two sad nights in rocke lay coffin'd dead,
And with an iron guard inuironed.
Life out of death, light out of darknesse springs,
From a base iaile foorth comes the King of kings ;
What late was mortall, thrall'd to euery woe
That lackeyes life, or vpon sence doth grow,

Immortall is, of an eternall stampe,
Farre brighter beaming than the morning lampe.
So from a blacke ecclipse out-peeres the sunne ;
Such, when a huge of dayes haue on her runne,
In a farre forest in the pearly east,
And shee her selfe hath burnt and spicie nest,
The lonlie bird, with youthfull pennes and combe,
Doth soare from out her cradle and her tombe ;
So a small seede that in the earth lies hidde
And dies, reuiuing burstes her cloddie side,
Adorn'd with yellow lockes, of new is borne,
And doth become a mother great with corne,
Of graines brings hundreths with it, which when old
Enrich the furrowes with a sea of gold.
    Haile holy victor, greatest victor haile,
That hell dost ransacke, against death preuaile,
O how thou long'd for comes ! with iubeling cries
The all-triumphing palladines of skies
Salute thy rising ; earth would ioyes no more
Beare, if thou rising didst them not restore :
A silly tombe should not his flesh enclose,
Who did heauen's trembling tarasses dispose ;
No monument should such a iewell hold,
No rocke, though rubye, diamond, and gold.
Thou onely pittie didst vs, humane race,
Bestowing on vs of thy free-giuen grace
More than wee forfaited and loosed first,
In Eden's rebell when wee were accurst.
Then earth our portion was, earth's ioyes but giuen,
Earth and earth's blisse thou hast exchang'd with heauen.
O what a hight of good vpon vs streames
From the great splendor of thy bountie's beames !

When wee deseru'd shame, horrour, flames of wrath,
Thou bled our wounds, and suffer didst our death ;
But, Father's iustice pleas'd, hell, death o'rcome,
In triumph now thou risest from thy tombe,
With glories which past sorrowes contervaile ;
Haile, holy victor ! greatest victor, haile !
   Hence, humble sense, and hence yee guides of sense,
Wee now reach heauen ; your weake intelligence,
And searching pow'rs were in a flash made dim,
To learne from all eternitie that him
The Father bred, then that hee heere did come,
His bearer's parent, in a virgin's wombe ;
But then when sold, betray'd, scourg'd, crown'd with thorne,
Naill'd to a tree, all breathlesse, bloodlesse, torne,
Entomb'd, him rising from a graue to finde,
Confounds your cunning, turnes like moles you blinde.
Death, thou that heretofore still barren wast,
Nay, didst each other birth eate vp and waste,
Imperious, hatefull, pittilesse, vniust,
Vnpartiall equaller of all with dust,
Stern executioner of heauenly doome,
Made fruitfull, now life's mother art become,
A sweete releife of cares the soule molest,
An harbinger to glory, peace, and rest,
Put off thy mourning weedes, yeeld all thy gall
To daylie-sinning life, proud of thy fall ;
Assemble thy captiues, bid all hast to rise,
And euerie corse, in earth-quakes where it lies,
Sound from each flowrie graue, and rockie iaile,
Haile, holy victor, greatest victor, haile !
   The world, that wanning late and faint did lie,
Applauding to our ioyes thy victorie,

To a yong prime essayes to turne againe,
And as ere soyl'd with sinne yet to remaine,
Her chilling agues shee beginnes to misse,
All blisse returning with the Lord of blisse.
With greater light heauen's temples opened shine,
Mornes smiling rise, euens blushing doe decline,
Cloudes dappled glister, boisterous windes are calme,
Soft zephires doe the fields with sighes embalme,
In ammell blew the sea hath husht his roares,
And with enamour'd curles doth kisse the shoares :
All-bearing earth, like a new-married queene,
Her beauties hightenes, in a gowne of greene
Perfumes the aire, her meades are wrought with flowres,
In colours various, figures, smelling, powres ;
Trees wanton in the groues with leauie lockes,
Her hilles empampred stand, the vales, the rockes
Ring peales of ioy, her floods, her christall bookes,
The meadowes' tongues, with many maz-like crookes,
And whispering murmures, sound vnto the maine,
That world's pure age returned is againe.
The honny people leaue their golden bowres,
And innocently pray on budding flowres ;
In gloomy shades, pearcht on the tender sprayes,
The painted singers fill the aire with layes :
Seas, floods, earth, aire, all diuerslie doe sound,
Yet all their diuerse notes haue but one ground,
Re-ecchoed here downe from heauen's azure vaile,
Haile, holy victor, greatest victor, haile !
    O day ! on which deathe's adamantine chaine
The Lord did breake, ransacking Satan's raigne,
And in triumphing pompe his trophees rear'd,
Bee thou blest euer, hence-foorth still endear'd

With name of his owne day : the law to grace,
Types to their substance yeelde, to thee giue place
The olde new-moones, with all festiuall dayes,
And what aboue the rest deserueth praise,
The reuerent Saboth ; what could else they bee
Than golden heraulds, telling what by thee
Wee should enjoy ?   Shades past, now shine thou cleare,
And hence-foorth bee thou empresse of the yeare,
This glorie of thy sister's sex to winne
From worke on thee, as other dayes from sinne,
That man-kind shall forbeare, in euerie place
The prince of planets warmeth in his race,
And farre beyond his pathes in frozen climes :
And may thou bee so blest to out-date times,
That when heauen's quire shall blaze in accents lowd
The manie mercies of their soueraigne good,
How hee on thee did sinne, death, hell destroy,
It may bee aye the antheme of their ioy.

AN HYMNE OF THE ASCENSION.

BRIGHT portalles of the skie,
  Emboss'd with sparkling starres,
  Doores of eternitie,
  With diamantine barres,
  Your arras rich vp-hold,
  Loose all your bolts and springs,
  Ope wyde your leaues of gold,
That in your roofes may come the King of kings.
Scarff'd in a rosie cloud,
  Hee doth ascend the aire,
  Straight doth the moone him shrowd
  With her resplendant haire ;
  The next enchristall'd light
  Submits to him its beames,
  And hee doth trace the hight
Of that faire lamp which flames of beautie streames.
Hee towers those golden bounds
  Hee did to sunne bequeath,
  The higher wand'ring rounds
  Are found his feete beneath ;
  The milkie-way comes neare,
  Heauen's axell seemes to bend,
  Aboue each turning spheare
That roab'd in glorie heauen's King may ascend.
O well-spring of this all,
  Thy father's image viue,
  Word, that from nought did call
  What is, doth reason, liue,
  The soule's eternall foode,

Earth's ioy, delight of heauen!
All truth, loue, beautie, good,
  To thee, to thee bee praises euer giuen.
What was dismarshall'd late
  In this thy noble frame,
  And lost the prime estate,
  Hath re-obtain'd the same,
  Is now most perfect seene ;
  Streames which diuerted were,
  And troubled strayed vncleene,
  From their first source, by thee home turned are.
By thee that blemish old
  Of Eden's leprous prince,
  Which on his race tooke hold,
  And him exyl'd from thence,
  Now put away is farre ;
  With sword, in irefull guise,
  No cherub more shall barre
  Poore man the entries into Paradise.
By thee those spirits pure,
  First children of the light,
  Now fixed stand and sure
  In their eternall right ;
  Now humane companies
  Renew their ruin'd wall ;
  Fall'n man as thou mak'st rise,
  Thou giu'st to angels that they shall not fall.
By thee that prince of sinne
  That doth with mischiefe swell,
  Hath lost what hee did winne,
  And shall endungeon'd dwell ;

          x

His spoyles are made thy pray,
His phanes are sackt and torne,
His altars raz'd away,
And what ador'd was late, now lyes a scorne.
These mansions pure and cleare,
Which are not made by hands,
Which once by him joy'd were,
And his, then not stain'd, bands,
Now forefait'd, dispossest,
And head-long from them throwne,
Shall Adam's heires make blest,
By thee, their great Redeemer, made their owne.
O well-spring of this all,
Thy father's image viue,
Word, that from nought did call
What is, doth reason, liue;
Whose worke is but to will,
God's coeternall sonne,
Great banisher of ill!
By none but thee could these great deedes bee done.
Now each etheriall gate
To him hath opened bin,
And glorie's King in state
His pallace enters in;
Now com'd is this high prest,
In the most holie place,
Not without blood addrest,
With glorie heauen, the earth to crowne with grace.
Starres which all eyes were late,
And did with wonder burne,
His name to celebrate,
In flaming tongues them turne;

Their orbye christales moue
  More actiue than before,
  And entheate from aboue,
  Their soueraigne prince laude, glorifie, adore.
The quires of happie soules,
  Wakt with that musicke sweete,
  Whose descant care controules,
  Their Lord in triumph meete;
  The spotlesse sprightes of light
  His trophees doe extole,
  And, archt in squadrons bright,
  Greet their great victor in his Capitole.
O glorie of the heauen!
  O sole delight of earth!
  To thee all power bee giuen
  God's vncreated birth;
  Of man-kind louer true,
  Indeerer of his wrong,
  Who dost the world renew,
  Still bee thou our saluation and our song.
From top of Oliuet such notes did rise,
When man's Redeemer did transcend the skies.

MAN'S KNOWLEDGE, IGNORANCE IN THE MISTERIES OF GOD.

BENEATH a sable vaile, and shadowes deepe,
Of vnaccessible and dimming light,
In silence ebane clouds more blacke than night,
The world's great King his secrets hidde doth keepe:
Through those thicke mistes when any mortall wight
Aspires, with halting pace, and eyes that weepe,
To pore, and in his misteries to creepe,
With thunders hee and lightnings blastes their sight.
O sunne invisible, that dost abide
Within thy bright abysmes, most faire, most darke,
Where with thy proper rayes thou dost thee hide!
O euer-shining, neuer full-seen marke!
  To guide mee in life's night, thy light mee show,
  The more I search, of thee the lesse I know.

CONTEMPLATION OF INVISIBLE EXCELLENCIES ABOUE,
BY THE VISIBLE BELOW.

IF with such passing beautie, choise delights,
The architect of this great round did frame
This pallace visible, (short listes of fame,
And sillie mansion but of dying wights,)
How many wonders, what amazing lights,
Must that triumphing seat of glorie clame,
That doth transcend all this great all's vaste hights,
Of whose bright sunne ours heere is but a beame?
O blest abod! O happie dwelling-place,
Where visiblie th' Invisible doth raigne,
Blest people which doe see true beautie's face,
With whose farre dawnings scarce he earth doth daigne!
  All ioy is but annoy, all concord strife,
  Match'd with your endlesse blisse and happie life.

THE DIFFERENCE BETWEENE EARTHLIE AND HEAUENLIE LOUE.

LOUE, which is here a care,
That wit and will doth marre,
Vncertaine truce, and a most certaine warre;
A shrill tempestuous winde,
Which doth disturbe the minde,
And like wilde waues our designes all commoue;
Among those powres aboue,
Which see their Maker's face,
It a contentment is, a quiet peace,
A pleasure voide of griefe, a constant rest,
Eternall ioy, which nothing can molest.

EARTH AND ALL ON IT CHANGEABLE.

THAT space, where raging waues doe now diuide
From the great continent our happie isle,
Was some-time land; and where tall shippes doe glide,
Once with deare arte the crooked plough did tyle:
Once those faire bounds stretcht out so farre and wide,
Where townes, no, shires enwall'd, endeare each mile,
Were all ignoble sea, and marish vile,
Where Proteus' flockes danc'd measures to the tyde.
So age, transforming all, still forward runnes,
No wonder though the earth doth change her face,
New manners, pleasures new, turne with new sunnes,
Lockes now like gold grow to an hoarie grace;
 Nay, minde's rare shape doth change; that lyes despis'd
 Which was so deare of late, and highlie pris'd.

THE WORLD A GAME.

This world a hunting is,
The pray poore man, the Nimrod fierce is death,
His speedie grei-hounds are
Lust, sicknesse, enuie, care,
Strife that neere falles amisse,
With all those ills which haunt vs while wee breath.
Now, if by chance wee flie
Of these the eager chase,
Old age with stealing pace
Castes vp his nets, and there wee panting die.

THE COURT OF TRUE HONOUR.

Why, worldlings, do ye trust fraile honour's dreams,
And leane to guilted glories which decay?
Why doe yee toyle to registrate your names
On ycie pillars, which soone melt away?
True honour is not here; that place it clames,
Where blacke-brow'd night doth not exile the day,
Nor no farre-shining lamp diues in the sea,
But an eternall sunne spreades lasting beames:
There it attendeth you, where spotlesse bands
Of spirits stand gazing on their soueraigne blisse,
Where yeeres not hold it in their canckring hands,
But who once noble, euer noble is.
    Looke home, lest hee your weakned wit make thrall,
    Who Eden's foolish gard'ner earst made fall.

AGAINST HYPOCRISIE.

AS are those apples, pleasant to the eye,
But full of smoke within, which vse to grow
Neere that strange lake, where God powr'd from the skie
Huge showres of flames, worse flames to ouer-throw ;
Such are their workes that with a glaring show
Of humble holinesse, in vertue's dye
Would colour mischiefe, while within they glow
With coales of sinne, though none the smoake descrie.
Ill is that angell which earst fell from heauen,
But not more ill than hee, nor in worse case,
Who hides a traitrous minde with smiling face,
And with a doue's white feather maskes a rauen.
  Each sinne some colour hath it to adorne,
  Hypocrisie all-mighty God doth scorne.

CHANGE SHOULD BREEDE CHANGE.

NEW doth the sunne appeare,
The mountaines' snowes decay,
Crown'd with fraile flowres foorth comes the babye yeare.
My soule, time postes away,
And thou yet in that frost
Which flowre and fruit hath lost,
As if all heere immortall were, dost stay :
For shame, thy powers awake,
Looke to that heauen which neuer night makes blacke,
And there, at that immortall sunne's bright rayes,
Decke thee with flowers which feare not rage of dayes.

THE PRAISE OF A SOLITARIE LIFE.

THRICE happie hee, who by some shadie groue,
Farre from the clamorous world, doth liue his owne,
Though solitarie, who is not alone,
But doth conuerse with that eternall loue.
O how more sweete is bird's harmonious moane,
Or the hoarse sobbings of the widow'd doue,
Than those smooth whisperings neere a prince's throne,
Which good make doubtfull, doe the euill approue!
O how more sweet is zephire's wholesome breath,
And sighes embalm'd, which new-borne flow'rs vnfold,
Than that applause vaine honour doth bequeath!
How sweete are streames to poison drunke in gold!
  The world is full of horrours, troubles, slights,
  Woods' harmelesse shades haue only true delightes

TO A NIGHTINGALE.

SWEET bird, that sing'st away the early howres,
Of winters past or comming void of care,
Well pleased with delights which present are,
Faire seasones, budding sprayes, sweet-smelling flowers ;
To rocks, to springs, to rils, from leauy bowres
Thou thy Creator's goodnesse dost declare,
And what deare gifts on thee hee did not spare,
A staine to humane sence in sinne that lowres.
What soule can be so sicke, which by thy songs,
Attir'd in sweetnesse, sweetly is not driuen
Quite to forget earth's turmoiles, spights, and wrongs,
And lift a reuerend eye and thought to heauen ?
  Sweet artlesse songstarre, thou my minde dost raise
  To ayres of spheares, yes, and to angels' layes.

CONTENT AND RESOLUTE.

As when it hap'neth that some louely towne,
Vnto a barbarous besieger falles,
Who there by sword and flame himselfe enstalles,
And, cruell, it in teares and blood doth drowne;
Her beauty spoyl'd, her citizens made thralles,
His spight yet so cannot her all throw downe,
But that some statue, arch, phan of renowne
Yet lurkes vnmaym'd within her weeping walles:
So, after all the spoile, disgrace, and wrake,
That time, the world, and death could bring combin'd,
Amidst that masse of ruines they did make,
Safe and all scarre-lesse yet remaines my minde:
    From this so high transcending rapture springes,
    That I, all else defac'd, not enuie kinges.

DEATHE'S LAST-WILL.

MORE oft than once death whisper'd in mine eare,
Graue what thou heares in diamond and gold;
I am that monarch whom all monarches feare,
Who hath in dust their farre-stretch'd pride vproll'd;
All, all is mine beneath moone's siluer spheare,
And nought, saue vertue, can my power with-hold:
This, not belieu'd, experience true thee told,
By danger late when I to thee came neare.
As bugbeare then my visage I did show,
That of my horrours thou right vse mightst make,
And a more sacred path of liuing take:
Now still walke armed for my ruthlesse blow,
    Trust flattering life no more, redeeme time past,
    And liue each day as if it were thy last.

Y

THE BLESSEDNESSE OF FAITHFULL SOULES BY DEATH.

LET vs each day enure our selues to dye,
If this, and not our feares, be truely death,
Aboue the circles both of hope and faith
With faire immortall pinniones to flie ;
If this be death, our best part to vntie,
By ruining the iaile, from lust and wrath,
And euery drowsie languor heere beneath,
It turning deniz'd citizen of skie ;
To haue more knowledge than all bookes containe,
All pleasures euen surmounting wishing powre,
The fellowship of God's immortall traine,
And these that time nor force shall e're deuoure ;
   If this be death, what ioy, what golden care
   Of life can with death's ouglinesse compare?

AN HYMNE OF TRUE HAPPINESSE.

   AMIDST the azure cleare
  Of Iordan's sacred streames,
  Iordan of Libanon the of-spring deare,
  When zephire's flowers vnclose,
  And sunne shines with new beames,
  With graue and stately grace a nimphe arose.
Vpon her head she ware
  Of amaranthes a crowne,
  Her left hand palmes, her right a brandon bare,
  Vnvail'd skinne's whitenesse lay,
  Gold haires in curles hang downe,
  Eyes sparkled ioy, more bright than starre of day.

The flood a throne her rear'd
  Of waues, most like that heauen
  Where beaming starres in glorie turne ensphear'd ;
  The aire stood calme and cleare,
  No sigh by windes was giuen,
  Birdes left to sing, heards feed, her voyce to heare.
World-wand'ring sorrie wights,
  Whom nothing can content
  Within those varying listes of dayes and nights,
  Whose life, ere knowne amisse,
  In glittering griefes is spent,
  Come learne, said shee, what is your choisest blisse ;
From toyle and pressing cares
  How yee may respit finde,
  A sanctuarie from soule-thralling snares,
  A port to harboure sure
  In spight of waues and winde,
  Which shall, when time's houre-glasse is runne, endure.
Not happie is that life
  Which yee as happie hold,
  No, but a sea of feares, a field of strife,
  Charg'd on a throne to sit
  With diadems of gold,
  Preseru'd by force, and still obseru'd by wit ;
Huge treasures to enioy,
  Of all her gemmes spoyle Inde,
  All Seres' silke in garments to imploy,
  Deliciously to feed,
  The Phenix' plumes to finde
  To rest vpon, or decke your purple bed ;

Fraile beautie to abuse,
   And, wanton Sybarites,
   On past or present touch of sense to muse;
   Neuer to heare of noise
   But what the eare delites,
   Sweet musick's charmes, or charming flatterer's voice.
Nor can it blisse you bring,
   Hidde nature's depthes to know,
   Why matter changeth, whence each forme doth spring;
   Nor that your fame should range,
   And after-worlds it blow
   From Tanäis to Nile, from Nile to Gange.
All these haue not the powre
   To free the minde from feares,
   Nor hiddeous horror can allay one howre,
   When death in steele doth glance,
   In sicknesse lurke or yeares,
   And wakes the soule from out her mortall trance.
No, but blest life is this,
   With chaste and pure desire,
   To turne vnto the load-starre of all blisse,
   On God the minde to rest,
   Burnt vp with sacred fire,
   Possessing him, to bee by him possest.
When to the baulmie east
   Sunne doth his light impart,
   Or when hee diueth in the lowlie west,
   And rauisheth the day,
   With spotlesse hands and hart
   Him chearefully to praise, and to him pray;
To heed each action so,
   As euer in his sight,

More fearing doing ill than passiue woe ;
Not to seeme other thing
    Than what yee are aright,
Neuer to doe what may repentance bring ;
Not to bee blowne with pride,
    Nor mou'd at glorie's breath,
    Which shadow-like on wings of time doth glide ;
So malice to disarme,
    And conquere hastie wrath,
    As to doe good to those that worke your harme ;
To hatch no base desires,
    Or gold or land to gaine,
    Well pleas'd with what by vertue one acquires ;
To haue the wit and will
    Consorting in one straine,
    Than what is good to haue no higher skill ;
Neuer on neighbour's well
    With cocatrice's eye
    To looke, and make an other's heauen your hell ;
Not to be beautie's thrall,
    All fruitlesse loue to flie,
    Yet louing still a loue transcending all ;
A loue which, while it burnes
    The soule with fairest beames,
    In that vncreated sunne the soule it turnes,
    And makes such beautie proue,
    That, if sense saw her gleames,
    All lookers on would pine and die for loue.
Who such a life doth liue,
    Yee happie euen may call,
    Ere ruthlesse death a wished end him giue,
    And after then when giuen,

More happie by his fall,
For humanes, earth, enioying angels, heauen.
Swift is your mortall race,
   And glassie is the field,
   Vaste are desires not limited by grace,
   Life a weake tapper is ;
   Then, while it light doth yeeld,
   Leaue flying ioyes, embrace this lasting blisse.
This when the nimph had said,
   Shee diu'd within the flood,
   Whose face with smyling curles long after staid :
   Then sighes did zephyres presse,
   Birdes sang from euery wood,
   And ecchoes rang, This was true happinesse.

AN HYMNE OF THE

FAIREST FAIRE.

___

AN HYMNE OF THE NATURE, ATRIBUTES, AND WORKES OF GOD.

I FEELE my bosome glow with wontlesse fires,
Rais'd from the vulgar prease my mind aspires,
Wing'd with high thoghts, vnto his praise to clime,
From deepe eternitie who call'd foorth time ;
That essence which not mou'd makes each thing moue,
Vncreated beautie, all-creating loue :
But by so great an object, radient light,
My heart appall'd, enfeebled restes my sight,
Thicke cloudes benighte my labouring ingine,
And at my high attempts my wits repine.
If thou in mee this sacred rapture wrought,
My knowledge sharpen, sarcells lend my thought ;
Grant mee, time's Father, world-containing King,
A pow'r, of thee in pow'rfull layes to sing,
That as thy beautie in earth liues, heauen shines,
So it may dawne or shadow in my lines.
  As farre beyond the starrie walles of heauen,
As is the loftiest of the planets seuen,
Sequestred from this earth, in purest light,
Out-shining ours, as ours doth sable night,
Thou, all-sufficient, omnipotent,
Thou euer-glorious, most excellent,

God various in names, in essence one,
High art enstalled on a golden throne,
Out-reaching heauen's wide vastes, the bounds of nought,
Transcending all the circles of our thought:
With diamantine scepter in thy hand,
There thou giu'st lawes, and dost this world command,
This world of concords rais'd vnliklie-sweete,
Which like a ball lyes prostrate to thy feete.
　　If so wee may well say, (and what wee say,
Heere wrapt in flesh, led by dimme reason's ray,
To show by earthlie beauties which wee see,
That spirituall excellence that shines in thee,
Good Lord, forgiue,) not farre from thy right side,
With curled lockes youth euer doth abide;
Rose-cheeked youth, who, garlanded with flowres
Still blooming, ceasleslie vnto thee powres
Immortall nectar, in a cuppe of gold,
That by no darts of ages thou grow old,
And, as ends and beginnings thee not clame,
Successionlesse that thou bee still the same.
　　Neare to thy other side resistlesse might,
From head to foote in burnisht armour dight,
That ringes about him, with a wauing brand,
And watchfull eye, great sentinell doth stand;
That neither time nor force in ought impaire
Thy workmanshippe, nor harme thine empire faire,
Soone to giue death to all againe that would
Sterne discord raise, which thou destroy'd of old;
Discord that foe to order, nurse of warre,
By which the noblest things dimolisht are;
But, catife, shee no treason doth deuise,
When might to nought doth bring her enterprise,

Thy all-vpholding might her malice raines,
And her in hell throwes bound in iron chaines.
    With lockes in waues of gold that ebbe and flow
On yuorie necke, in robes more white than snow,
Truth stedfastlie before thee holdes a glasse,
Indent'd with gemmes, where shineth all that was,
That is, or shall bee : heere, ere ought was wrought,
Thou knew all that thy pow'r with time forth-brought,
And more, things numberlesse which thou couldst make,
That actuallie shall neuer beeing take :
Heere, thou beholdst thy selfe, and, strange, dost proue
At once the beautie, louer, and the loue.
    With faces two, like sisters, sweetlie faire,
Whose blossomes no rough autumne can impaire,
Stands Prouidence, and doth her lookes disperse
Through euerie corner of this vniuerse ;
Thy prouidence at once which generall things
And singulare doth rule, as empires kings ;
Without whose care this world, lost, would remaine
As shippe without a maister in the maine,
As chariot alone, as bodies proue
Depriu'd of soules by which they bee, liue, moue.
    But who are they which shine thy throne so neare,
With sacred countenance, and looke seuere ?
This in one hand a pond'rous sword doth hold,
Her left stayes charg'd with ballances of gold ;
That with browes girt with bayes, sweete-smiling face,
Doth beare a brandon with a babish grace ;
Two milke-white winges him easilie doe moue.
O shee thy justice is, and this thy loue !
By this thou brought this engine great to light,
By that it fram'd in number, measure, weight,

Z

That destine doth reward to ill and good ;
But sway of iustice is by loue with-stood,
Which did it not relent and mildlie stay,
This world ere now had had its funerall day.
   What bands enclustred neare to these abide,
Which into vaste infinitie them hide ;
Infinitie that neither doth admit
Place, time, nor number to encroach on it ?
Heere bountie sparkleth, heere doth beautie shine,
Simplicitie more white than gelsemine,
Mercie with open wings, ay-varied blisse,
Glorie, and ioy that blesse's darling is.
   Ineffable, all-pow'rfull God, all-free,
Thou onelie liu'st, and each thing liues by thee ;
No ioy, no, nor perfection to thee came
By the contriuing of this world's great frame ;
Ere sunne, moone, starres beganne their restlesse race,
Ere paint'd with purple light was heauen's round face,
Ere aire had clouds, ere clouds weept down their showrs,
Ere sea embraced earth, ere earth bare flowres,
Thou happie liu'd ; world nought to thee supply'd,
All in thy selfe thy selfe thou satisfy'd :
Of good no slender shadow doth appeare,
No age-worne tracke in thee which shin'd not cleare ;
Perfection's summe, prime-cause of euerie cause,
Midst, end, beginning, where all good doth pause.
Hence of thy substance, differing in nought,
Thou in eternitie thy sonne foorth brought,
The onelie birth of thy vnchanging minde,
Thine image, paterne-like, that euer shin'd ;
Light out of light, begotten not by will,
But nature, all and that same essence still

Which thou thy selfe ; for thou dost nought possesse
Which hee hath not, in ought nor is hee lesse
Than thou his great begetter : of this light,
Eternall, double, kindled was thy spright
Eternallie, who is with thee the same,
All-holie gift, embassadour, knot, flame.
Most sacred Triade ! O most holie One !
Vnprocreat'd Father, euer-procreat'd Sonne,
Ghost breath'd from both, you were, are, aye shall bee,
Most blessed, three in one, and one in three,
Vncomprehensible by reachlesse hight,
And vnperceiued by excessiue light.
So in our soules, three and yet one are still,
The vnderstanding, memorie, and will :
So, though vnlike, the planet of the dayes,
So soone as hee was made begate his rayes,
Which are his of-spring, and from both was hurl'd
The rosie light which comfort doth the world,
And none fore-went an other : so the spring,
The well-head, and the streame which they foorth bring,
Are but one selfe-same essence, nor in ought
Doe differ, saue in order, and our thought
No chime of time discernes in them to fall,
But three distinctlie bide one essence all.
But these expresse not thee ; who can declare
Thy beeing ? Men and angels dazel'd are :
Who force this Eden would with wit or sence,
A cherubin shall finde to barre him thence.
    All's architect, lord of this uniuerse,
Wit is ingulph'd that would thy greatnesse pierce.
Ah ! as a pilgrime who the Alpes doth passe,
Or Atlas' temples crown'd with winter's glasse,

The ayrie Caucasus, the Apennine,
Pyrenes' cliftes where sunne doth neuer shine,
When hee some heapes of hilles hath ouer-went,
Beginnes to thinke on rest, his iourney spent,
Till, mounting some tall mountaine, hee doe finde
More hights before him than hee left behinde :
With halting pace, so while I would mee raise
To the vnbounded circüits of thy praise,
Some part of way I thought to haue o're-runne,
But now I see how scarce I haue begunne,
With wonders new my spirits range possest,
And wandring waylesse in a maze them rest.
    In those vaste fieldes of light, etheriall plaines,
Thou art attended by immortall traines
Of intellectuall pow'rs, which thou brought forth,
To praise thy goodnesse, and admire thy worth ;
In numbers passing other creatures farre,
Since most in number noblest creatures are,
Which doe in knowledge vs no lesse out-runne,
Than moone doth starres in light, or moone the sunne.
Vnlike, in orders rang'd and manie a band,
(If beautie in disparitie doth stand,)
Arch-angels, angels, cherubes, seraphines,
And what with name of thrones amongst them shines,
Large-ruling princes, dominations, powres,
All-acting vertues of those flaming towres :
These fred of vmbrage, these of labour free,
Rest rauished with still beholding thee ;
Inflam'd with beames which sparkle from thy face,
They can no more desire, farre lesse embrace.
    Low vnder them, with slow and staggering pace,
Thy hand-maide Nature thy great steppes doth trace,

The source of second causes, golden chaine
That linkes this frame, as thou it doth ordaine ;
Nature gaz'd on with such a curious eye,
That earthlings oft her deem'd a deitye.
By nature led, those bodies faire and greate,
Which faint not in their course, nor change their state,
Vnintermixt, which no disorder proue,
Though aye and contrarie they alwayes moue ;
The organes of thy prouidence diuine,
Bookes euer open, signes that clearelie shine,
Time's purpled maskers then doe them aduance,
As by sweete musicke in a measur'd dance.
Starres, hoste of heauen, yee firmament's bright flow'rs,
Cleare lampes which ouer-hang this stage of ours,
Yee turne not there to decke the weeds of night,
Nor pageant-like to please the vulgare sight,
Great causes sure yee must bring great effectes,
But who can descant right your graue aspects ?
Hee onlie who you made, deciphere can
Your notes ; heauen's eyes, yee blinde the eyes of man.
    Amidst these saphire farre-extending hights,
The neuer-twinkling, euer-wand'ring lights
Their fixed motions keepe ; one drye and cold,
Deep-leaden colour'd, slowlie there is roll'd,
With rule and line for time's steppes measur'd euen,
In twice three lustres hee but turnes his heauen.
With temperate qualities and countenance faire,
Still mildelie smiling, sweetlie debonnaire,
An other cheares the world, and way doth make
In twice six autumnes through the zodiacke.
But hote and drye, with flaming lockes and browes
Enrag'd, this in his red pauillion glowes:

Together running with like speede, if space,
Two equallie in hands atchieue their race;
With blushing face this oft doth bring the day,
And vsheres oft to statelie starres the way;
That various in vertue, changing, light,
With his small flame engemmes the vaile of night.
Prince of this court, the sunne in triumph rides,
With the yeare snake-like in her selfe that glides;
Time's dispensator, faire life-giuing source,
Through skie's twelue posts as hee doth runne his course,
Heart of this all, of what is knowne to sence
The likest to his Maker's excellence;
In whose diurnall motion doth appeare
A shadow, no, true pourtrait of the yeare.
The moone moues lowest, siluer sunne of night,
Dispersing through the world her borrow'd light,
Who in three formes her head abroad doth range,
And onelie constant is in constant change.
　Sad queene of silence, I neere see thy face
To waxe, or waine, or shine with a full grace,
But straight amaz'd on man I thinke, each day
His state who changeth, or if hee find stay,
It is 'in drearie anguish, cares, and paines,
And of his labours death is all the gaines.
Immortall monarch, can so fond a thought
Lodge in my brest, as to trust thou first brought
Heere in earth's shadie cloister wretched man,
To sucke the aire of woe, to spend life's span
Midst sighes and plaints, a stranger vnto mirth,
To giue himselfe his death rebuking birth;
By sense and wit of creatures made king,
By sense and wit to liue their vnderling;

And, what is worst, haue eaglet's eyes to see
His owne disgrace, and know an high degree
Of blisse, the place, if thereto hee might clime,
And not liue thralled to imperious time?
Or, dotard, shall I so from reason swerue,
To deeme those lights which to our vse doe serue,
For thou dost not them need, more noblie fram'd
Than vs, that know their course, and haue them nam'd?
No, I neere thinke but wee did them surpasse
As farre as they doe asterismes of glasse,
When thou vs made : by treason high defil'd,
Thrust from our first estate, wee liue exil'd,
Wand'ring this earth, which is of death the lot,
Where he doth vse the pow'r which he hath got,
Indifferent umpire vnto clownes and kings,
The supreame monarch of all mortall things.
    When first this flowrie orbe was to vs giuen,
It but in place disualu'd was to heauen ;
These creatures which now our soueraignes are,
And as to rebelles doe denounce vs warre,
Then were our uassalles ; no tumultuous storme,
No thunders, quakings, did her forme deforme ;
The seas in tumbling mountaines did not roare,
But like moist christall whispered on the shoare ;
No snake did met her meads, nor ambusht lowre
In azure curles beneath the sweet-spring flowre ;
The nightshade, henbane, naple, aconite,
Her bowels then not bare, with death to smite
Her guiltlesse brood ; thy messengers of grace,
As their high rounds, did haunte this lower place.
O ioy of ioyes ! with our first parents thou
To commune then didst daigne, as friends doe now :

Against thee wee rebell'd, and iustly thus
Each creature rebelled against vs;
Earth, reft of what did chiefe in her excell,
To all became a iaile, to most a hell,
In time's full terme vntill thy sonne was giuen,
Who man with thee, earth reconcil'd with heauen.
    Whole and entire, all in thy selfe thou art,
All-where diffus'd, yet of this all no part;
For infinite, in making this faire frame,
Great without quantitie, in all thou came,
And filling all, how can thy state admit
Or place or substance to be voide of it?
Were worlds as many as the raies which streame
From heauen's bright eyes, or madding wits do dreame,
They would not reele in nought, nor wandring stray,
But draw to thee, who could their centers stay;
Were but one houre this world disioyn'd from thee,
It in one houre to nought reduc'd should bee,
For it thy shaddow is; and can they last,
If seuer'd from the substances them cast?
O only blest, and author of all blisse,
No, blisse it selfe, that all-where wished is,
Efficient, exemplarie, finall good,
Of thine owne selfe but onely vnderstood!
Light is thy curtaine, thou art light of light,
An euer-waking eye still shining bright;
In-looking all, exempt of passiue powre
And change, in change since death's pale shade doth lowre:
All times to thee are one, that which hath runne,
And that which is not brought yet by the sunne,
To thee are present, who dost alwayes see
In present act what past is, or to bee.

Day-liuers, wee rememberance doe losse
Of ages worne, so miseries vs tosse,
(Blinde and lethargicke of thy heauenly grace,
Which sinne in our first parents did deface,
And euen while embryones curst by iustest doome,)
That wee neglect what gone is or to come:
But thou in thy great archieues scrolled hast,
In parts and whole, what euer yet hath past,
Since first the marble wheeles of time were roll'd,
As euer liuing, neuer waxing old,
Still is the same thy day and yesterday,
An vn-diuided now, a constant ay.
    O King, whose greatnesse none can comprehend,
Whose boundlesse goodnesse doth to all extend,
Light of all beautie, ocean without ground,
That standing flowest, giuing dost abound ;
Rich palace, and indweller euer blest,
Neuer not working, euer yet in rest !
What wit ʳannot conceiue, words say of thee,
Heere where as in a mirrour wee but see
Shadowes of shadowes, atomes of thy might,
Still owlie eyed when staring on thy light,
Grant that released from this earthly iaile,
And fred of clouds which heere our knowledge vaile,
In heauen's high temples, where thy praises ring,
I may in sweeter notes heare angels sing.

                         2 A

A PRAYER FOR MANKINDE.

GREAT God, whom wee with humble thoughts adore,
Eternall, infinite, almightie King,
Whose dwellings heauen transcend, whose throne before
Archangells serue, and seraphines doe sing ;
Of nought who wrought all that with wond'ring eyes
Wee doe behold within this spacious round,
Who makes the rockes to rocke, to stand the skies,
At whose command clouds dreadfull thunders sound !
Ah ! spare vs wormes, weigh not how wee, alas !
Euill to our selues, against thy lawes rebell ;
Wash of those spots which still in minde's cleare glasse,
Though wee be loath to looke, wee see too well.
Deseru'd reuenge O ! doe not, doe not take ;
Doe thou reuenge, what shall abide thy blow ?
Passe shall this world, this world which thou didst make,
Which should not perish till thy trumpet blow.
What soule is found whom parents' crime not staines,
Or what with its owne sinne destain'd is not ?
Though iustice rigor threaten, ah ! her raines
Let mercy guide, aud neuer bee forgot.
     Lesse are our faults farre, farre than is thy loue,
O ! what can better seeme thy grace diuine,
Than they, that plagues deserue, thy bounty proue,
And where thou showre may'st vengeance, faire to shine ?
Then looke and pittie, pittying forgiue
Vs guiltie slaues, or seruants, now in thrall ;
Slaues, if, alas ! thou looke how wee doe liue,
Or doing ill, or doing nought at all ;

Of an vngratefull minde a foule effect :
But if thy giftes, which amplie heretofore
Thou hast vpon vs powr'd, thou dost respect,
Wee are thy seruants, nay, than seruants more,
Thy children, yes, and children dearely bought ;
But what strange chance vs of this lot bereaues ?
Poore worthles wights how lowlie are wee brought,
Whom grace made children, sinne hath turned slaues ?
Sinne hath turn'd slaues, but let those bands grace breake,
That in our wrongs thy mercies may appeare,
Thy wisedome not so meane is, pow'r so weake,
But thousand wayes they can make worlds thee feare.
   O wisedome boundlesse ! O miraculous grace !
Grace, wisedome which make winke dimme reason's eye,
And could heauen's King bring from his placelesse place,
On this ignoble stage of care to die,
To dye our death, and with the sacred streame
Of bloud and water guishing from his side,
To put away each odious act and blame
By vs contriu'd, or our first parents' pride.
Thus thy great loue and pitty, heauenly King,
Loue, pitty, which so well our losse preuent,
Of euill it selfe, loe ! could all goodnesse bring,
And sad beginning cheare with glad euent :
O loue and pitty, ill-knowne of these times !
O loue and pittie, carefull of our neede !
O bounties, which our execrable crimes,
Now numberlesse, contend neere to exceed !
Make this excessiue ardour of thy loue
So warme our coldnesse, so our lifes renew,
That wee from sinne, sinne may from vs remoue,
Wit may our will, faith may our wit subdue.

Let thy pure loue burne vp all worldly lust,
Hell's pleasant poison killing our best part,
Which makes vs ioye in toyes, adore fraile dust
In stead of thee, in temple of our heart.
   Grant when at last our soules these bodies leaue,
Their loathsome shops of sinne, and mansions blinde,
And doome before thy royall seat receaue,
They may a sauiour, not a iudge thee finde.

THE SHADOW OF THE
IVDGEMENT.

AN ESSAY OF THE GREAT AND GENERALL IUDGEMENT
OF THE WORLD.

Aʙᴏᴜᴇ those boundlesse bounds where starrs do moue,
The seeling of the christall round aboue,
And raine-bow-sparkling arch of diamond cleare,
Which crownes the azure of each vnder spheare,
In a rich mansion radiant with light,
To which the sunne is scarce a taper bright,
Which, though a bodie, yet so pure is fram'd,
That almost spirituall it may bee nam'd ;
Where blisse aboundeth, and a lasting may,
All pleasures heightning, flourisheth for ay,
The King of ages dwells.   About his throne,
Like to those beames day's golden lamp hath on,
Angelike splendors glance, more swift than ought
Reueal'd to sence, nay, than the winged thought,
His will to practise : here doe seraphines
Burne with immortall loue, there cherubines
With other noble people of the light,
As eaglets in the sunne, delight their sight ;
Heauen's ancient denizones, pure actiue powres,
Which, fred of death, that cloister high embowres,
Etheriall princes, euer-conquering bandes,
Blest subjectes acting what their king commandes ;

Sweet quiristers, by whose melodious straines
Skies dance, and earth vntyr'd their brawle sustaines:
Mixed among whose sacred legiones deare
The spotlesse soules of humanes doe appeare,
Deuesting bodies which did cares deuest,
And there liue happie in eternall rest.
   Hither, sure-charg'd with griefe, fraught with annoy,
Sad spectacle into that place of ioy,
Her haire disordered dangling o're her face,
Which had of pallid violets the grace,
The crimsin mantle wont her to adorne
Cast loose about, and in large peeces torne,
Sighes breathing forth, and from her heauie eyne
Along her cheekes distilling christall brine,
Which downe-wards to her yuorie brest was driuen,
And had bedewed the milkie-way of heauen,
Came Pietie: at her left hand neare by
A wailing woman bare her company,
Whose tender babes her snowie necke did clip,
And now hang on her pappe, now by her lip:
Flames glanc'd her head aboue, which once did glow,
But late looke pale, a poore and ruthfull show:
Shee sobbing shrunke the throne of God before,
And thus beganne her case to him deplore.
   Forlorne, wretch'd, desolate, to whom should I
My refuge haue, below or in the skie,
But vnto thee? See, all-beholding King,
That seruant, no, that darling thou didst bring
On earth, lost man to saue from hell's abisme,
And raise vnto these regiones aboue tyme,
Who made thy name so truelie bee implor'd,
And by the reuerent soule so long ador'd;

Her banisht now see from these lower boundes,
Behold her garments' shreedes, her bodie's woundes;
Looke how her sister Charitie there standes,
Proscrib'd on earth, all maim'd by wicked handes:
Mischeefe there mountes to such an high degree,
That there now none is left who cares for mee.
There dwelles idolatrie, there atheisme raignes,
There man in dombe, yet roaring sinnes him staines;
So foolish, that hee puppets will adore
Of mettall, stone, and birds, beastes, trees, before
Hee once will to thy hollie seruice bow,
And yeelde thee homage. Ah, alas! yee now
To those black sprightes, which thou dost keepe in chaines,
Hee vowes obedience, and with shamefull paines
Infernall horroures courtes; case fond and strange!
To bane than blisse desiring more the change.
Thy charitie, of graces once the cheife,
Did long tyme find in hospitalls reliefe ;
Which now lye leuell'd with the lowest ground,
Where sad memorialls scarce are of them found ;
Then, vagabounding, temples her receau'd,
Where my poore cells afforded what she crau'd;
But now thy temples raz'd are, humane blood
Those places staines, late where thy altares stood:
Tymes are so horrid, to implore thy name
That it is held now on the earth a blame.
Now doth the warriour with his dart and sword
Write lawes in blood, and vent them for thy word:
Relligion, faith pretending to make knowne,
All haue all faith, religion quite o'rthrowne ;
Men awlesse, lawlesse liue, most woefull case !
Men, no more men, a God-contemning race.

Scarce had shee said, when from the nether world,
Like to a lightning through the welken hurl'd,
That scores with flames the way, and euerie eye
With terrour dazelles as it swimmeth by,
Came Iustice : to whom angels did make place,
And Truth her flying foote-steppes straight did trace.
Her sword was lost, the precious weights shee bare
Their beame had torne, scales rudlie bruised were :
From off her head was reft her golden crowne,
In ragges her vaile was rent and starre-spangl'd gowne,
Her teare-wette lockes hange o're her face, which made
Betweene her and the mightie King a shade.
Iust wrath had rais'd her colour, (like the morne
Portending clouds' moist embryones to bee borne,)
Of which shee taking leaue, with heart swollen great,
Thus stroue to plaine before the throne of state :
    Is not the earth thy worke-man-ship, great King ?
Didst thou not all this all from nought once bring,
To this rich beautie which doth on it shine,
Bestowing on each creature of thine
Some shadow of thy bountie ? Is not man
Thy vassall, plac'd to spend his life's short span
To doe thee homage ? And then didst not thou
A queene installe mee there, to whom should bow
Thy earth's endwellers, and to this effect
Put in my hand thy sword ? O high neglect !
Now wretched earthlings, to thy great disgrace,
Peruerted haue my pow'r, and doe deface
All reuerent trackes of iustice ; now the earth,
Is but a frame of shame, a funerall harth,
Where euerie vertue hath consumed beene,
And nought, no not their dust, restes to be seene :

Long hath it mee abhor'd, long chased mee ;
Expelled last, heere I haue fled to thee,
And foorth-with rather would to hell repaire
Than earth, sith iustice execute is there.
All liue on earth by spoyle ; the host his guest
Betrayes ; the man of her lyes in his brest
Is not assured ; the sonne the father's death
Attempts, and kinred kinred reaue of breath
By lurking meanes, of such age few makes sicke,
Since hell disgorg'd her banefull arsenicke.
Whom murthers, foule assasinates defile,
Most who the harmelesse innocent beguile,
Who most can rauage, robe, ransacke, blasphame,
Is held most vertuous, hath a worthie's name ;
So on emboldned malice they relye,
That, madding, thy great puissance they defye :
Earst man resembl'd thy pourtrait, soyl'd by smooke
Now like thy creature hardlie doth hee looke.
Olde nature heere, (shee pointed where there stood
An aged ladie in a heauie mood,)
Doth breake her staffe, denying humane race
To come of her, things borne to her disgrace.
The doue the doue, the swan doth loue the swan,
Nought so relentlesse vnto man as man.
O ! if thou mad'st this world, gouern'st it all,
Deserued vengeance on the earth let fall ;
The periode of her standing perfect is,
Her houre-glasse not a minute short doth misse.
The end, O Lord, is come ; then let no more
Mischiefe still triumph, bad the good deuoure,
But of thy word sith constant, true thou art,
Giue good their guerdon, wicked due desart.

Shee said : through out the shining palace went
A murmure soft, such as a-farre is sent
By musked zephires' sighes along the maine,
Or when they curle some flowrie lea and plaine ;
One was their thought, one their intention, will,
Nor could they erre, truth there residing still :
All, mou'd with zeale, as one with cryes did pray,
Hasten, O Lord, O hasten the last day.
  Looke how a generous prince, when hee doth heare
Some louing citie, and to him most deare,
Which wont with giftes and showes him intertaine,
And as a father's, did obey his raigne,
A rout of slaues and rascall foes to wracke,
Her buildings ouer-throw, her richesse sacke,
Feeles vengefull flames within his bosome burne,
And a just rage all respects ouer-turne :
So seeing earth, of angels once the inne,
Mansion of saintes, deflowred all by sinne,
And quite confus'd by wretches heere beneath,
The world's great soueraigne moued was to wrath :
Thrice did hee rouse himselfe, thrice from his face
Flames sparkle did throughout the heauenlie place.
The starres, though fixed, in their rounds did quake,
The earth, and earth-embracing sea did shake :
Carmell and Hæmus felt it, Athos' topes
Affrighted shrunke, and neare the Æthiope's
Atlas, the Pyrenees, the Appennine,
And loftie Grampius, which with snow doth shine.
Then to the synode of the sprights hee swore,
Man's care should end, and tyme should bee no more ;
By his owne selfe hee swore of perfect worth,
Straight to performe his word sent angels forth.

There lyes an island, where the radiant sunne,
When hee doth to the northerne tropicke runne,
Of sex long monethes makes one tedious day ;
And when through southerne signes he holds his way,
Sex monethes turneth in one loathsome night,
(Night neither heere is faire, nor day hote-bright,
But halfe white and halfe more ;) where sadlie cleare
Still coldlie glance the beames of either beare,
The frostie Groen-land.   On the lonlie shore
The ocean in mountaines hoarse doth roare,
And ouer-tumbling, tumbling ouer rockes,
Castes various raine-bowes, which in froth he choakes ;
Gulfes all about are shrunke most strangelie steepe,
Than Nilus' cataractes more vaste and deepe.
To the wilde land beneath to make a shade,
A mountaine lifteth vp his crested head :
His lockes are yce-sheekles, his browes are snow,
Yet, from his burning bowelles deepe below,
Cometes, farre-flaming pyramides are driuen,
And pitchie meteores, to the cope of heauen.
No summer heere the loulie grasse forth bringes,
Nor trees, no, not the deadlie cypresse springes.
Caue-louing eccho, daughter of the aire,
By humane voyce was neuer wak'ned heere :
In stead of night's blake birdes, and plaintfull owle,
Infernall furies heere doe yell and howle.
A mouth yawnes in this hight so blacke obscure
With vapours, that no eye it can endure :
Great Ætna's cauernes neuer yet did make
Such sable dampes, though they bee hideous blacke ;
Sterne horroures heere eternallie doe dwell,
And this gulfe destine for a gate to hell.

Forth from this place of dread, earth to appall,
Three Furies rushed at the angel's call.
One with long tresses doth her visage maske,
Her temples clouding in a horrid caske ;
Her right hand swinges a brandon in the aire,
Which flames and terrour hurleth euery where ;
Ponderous with darts, her left doth beare a shield,
Where Gorgone's head lookes grimme in sable field ;
Her eyes blaze fire and blood, each haire stilles blood,
Blood trilles from either pappe ; and where shee stood,
Blood's liquid corrall sprang her feete beneath,
Where shee doth streach her arme is blood and death.
Her Stygian head no sooner shee vpreares,
When earth of swords, helmes, lances, straight appeares
To bee deliuered, and from out her wombe
In flame-wing'd thunderes artellerie doth come ;
Floodes, siluer streames doe take a blushing dye,
The plaines with breathlesse bodies buried lye ;
Rage, wronge, rapte, sacriledge doe her attend,
Feare, discorde, wracke, and woes which haue none end :
Towne is by towne, and prince by prince with-stood,
Earth turnes an hideous shambles, a lake of blood.
    The next with eyes sunke hollow in her braines,
Lean face, snarl'd haire, with blacke and emptie veines,
Her dry'd-vp bones scarce couered with her skinne,
Bewraying that strange structure built within,
Thigh-bellilesse, most gastlie to the sight,
A wasted skeliton resembleth right.
Where shee doeth roame, in aire faint doe the birdes,
Yawne doe earth's ruthlesse brood and harmelesse heards,
The woods wilde forragers doe howle and roare,
The humid swimmers dye along the shoare ;

In townes, the liuing doe the dead vp-eate,
Then dye themselues ; alas ! and wanting meate,
Mothers not spare the birth of their owne wombes,
But turne those nestes of life to fatall tombes.
 Last did a saffron-colour'd hagge come out,
With vncomb'd haire, browes banded all about
With duskie cloudes, in ragged mantle cled,
Her breath with stinking fumes the aire be-spred ;
In either hand shee held a whip, whose wyres
Still'd poyson, blaz'd with Phlegethontall fyres.
Relentlesse, shee each state, sex, age defiles,
Earth streames with goares, burnes with inuenom'd biles ;
Where shee repaires, townes doe in desartes turne,
The liuing haue no pause the dead to mourne ;
The friend, ah ! dares not locke the dying eyes
Of his belou'd, the wyfe the husband flies ;
Men basiliskes to men proue, and by breath
Than lead or steale bring worse and swifter death :
No cypresse, obsequies, no tombe they haue,
The sad heauen mostlie serues them for a graue.
 These ouer earth tumultuouslie doe runne,
South, north, from rising to the setting sunne ;
They some time parte, yet, than the windes more fleete,
Forth-with together in one place they meete.
Great Quinzai yee it know, Susania's pride,
And you where statelie Tiber's streames doe glide,
Memphis, Parthenope, yee too it know,
And where Euripus' seuen-folde tyde doth flow :
Yee know it, empresses on Tames, Rosne, Seine,
And yee faire queenes by Tagus, Danube, Reine.
Though they doe scoure the earth, roame farre and large,
Not thus content the angels leaue their charge :

Wee of her wracke these slender signes may name,
By greater they the iudgement doe proclame.
    This center's center with a mightie blow
One bruiseth, whose crackt concaues lowder low
And rumbel, than if all the artellerie
On earth discharg'd at once were in the skie ;
Her surface shakes, her mountaines in the maine
Turne topsituruie, of heights making plaine :
Townes them ingulfe, and late where towres did stand,
Now nought remaineth but a waste of sand ;
With turning eddyes seas sinke vnder ground,
And in their floting depthes are valleyes found ;
Late where with foamie crestes waues tilted waues,
Now fishie bottomes shine and mossie caues.
The mariner castes an amazed eye
On his wing'd firres, which bedded hee findes lye,
Yet can hee see no shore ; but whilst hee thinkes,
What hideous creuesse that hudge current drinkes,
The streames rush backe againe with storming tyde,
And now his shippes on cristall mountaines glyde,
Till they bee hurl'd farre beyond seas and hope,
And setle on some hill or palace tope,
Or, by triumphant surges ouer-driuen,
Show earth their entrailles, and their keeles the heauen.
    Skie's clowdie tables some doe paint with fights
Of armed squadrones, justling steedes and knights,
With shining crosses, iudge, and saphire throne ;
Arraigned criminelles to howle and groane,
And plaintes send forth are heard ; new worlds seene, shine
With other sunnes and moones, false starres decline,
And diue in seas ; red comets warme the aire,
And blaze, as other worlds were judged there.

Others the heauenlie bodies doe displace,
Make sunne his sister's stranger steppes to trace ;
Beyond the course of spheares hee driues his coach,
And neare the cold Arcturus doth approach ;
The Sythian amaz'd is at such beames,
The Mauritanian to see ycie streames ;
The shadow which ere-while turn'd to the west,
Now wheeles about, then reeleth to the east :
New starres aboue the eight heauen sparkle cleare,
Mars chopes with Saturne, Ioue claimes Marses spheare ;
Shrunke nearer earth, all blackned now and broone,
In maske of weeping cloudes appeares the moone.
There are noe seasons ; autumne, summer, spring
Are all sterne winter, and no birth forth bring :
Red turnes the skie's blew curtaine o're this globe,
As to propine the iudge with purple robe.
    At first, entraunc'd, with sad and curious eyes
Earth's pilgrimes stare on those strange prodigies ;
The starre-gazer this round findes truely moue
In partes and whole, yet by no skill can proue
The firmament's stay'd firmenesse. They which dreame
An euerlastingnesse in world's vaste frame,
Thinke well some region where they dwell may wracke,
But that the whole nor time nor force can shake ;
Yet, franticke, muse to see heauen's statly lights,
Like drunkards, waylesse reele amidst their heights.
Such as doe nationes gouerne, and command
Vastes of the sea and emperies of land,
Repine to see their countries ouer-throwne,
And finde no foe their furie to make knowne.
Alas! say they, what bootes our toyles and paines ?
Of care on earth is this the furthest gaines ?

No richesse now can bribe our angrye fate,
O no! to blaste our pride the heauenes do threate;
In dust now must our greatnesse buried lye,
Yet is it comfort with the world to dye.
As more and more the warning signes encrease,
Wild dread depriues lost Adame's race of peace;
From out their grandame earth they faine would flie,
But whither know not, heauens are farre and hie;
Each would bewaile and mourne his own distresse,
But publicke cryes doe priuate teares suppresse;
Lamentes, plaintes, shreekes of woe disturbe all eares,
And feare is equall to the paine it feares.
   Amidst this masse of crueltie and slights,
This galley full of God-despising wights,
This iaile of sinne and shame, this filthie stage
Where all act folly, miserie, and rage;
Amidst those throngs of old prepar'd for hell,
Those numbers which no Archimede can tell,
A silly crue did lurke, a harmlesse rout
Wand'ring the earth, which God had chosen out
To liue with him, (few roses which did blow
Among those weedes earthe's garden ouer-grow;
A deaw of gold still'd on earthe's sandy mine,
Small diamondes in world's rough rocks which shine,)
By purple tyrants which persued and chas'd,
Liu'd recluses, in lonlie islands plac'd;
Or did the mountaines haunte, and forests wild,
Which they than townes more harmelesse found and mild;
Where many an hymne they to their Maker's praise
Teacht groues and rocks, which did resound their layes:
Nor sword nor famine, nor plague poisoning aire,
Nor prodigies appearing euery where,

Nor all the sad disorder of this all,
Could this small handfull of the world appall.
But as the flowre, which during winter's cold
Runnes to the roote, and lurkes in sap vp-rol'd,
So soone as the great planet of the yeare
Beginnes the twinnes' deare mansion to cleare,
Liftes vp its fragrant head, and to the field
A spring of beauty and delight doth yeeld;
So at those signes and apparitiones strange,
Their thoughts, lookes, gestures did beginne to change,
Ioy makes their hands to clap, their hearts to dance,
In voice turnes musicke, in their eyes doth glance.
    What can, say they, these changes else portend,
Of this great frame saue the approaching end?
Past are the signes, all is perform'd of old
Which the Almightie's heraulds vs fore-told.
Heauen now no longer shall of God's great power
A turning temple be, but fixed tower;
Burne shall this mortall masse amidst the aire,
Of diuine iustice turn'd a trophee faire:
Neare is the last of dayes, whose light enbalmes
Past griefes, and all our stormy cares becalmes.
O happy day! O chearefull holy day,
Which night's sad sables shall not take away!
Farewell, complaintes, and yee yet doubtfull thoughts,
Crown now your hopes with comforts long time sought;
Wypt from our eyes now shall be euerie teare,
Sighes stopt, since our saluation is so neare.
What long wee long'd for, God at last hath giuen,
Earth's chosen bands to ioyne with those of heauen;
Now noble soules a guerdon just shall finde,
And rest and glorie bee in one combinde;

Now, more than in a mirrour, by these eyne
Euen face to face our Maker shall be seene :
O welcome wonder of the soule and sight !
O welcome obiect of all true delight !
Thy triumphes and returne wee did expect,
Of all past toyles to reape the deare effect :
Since thou art iust, performe thy holy word,
O come still hop'd for, come, long wish'd for Lord !
    While thus they pray, the heauens in flames appeare,
As if they shew fire's elementall spheare ;
The earth seemes in the sunne, the welken gone ;
Wonder all hushes ; straight the aire doth grone
With trumpets, which thrice-lowder sounds doe yeeld
Than deafening thunders in the airie field.
Created nature at the clangor quakes,
Immur'd with flames, earth in a palsey shakes,
And from her wombe the dust in seuerall heapes
Takes life, and mustereth into humane shapes :
Hell burstes, and the foule prisoners there bound
Come howling to the day, with serpentes crown'd.
Milliones of angels in the loftie hight,
Cled in pure gold and the electar bright,
Ushering the way still where the iudge should moue,
In radiant raine-bowes vaulte the skies aboue,
Which quickly open, like a curtaine driuen,
And, beaming glorie, show the King of Heauen.
    What Persian prince, Assirian most renown'd,
What Sythian with conquering squadrones crown'd,
Ent'ring a breached citie, where conspire
Fire to drie blood, and blood to quench out fire,
Where cutted carcasses' quicke members reele,
And by their ruine blunts the reeking steele,

Resembleth now the euer-liuing King ?
What face of Troy, which doth with yelling ring,
And Grecian flames transported in the aire,
What dreadfull spectacle of Carthage faire,
What picture of rich Corinthe's tragicke wracke,
Or of Numantia the hideous sacke,
Or these together showne, the image, face,
Can represent of earth, and plaintfull case,
Which must lye smoking in the world's vast wombe,
And to it selfe both fewell be and tombe ?
    Neare to that sweet and odoriferous clime,
Where the all-cheering emperour of tyme
Makes spring the casia, narde, and fragrant balmes,
And euerie hill and collin crownes with palmes ;
Where incense sweats, where weeps the precious mirre,
And cedars ouer-tope the pine and firre ;
Neare where the aged phœnix, ty'rd of breath,
Doth build her nest, and takes new life in death ;
A valley into wide and open feildes
Farre it extendeth,   *   *   *   *

THE REST IS DESIRED.

A

CYPRESSE

GROVE:

BY

W. D.

A CYPRESSE GROVE.

Thovgh it hath beene doubted if there bee in the soule
such imperious and superexcellent power, as that it can,
by the vehement and earnest working of it, deliuer knowledge to an other without bodilie organes, and by onelie
conceptions and ideas produce reall effects; yet it hath
beene euer, and of all, held as infalible and most certaine, that it often, either by outward inspiration or some
secret motion in it selfe, is augure of its owne misfortunes,
and hath shadowes of approaching dangers presented
vnto it before they fall forth. Hence so manie strange
apparitions and signes, true visions, vncouth heauinesse,
and causelesse languishings : of which to seeke a reason,
vnlesse from the sparkling of God in the soule, or from
the God-like sparkles of the soule, were to make reason
vnreasonable, by reasoning of things transcending her
reach.

Hauing, when I had giuen my selfe to rest in the quiet solitarinesse of the night, found often my imagination troubled with a confused feare, no, sorrow or horror, which interrupting sleepe, did astonish my senses, and rouse mee, all appalled and transported, in a sudden agonie and amazednesse ; of such an vnaccustomed perturbation, not knowing, nor beeing able to diue into any apparent cause, carried away with the streame of my then doubting thoughts, I beganne to ascribe it to that secret fore-knowledge and presaging power of the profeticke minde, and to interpret such an agonie to bee to the spirit, as a sudden faintnesse and vniuersall wearinesse vseth to bee to the bodie, a signe of following sicknesse ; or, as winter lightninges, earth-quakes, and monsteres proue to common-wealthes and great cities, herbingers of wretched euents, and emblemes of their hidden destinies.

Heerevpon, not thinking it strange if whatsoeuer is humaine should befall mee, knowing how Prouidence ouer-commeth griefe, and discountenances crosses ; and that as wee should not despaire in euills which may happen vs, wee should not bee too confident, nor too much leane to those goods wee enjoye, I beganne to turne ouer in my remembrance all that could afflict miserable mortalitie, and to fore-cast euerie accident which could beget gloomie and sad apprehensions, and with a maske of horrour shew it selfe to humaine eyes ; till in the end, as by vnities and points mathematicians are brought to great numbers and huge greatnesse, after manie fantasticall glances of the woes of mankind, and those encombrances which follow vpon life, I was brought to thinke, and with amazement, on the last of humaine terrors, or as one tearmed it, the last of all dreadfull and terrible euils, DEATH. For to easie censure it would appeare that the soule, if it can fore-see that diuorcement which it is to haue from the bodie, should not without great reason bee thus ouer-grieued, and plunged in inconsolable and vn-accustumed sorrow; considering their neare vnion, long familiaritie and loue, with the great change, paine, vglinesse, which are apprehended to bee the inseperable attendants of death.

They had their beeing together; partes they are of one reasonable creature; the harming of the one is the weakning of the working of the other. What sweete contentments doeth the soule enjoye by the senses? They are the gates and windowes of its knowledge, the organes of its delight. If it bee tideous to an excellent player on the lute to endure but a few monethes the want of one, how much more must the beeing without such noble tooles and engines bee plaintfull to the soule? And if two pilgrimes, which have wandred some little peece of ground together, haue an heartsgriefe when they are neare to parte, what must the sorrow bee at the parting of two so louing friendes and neuer-loathing louers as are the bodie and soule?

Death is the sade estranger of acquantance, the eternall diuorcer of mariage, the rauisher of the children from their parentes, the stealer of parents from the children, the interrer of fame, the sole cause of forgetfulnesse, by which the liuing talke of those gone away as of so manie shadowes, or fabulous paladines. All strength by it is enfeebled, beautie turned in deformitie and rottennesse, honour in contempt, glorie into basenesse: it is the vnreasonable breaker off of all the actions of vertue, by

2 D

which wee enjoye no more the sweete pleasures on earth, neither contemplate the statelie reuolutions of the hea- uens ; sunne perpetuallie setteth, starres neuer rise vnto vs. It in one moment depriueth vs of what with so great toyle and care in manie yeeres wee haue heaped toge- ther: by this are successions of linages cut short, king- domes left heirelesse, and greatest states orphaned. It is not ouercome by pride, smoothed by gawdie flatte- rie, tamed by intreaties, bribed by benefites, softned by lamentations, diuerted by time. Wisedome, saue this, can alter and helpe anie thing. By death wee are exiled from this faire citie of the world ; it is no more a world vnto vs, nor wee anie more people into it. The ruines of phanes, palaces, and other magnificent frames, yeeld a sad prospect to the soule ; and how should it consider the wracke of such a wonderfull maister-piece as is the bo- die, without horrour ?

Though it cannot well and altogether bee denyed, but that death naturallie is terrible and to bee abhorred, it beeing a priuation of life, and a not beeing, and euerie priuation beeing abhorred of nature, and euill in it selfe, the feare of it too beeing ingenerate vniuersalie in all creatures ; yet I haue often thought that euen natural- lie, to a minde by onelie nature resolued and prepared, it is more terrible in conceite than in veritie, and at the first glance than when well pryed into ; and that rather by the weaknesse of our fantasie, than by what is in it ; and that the marble colours of obsequies, weeping, and fu- nerall pompe, with which wee our selues limne it forth, did adde much more gastlinesse vnto it than otherwayes it hath. To auerre which conclusion, when I had recol- lected my ouer-charged spirits, I began thus with my selfe.

If on the great theater of this earth, amongst the numberlesse number of men, to die were onelie proper to thee and thine, then vndoubtedlie thou hadst reason to grudge at so seuere and partiall a law. But since it is a necessitie, from the which neuer an age by-past hath beene exempted, and vnto which these which bee, and so manie as are to come, are thralled, no consequent of life beeing more common and familiar, why shouldst thou, with vnprofitable and nothing-auailing stubburn-nesse, oppose to so vneuitable and necessarie a condition? This is the high-way of mortalitie, our generall home: behold, what millions haue trode it before thee, what multitudes shall after thee, with them which at that same instant runne! In so vniuersall a calamitie, if death be one, priuate complaints cannot bee heard: with so manie royall palaces, it is small lose to see thy poore caban burne. Shall the heauens stay their euer-rolling wheeles, (for what is the motion of them but the motion of a swift and euer-whirling wheele, which twinneth forth and againe vp-windeth our life?) and hold still time to pro-long thy miserable dayes, as if the highest of their working were to doe homage vnto thee? Thy death is a peece of the order of this all, a part of the life of this world; for while the world is the world, some creatures must dye, and others take life. Eternall things are raised farre aboue this orbe of generation and corruption, where the first matter, like a still-flowing and ebbing sea, with di-uerse waues, but the same water, keepeth a restlesse and neuer-tyring current: what is below in the vniuersality of the kind, not in it selfe, doeth abide; MAN a long line of yeeres hath continued, THIS MAN euerie hundreth is swipt away. This aire-encircled globe is the sole region of

death, the graue, where euerie thing that taketh life must
rotte, the listes of fortune and change, onelie glorious in the inconstancie and varying alterationes of it ;
which, though manie, seeme yet to abide one, and being
a certaine entire one, are euer manie.   The neuer-agree-
ing bodies of the elementall brethren turne one in another : the earth changeth her countenance with the seasons, some-times looking colde and naked, other tymes
hote and flowrie ; nay, I can not tell how, but euen the
lowest of those celestiall bodies, that mother of moneths,
and empresse of seas and moisture, as if shee were a
mirrour of our constant mutabilitie, appeareth, by her
great nearnesse vnto vs, to participate of our alterations,
neuer seeing vs twice with that same face, now looking
blacke, then pale and wanne, sometimes againe in the
perfection and fulnesse of her beautie shining ouer vs.
Death heere no lesse than life doth acte a part ; the taking
away of what is olde, beeing the making way for what
is young.   This earth is as a table-booke, and men are
the notes, the first are washen out, that new may be written in.   They which forewent vs did leaue a roome
for vs, and should wee grieue to doe the same to these
which should come after vs ? Who beeing admitted to
see the exquisite rarities of some antiquarie's cabinet is
grieued, all viewed, to haue the courtaine drawen, and
giue place to new pilgrimes ? And when the Lord
of this vniuerse hath shewed vs the various wonders of
his amazing frame, should wee take it to heart, when
hee thinketh time to dislodge? This is his vnalterable
and vneuitable decree : as wee had no part of our will
in our entrance into this life, wee should not presume
of anie in our leauing it, but soberlie learne to will that

which hee wills, whose verie willing giueth beeing to
all that it wills ; and adoring the orderer, not repine at
the order and lawes, which all-where and all-wayes are
so perfectlie established, that who would essay to alter and
amend anie of them, hee should either make them worse,
or desire thinges beyond the leuell of possibilitie. All that
is necessarie and conuenient for vs they haue bestowed
vpon vs, and freelie granted; and what they haue not
bestowed nor granted vs, neither is it necessarie nor conuenient that wee should haue it.

If thou doest complaine that there shall bee a time
in the which thou shalt not bee, why doest thou not
too grieue that there was a time in the which thou
wast not, and so that thou art not as olde as that en-
lifening planet of time ? For, not to haue beene a thousand yeeres before this moment, is as much to bee deplo-
red as not to bee a thousand after it, the effect of them
both beeing one ; that will bee after vs which long long
ere wee were was. Our children's children haue that
same reason to murmure that they were not young men
in our dayes, which wee now to complaine that wee shall
not be old in theirs. The violets haue their time, though
they empurple not the winter, and the roses keepe their
season, though they discouer not their beautie in the spring.

Empires, states, kingdomes haue, by the doome of the
supreame prouidence, their fatall periods; great cities lye
sadlie buried in their dust ; artes and sciences haue not
onelie their ecclipses, but their wainings and deathes ; the
gastlie wonders of the world, raised by the ambition of
ages, are ouerthrowne and trampled ; some lights aboue,
deseruing to be intitled starres, are loosed, and neuer
more seene of vs ; the excellent fabrike of this vniuerse

it selfe shall one day suffer ruine, or a change like a ruine ;
and poore earthlings thus to bee handled complaine !

But is this life so great a good that the lose of it
should bee so deare vnto man ? If it be, the meanest creatures of nature thus bee happie, for they liue no lesse
than hee. If it bee so great a felicitie, how is it esteemed
of man himselfe at so small a rate, that for so poore gaines,
nay, one disgracefull word, hee will not stand to loose it ?
What excellencie is there in it, for the which hee should
desire it perpetuall, and repine to bee at rest, and returne
to his olde grand-mother dust? Of what moment are
the labours and actions of it, that the interruption and
leauing off of them should bee to him so distastfull, and
with such grudging lamentations receiued ?

Is not the entring into life weaknesse, the continuing
sorrow ? In the one, hee is exposed to all the injuries of
the elementes, and, like a condemned trespasser, as if it
were a fault to come to light, no sooner borne than fast
manacled and bound ; in the other, hee is restlesslie, like
a ball, tossed in the tinnise-court of this world. When
hee is in the brightest meridiane of his glorie, there need-
eth nothing to destroy him, but to let him fall his owne
hight : a reflexe of the sunne, a blast of winde, nay, the
glance of an eye is sufficient to vndoe him. Howe can
that be anie great matter, of which so small instrumentes
and slender actions are maisters ?

His bodie is but a masse of discording humours, composed and elemented by the conspiring influences of superior lights, which, though agreeing for a trace of tyme,
yet can neuer be made vniforme and kept in a just proportion. To what sickenesse is it subject vnto, beyond those
of the other sensible creatures, no parte of it beeing

which is not particularlie infected and afflicted by some
one, nay, euerie part with many, yea, so many, that the
maisters of that arte can scarce number or name them?
So that the life of diuerse of the meanest creatures of
nature hath, with great reason, by the most wise beene
preferred to the naturall life of man; and wee should
rather wonder how so fragill a matter should so long endure, than how so soone dissolue and decay.

Are the actiones of the most part of men much
differing from the exercise of the spider, that pitcheth
toyles, and is tapist, to pray on the smaller creatures, and for
the weauing of a scornefull webbe euiscerateth it selfe
manie dayes, which when with much industerie finished,
a little puffe of winde carrieth away both the worke and
the worker? Or are they not like the playes of children,
or, to hold them at their highest rate as is a May-game,
a maske, or what is more earnest, some studie at chesse?
Euerie day wee rise and lye downe, apparrell our bodies
and disapparrell them, make them sepulchers of dead
creatures, wearie them, and refresh them; which is a circle
of idle trauells and laboures, like Penelope's taske, vn-
profitablie renewed. Some time wee are in a chase after
a fading beautie; now wee seeke to enlarge our boundes,
increase our treasure, liuing poorelie, to purchase what
wee must leaue to those wee shall neuer see, or, happelie,
to a foole or a prodigall heire. Raised with the wind of
ambition, wee courte that idle name of honour, not
considering how they mounted aloft in the highest ascendant of earthlie glorie, are but tortured ghostes,
wandring with golden fetters in glistering prisones, hauing feare and dangers their vnseparable executioners
in the midst of multitudes rather guarded than regarded.

They whom opacke imaginations and inward thought-
fulnesse, haue made wearie of the world's eye, though
they haue with-drawne themselues from the course of
vulgare affaires, by vaine contemplationes, curious
searches, thinke their life away, are more disquieted, and
liue worse than others, their wit beeing too sharpe
to giue them a true taste of present infelicities, and
to agrauate their woes ; while they of a more shallow
and blunt conceit, haue want of knowledge and ignorance of themselues, for a remedie and antidote
against all the greeuances and incombrances of life.

What camelion, what Euripe, what raine-bow, what
moone doth change so oft as man ? Hee seemeth not the
same person in one and the same day; what pleaseth him in
the morning, is in the euening distastfull vnto him. Yong,
hee scorneth his childish conceits, and wading deeper in
yeeres, (for yeeres are a sea, into which hee wadeth
vntill hee drowne,) hee esteemeth his youth vnconstancie,
rashnesse, follie : old, hee beginneth to pittie himselfe,
plaining because hee is changed, that the world is changed; like those in a ship, which, when they launce from the
shore, are brought to thinke the shore doeth flie from
them. Hee hath no sooner acquired what hee did desire,
but hee beginneth to enter into new cares, and desire
what hee shall neuer bee able to acquire. When hee
seemeth freed of euill in his owne estate, hee grudgeth
and vexeth himselfe at the happinesse and fortunes of
others. He is pressed with care for what is present, with
griefe for what is past, with feare for what is to come,
nay, for what will neuer come ; and as in the eye one
teare draweth another after it, so maketh hee one sorrow follow vpon a former, and euerie day lay vp stuffe of
griefe for the next.

The aire, the sea, the fire, the beasts bee cruell exe-cutioners of man; yet beastes, fire, sea, and aire, are pit-tifull to man in comparison of man, for moe men are de-stroyed by men, than by them all. What scornes, wrongs, contumelies, imprisonmentes, torments, poysons, re-ceiueth man of man! What ingines and new workes of death are daylie found out by man against man! What lawes to thrall his libertie, fantasies and bug-beares to infatuate and inueigle his reason! Amongst the beastes, is there anie that hath so seruile a lot in another's behalfe as man? Yet neither is content, nor hee who raign-eth, nor hee who serueth.

The halfe of our life is spent in sleepe, which hath such a resemblance to death, that often it separates the soule from the bodie, and teacheth it a sort of beeing aboue it, making it soare beyond the spheare of sensuall delightes, and attaine to knowledge, vnto which, while the bodie did awake, it dared scarce aspire. And who would not, rather than remaine chained in this loath-some galley of the world, sleepe euer, that is, dye, hauing all thinges at one stay, bee free from those vex-ationes, disasteres, contempts, indignities, and ma-nie manie anguishes, vnto which this life is enuassalled and made thrall? And, well looked vnto, our greatest contentment and happinesse heere seemeth rather to consist in an absence of miserie, than in the enjoying of any great good.

What haue the dearest fauoritès of the world, crea-ted to the paternes of the fairest ideas of mortalitie, to glorie in? Is it greatnesse? Who can bee great on so small a round as is this earth, and bounded with so short a course of time? How like is that to castles or

2 E

imaginarie cities raised in the skies by chaunce-meeting cloudes ; or to gyantes modelled, for a sport, of snow, which at the hoter lookes of the sunne melt away, and lye drowned in their owne moisture ? Such an impetuous vicissitude towseth the estate of this world. Is it knowledge ? But wee haue not yet attained to a perfect vnderstanding of the smallest flower, and why the grasse should rather bee greene than red. The element of fire is quite put out ; the aire is but water rarified ; the earth is found to moue, and is no more the center of the vniuerse, is turned into a magnes ; starres are not fixed, but swimme in the etheriall spaces ; cometes are mounted aboue the planetes. Some affirme there is another world of men and sensitiue creatures, with cities and palaces in the moone ; the sunne is lost, for it is but a light made of the conjunction of manie shining bodies together ; a clift in the lower heauens, through which the rayes of the highest defuse themselues, is obserued to haue spots. Thus sciences, by the diuerse motiones of this globe of the braine of man, are become opiniones, nay, errores, and leaue the imagination in a thousand labyrinthes. What is all wee knowe, compared with what wee knowe not ? Wee haue not yet agreed about the chiefe good and felicitie. It is perhaps artificiall cunning. How manie curiosities bee framed by the least creatures of nature, (who like a wise painter showeth in a small pourtrait more ingine than in a great,) vnto which the industrie of the most curious artizanes doeth not attaine ! Is it riches ? What are they but the idoles of fooles, the casting out of friendes, snares of libertie, bandes to such as haue them, possessing rather than possessed ; mettalles which nature hath hidde, fore-seeing the great

harmes they should occasion, and the onelie opinion of
man hath brought in estimation ? They are like to thornes
which laid on an open hand are easilie blowne away,
and wound the closing and hard-gripping.   Prodigalls
mis-spend them, wretches mis-keepe them : when wee
haue gathered the greatest aboundance, wee our selues
can enjoye no more of them than so much as belonges
to one man.   They take not away want but occasione
it ; what great and rich men doe by others, the meaner
and more contented sort doe by themselues.   Will some
talke of our pleasures ?   It is not, though in the fables,
told out of purpose, that Pleasure beeing called vp to
heauen, to disburthen her selfe and become more light,
did heere leaue her apparell, which Sorrow (then naked,
forsaken, and wandring,) finding, did afterwards attire her
selfe with : and if wee would say the truth of most of our
ioyes, wee must confesse them to bee but disguised sorrowes ; remorse euer ensueth them, and, beeing the
heires of displeasure, seldome doe they appeare, except
sadnesse and some wakning griefe hath reallie preceded
and fore-went them.   Will some ladies vaunt of their
beautie ? That is but skin-thicke, of two senses onelie
knowne, short euen of marble statues and pictures ; not
the same to all eyes, dangerous to the beholder, and
hurtfull to the possessour ; an enemie to chastitie, a
frame made to delight others more than those which haue
it, a superficiall varnish hiding bones and the braines,
thinges fearefull to bee looked vpon : growth in yeares
doeth blast it, or sicknesse or sorrow preuenting them.
Our strength matched with that of the vnreasonable
creatures is but weaknesse. All wee can set our eyes
vpon in these intricate mazes of life is but alchimie,

vaine perspectiue, and deceiuing shadowes, appearing
farre other wayes a-farre off than when enjoyed, and looked vpon at a neare distance. O! who, if before hee had
a beeing hee could haue knowledge of the manie-fold
miseries of it, would enter this woefull hospitall of the
world, and accept of life vpon such hard conditiones?

If death bee good, why should it bee feared, and if
it bee the worke of nature, how should it not be good?
For nature is an ordinance, disposition, and rule which
God hath established in creating this vniuerse, as is
the lawe of a king which can not erre. For how
should the maker of that ordinance erre, sith in him
there is no impotencie and weaknesse, by the which
hee might bring forth what is vnperfect, no peruersenesse
of will, of which might proceede any vicious action; no
ignorance, by the which hee might goe wrong in working, beeing most powerfull, most good, most wise,
nay, all-wise, all-good, all-powerfull? Hee is the
first orderer, and marshelleth euerie other order, the
highest essence, giuing essence to all other thinges,
of all causes the cause. Hee worketh powerfullie,
bounteouslie, wiselie, and maketh nature, his artificiall organ, doe the same. How is not death of nature, sith what is naturallie generate, is subject to corruption, and sith such an harmonie, which is life,
arising of the mixture of the foure elementes, which are
the ingredientes of our bodies, can not euer endure; the
contrarieties of their qualities, as a consuming rust in the
baser metalles, beeing an inward cause of a necessarie dis-
solution? O of fraile and instable thinges the constant,
firme, and eternall order! For euen in their changes they
keepe euer vniuersall, auncient, and vncorruptible lawes.

Againe, how can death bee euill, sith it is the thaw
of all these vanities which the frost of life bindeth together? If there bee a sacietie in life, then must there
not bee a sweetenesse in death? Man were an intolle-
rable thing were hee not mortall; the earth were not
ample enough to containe her of-spring if none dyed;
in two or three ages, without death, what an vnpleasant and lamentable spectacle were the most flow-
rishing cities! For, what should there bee to bee seene in
them, saue bodies languishing and courbing againe into
the earth, pale disfigured faces, skelitones in steade of
men; and what to bee heard but the exclamationes
of the yong, complaintes of the old, with the pittifull cryes of sicke and pining persons? There is almost
no infirmitie worse than age.

If there bee anie euill in death, it would appeare to
bee that paine and torment which wee apprehend to
arise from the breaking of those strait bands which keepe
the soule and bodie together, which, sith not without great
struggling and motion, seemeth to proue it selfe vehement
and most extreame. The senses are the onelie cause of
paine; but before the last trances of death they are so
brought vnder, that they haue no, or verie little strength,
and their strength lessening, the strength of paine too must
bee lessened. How should wee doubt but the weaknesse
of sense lesseneth paine, sith wee know that weakned
and maimed partes which receiue not nourishment, are a
great deale lesse sensible than the other partes of the bodie; and see that olde strengthlesse decrepit persons
leaue this world almost without paine, as in a sleepe? If
bodies of the most sound and wholesome constitution bee
these which most vehementlie feele paine, it must then

follow that they of a distempered and crasie constitution
haue least feeling of paine; and by this reason, all weake
and sicke bodies should not much feele paine; for if they
were not distempered and euill complexioned, they would
not bee sicke. That the sight, hearing, taste, smelling
leaue vs without paine, and vn-awares, we are vndoubtedlie
assured; and why should wee not thinke the same of the
feeling? That by which wee are capable of feeling, is
the vitall spirits animated by the braine, which in a man
in perfect health, by veines and arteres are spred and ex-
tended through the whole bodie, and hence it is that the
whole bodie is capable of paine; but, in dying bodies, wee
see that by pauses and degrees those partes which are furthest remoued from the heart become colde, and beeing
depriued of naturall heate, all the paine which they feele, is
that they doe feele no paine. Now, euen as ere the sicke
bee aware, the vitall spirits haue with-drawne themselues
from the whole extension of the bodie, to succour the
heart, (like distressed citizens, which, finding their walles
battered downe, flie to the defence of their cittadell,)
so doe they abandonne the heart without any sensible
touch; as the flame, the oyle failing, leaueth the weeke,
or as the light the aire which it doeth inuest. As to those
shrinking motions and convultions of sinewes and members, which appeare to witnesse greate paine, let one represent to himselfe the stringes of an high-tuned lute,
which breaking retire to their naturall windings, or a
peece of yce, that without any out-ward violence crack-
eth at a thaw: no otherwise doe the sinewes of the
bodie, finding themselues slacke and vnbended from the
braine, and their wonted labours and motions cease,
struggle, and seeme to stirre themselues, but without either

paine or sense. Sowning is a true pourtrait of death, or rather it is the same, beeing a cessation from all action, motion, and function of sense and life ; but in sowning
there is no paine, but a silent rest, and so deepe and sound
a sleepe, that the naturall is nothing in comparison of it.
What great paine then can there bee in death, which is
but a continued sowning, a sweete ignorance of cares,
and a neuer againe returning to the workes and dolorous
felicitie of life ? The wise and all prouident Creator
hath made death by many signes of paine appeare terrible, to the effect, that if man, for reliefe of miseries
and present euills, should haue vnto it recourse, it beeing
apparantlie a worser, hee should rather constantlie
indure what hee knoweth, than haue refuge vnto that
which hee feareth and knoweth not. The terrours of
death seeme the gardianes of life.

Now although death were an extreame paine, sith
it comes in an instant, what can it bee ? Why should
wee feare it, for, while wee are, it commeth not, and
it beeing come, wee are no more ? Nay, though it were
most painefull, long continuing, and terrible-vglie, why
should wee feare it, sith feare is a foolish passion but
where it may preserue ? But it can not preserue vs from
death, yea, rather feare maketh vs to meete with that
which wee would shunne, and banishing the comfortes
of present contentmentes, bringeth death more neare
vnto vs. That is euer terrible which is vnknowne : so
doe little children feare to goe in the darke, and their
feare is increased with tales.

But that perhaps which anguisheth thee most, is to
haue this glorious pageant of the world remoued from
thee in the prime and most delicious season of thy life ;

for, though to dye bee vsuall, to dye young may appeare
extraordinarie. If the present fruition of these things bee
vnprofitable and vaine, what can a long continuance of
them bee? If God had made life happier, hee had also made it longer. Stranger and newe halcyon, why
wouldst thou longer nestle amidst these vnconstant and
stormie waues? Hast thou not alreadie suffred enough
of this world, but thou must yet endure more? To
liue long, is it not to bee long troubled? But number thy
yeares, which are now   and thou shalt find,
that where as ten haue ouer-liued thee, thousands haue
not attained this age. One yeare is sufficient to beholde
all the magnificence of nature, nay, euen one day and
night; for more is but the same brought againe. This
sunne, that moone, these starres, the varying dance of
the spring, summer, autumne, winter, is that verie
same which the golden age did see. They which haue
the longest time lent them to liue in, haue almost no
part of it at all, measuring it, either by that space of time
which is past, when they were not, or by that which is
to come. Why shouldst thou then care whether thy
dayes be manie or few, which when prolonged to the
vttermost, proue, paralel'd with eternitie, as a teare is to
the ocean? To dye young, is to doe that soone, and
in some fewer dayes, which once thou must doe; it is
but the giuing ouer of a game, that, after neuer so manie
hazardes, must bee lost. When thou hast liued to that age
thou desirest, or one of Plato's yeares, so soone as the last
of thy dayes riseth aboue thy horizon, thou wilt then, as
now, demand longer respite, and expect more to come.
The oldest are most vnwilling to dye. It is hope of
long life that maketh life seeme short. Who will be-

hold, and with eyes of judgement behold, the manie changes depending on humaine affaires, with the af-
ter-claps of fortune, shall neuer lament to dye yong. Who
knoweth what alterations and sudden disasters in outward estate, or inward contentments, in this wildernesse
of the world, might haue befallen him who dyeth yong,
if hee had liued to bee olde? Heauen, fore-knowing im-
minent harmes, taketh those which it loueth to it selfe before they fall foorth. Death in youth is like the leauing a
supperfluous feast, before the drunken cups be presented,
and walke about. Pure, and, if wee may so say, virgine
soules carrie their bodies with no small agonies, and delight not to remaine long in the dregs of humane corruption, still burning with a desire to turne backe to the
place of their rest; for this world is their inne, and not
their home. That which may fall foorth euerie houre can
not fall out of time. Life is a iourney in a dustie way, the
furthest rest is death; in this some goe more heauilie bur-
thened than others : swift and actiue pilgrimmes come to
the end of it in the morning, or at noone, which tor-
toyse-paced wretches, clogged with the fragmentarie
rubbige of this world, scarce with great trauell crawle
vnto at mid-night. Dayes are not to bee esteemed after the
number of them, but after the goodnesse : more compasse
maketh not a spheare more compleate, but as round is a
little, as a large ring ; nor is that musician most praise-
worthie who hath longest played, but hee in measured accents who hath made sweetest melodie ; to liue long hath
often beene a let to liue well. Muse not how many yeares
thou mightst haue enjoyed life, but how sooner thou
mightst haue lossed it ; neither grudge so much that it is
no better, as comfort thy selfe that it hath beene no worse:

let it suffice that thou hast liued till this day, and, after the
course of this world, not for nought; thou hast had some
smiles of fortune, fauours of the worthiest, some friendes,
and thou hast neuer beene disfauoured of the heauen.

Though not for life it selfe, yet that to after-worlds thou
mightst leaue some monument that once thou wast, hap-
pilie in the cleare light of reason it would appeare that
life were earnestly to be desired : for sith it is denyed vs
to liue euer, said one, let vs leaue some worthy remembrance of our once heere beeing, and drawe out this
spanne of life to the greatest length, and so farre as is possible. O poore ambition! to what, I pray thee, mayst thou
concreded it? Arches and stately temples, which one
age doth raise, doth not another raze? Tombes and adopted pillars lye buried with those which were in them
buried. Hath not auarice defaced what religion did
make glorious? All that the hand of man can vpreare, is
either ouer-turned by the hand of man, or at length by
standing and continuing consumed; as if there were a
secret opposition in fate, the vneuitable decree of the
Eternall, to controule our industry, and conter-checke
all our deuices and proposing. Possessions are not en-
during; children lose their names, families glorying,
like marigolds in the sunne, on the highest top of
wealth and honour, no better than they which are
not yet borne, leauing off to bee. So doeth heauen
confound what wee endeauour by labour and arte to
distinguish. That renowne by papers, which is thought
to make men immortall, and which nearest doth approach the life of these eternall bodies aboue, how
slender it is the very word of paper doth import; and
what is it when obtained, but a flowrish of words, which

comming tymes may scorne? How many millions neuer heare the names of the most famous writers; and
amongst them to whom they are known, how few turne
ouer their pages; and of such as doe, how many sport
at their conceits, taking the verity for a fable, and oft
a fable for veritie, or, as wee doe pleasants, vse all for
recreation? Then the arising of more famous doth darken, put downe, and turne ignoble the glorie of the former, being held as garments worne out of fashion. Now,
when thou hast attained what praise thou couldst desire,
and thy fame is emblazoned in many stories, neuer after
to bee either shadowed or worne out, it is but an eccho,
a meere sound, a glow-worme, which seene a-farre
casteth some cold beames, but approached is found nothing, an imaginarie happinesse, whose good dependes
on the opinion of others. Desert and vertue for the
most part want monuments and memorie, seldome are
recorded in the volumnes of admiration, nay, are often branded with infamie, while statues and trophees
are erected to those whose names should haue beene
buried in their dust, and folded vp in the darkest clowds
of obliuion: so doe the rancke weeds in this garden
of the world choacke and ouer-run the swetest flowres.
Applause, whilst thou liuest, serueth but to make thee that
faire marke against which enuye and malice direct their
arrows, and when thou art wounded, all eyes are turned
towards thee, (like the sunne, which is most gazed on
in an ecclipse,) not for pittie or praise, but detraction:
at the best, it but resembleth that Siracusiane's spheare of
christall, not so faire as fraile; and, borne after thy death,
it may as well bee ascribed to some of those were in the
Trojan horse, or to such as are yet to bee borne an hun-

dreth yeares heareafter, as to thee, who nothing knowes,
and is of all vnknowne.   What can it auaile thee to bee
talked of, whilst thou art not?   Consider in what bounds
our fame is confined, how narrow the listes are of humane glorie, and the furthest shee can stretch her winges.
This globe of the earth and water, which seemeth huge
to vs, in respect of the vniuerse, compared with that
wide wide pauillion of heauen, is lesse than little, of no
sensible quantitie, and but as a point ; for the horizon
which boundeth our sight, deuideth the heauen as in two
halfes, hauing alwaies sixe of the zodiacke signes abouc,
and as many vnder it, which if the earth had any quantitie
compared to it, it could not doe.   More, if the earth were
not as a point, the starres could not still in all parts of it appeare to vs as of a like greatnes; for where the earth raised
it selfe in mountaines, wee beeing more neare to heauen,
they would appeare to vs of a greater quantity, and where
it is humbled in vallies, wee beeing further distant, they
would seeme vnto vs lesse : but the starres in all partes of
the earth appearing of a like greatnesse, and to euery part
of it, the heauen imparting to our sight the halfe of its inside, wee must auouch it to bee but as a point.   Well did
one compare it to an ant-hill, and men, the inhabi-
tants, to so manie pismires and grashoppers, in the toyle
and varietie of their diuersified studies.   Now of this
small indiuisible thing, thus compared, how much is couered with waters, how much not at all discouered,
how much vn-inhabited and desart, and how many millions of millions are they, which share the remnant amongst
them, in languages, customes, diuine rites differing, and
all almost to others vnknowne ? But let it bee granted that
glorye and fame are some great matter, are the life of the

dead, and can reach heauen it selfe, sith they are oft buried
with the honoured, and passe away in so fleet a reuoluti-
on of time, what great good can they haue in them ? How
is not glorie temporall, if it increase with yeares
and depend on time ? Then imagine mee, (for what cannot imagination reach vnto ?) one could bee famous in
all times to come, and ouer the whole world present,
yet shall hee bee for euer obscure and ignoble to those
mightie ones, which were onely heere-tofore esteemed
famous amongst the Assyrians, Persians, Romans. Againe,
the vaine affectation of man is so suppressed, that though
his workes abide some space, the worker is vnknowne :
the huge Egyptian pyramides, and that grot in Pausilipo,
though they haue wrestled with time, and worne vpon
the vaste of dayes, yet are their authores no more known,
than it is knowne by what strange earth-quackes and
deluges yles were diuided from the continent, or hilles
bursted foorth of the vallies. Dayes, monthes, and yeares
are swallowed vp in the great gulfe of tyme, which puts
out the eyes of all their glorie, and onelie a fattall obliuion remaines : of so manie ages past, wee may well figure
to our selues some likelie apparances, but can affirme little certaintie.

But, my soule, what aileth thee, to bee thus backward
and astonished at the remembrance of death, sith it doth
not reach thee, more than darknesse doth those farre-shin-
ning lampes aboue ? Rouse thy selfe for shame ; why
shouldst thou feare to bee without a bodie, sith thy Maker and the spirituall and supercelestiall inhabitantes haue
no bodies ? Hast thou euer seene any prisoner, who, when
the iaile gates were broken vp, and hee enfranchised and
set loose, would rather plaine and sit still on his fetters,

than seeke his freedome; or any mariner, who, in the midst of stormes arriuing neare the shore, would launch forth againe vnto the maine, rather than stricke saile and joyfullie enter the leas of a saue harbour? If thou rightlie know thy selfe, thou hast but small cause of anguish; for, if there bee any resemblance of that which is infinite, in what is finite, which yet by an infinite imperfection is from it distant, if thou bee not an image, thou art a shadow of that vnsearchable Trinitie in thy three essentiall powers, vnderstanding, will, memorie; which though three, are in thee but one, and abiding one, are distinctly three: but in nothing more comest thou neare that soueraigne good, than by thy perpetuitie, which who striue to improue, by that same doe it proue; like those that by arguing themselues to bee without all reason, by the verie arguing show how they haue some. For how can what is whollie mortall more thinke vpon, consider, or know that which is immortall, than the eye can know soundes, or the eare discerne of coloures? If none had eyes, who would euer dispute of light or shadow, and if all were deafe, who would descant of musicke? To thee nothing in this visible world is comparable; thou art so wonderfull a beautie, and so beautifull a wonder, that if but once thou couldst be gazed vpon by bodily eyes, euery heart would be inflamed with thy loue, and rauished from all seruile basenesse and earthlie desires. Thy being dependes not on matter; hence by thine vnderstanding dost thou dyue into the being of euerie other thing, and therein art so pregnant, that nothing by place, similitude, subject, time, is so conjoyned, which thou canst not separate; as what neither is, nor any wayes can exist, thou canst faine and giue an abstract being vnto. Thou seemest a world in thy selfe, containing heauen, starres, seas, earth, floodes, mountaines, forestes, and all that liues; yet rests thou not satiate with what is in thyselfe, nor with all in the wide vniuerse, because thou knowest their defectes, vntill thou raise thy selfe to the contemplation of that first illuminating intelligence, farre aboue time, and euen reaching eternitie it selfe, into which thou art transformed; for, by receiuing, thou beyond all other thinges art made that which thou receiuest. The more thou knowest the more apt thou art to know, not being amated with any object that excelleth in predominance, as sense by objectes sensible. Thy will is vncompellable, resisting force, daunting necessitie, despising danger, triumphing ouer affliction, vnmoued by pittie, and not constrained by all the toyles and disasters of life. What the artes-master of this vniuerse is in gouerning this vniuerse, thou art in the bodie; and as hee is whollie in euerie part of it, so art thou whollie in euerie part of the bodie; like vnto a mirrouer, euerie small parcell of which a-parte doeth represent and doe the same, what the whole did enteire and together. By thee man is that hymen of eternall and mortall thinges, that chaine together binding vnbodied and bodilie substances, without which the goodlie fabricke of this world were vnperfect. Thou hast not thy beginning from the fecunditie, power, nor action of the elementall qualities, beeing an immediate master-piece of that great Maker: hence, hast thou the formes and figures of all thinges imprinted in thee from thy first originall. Thou onelie at once art capable of contraries: of the three partes of time thou makest but one; thou knowest thy selfe so separate, absolute, and diuerse an essence from thy bodie, that thou disposest of it as it pleaseth thee, for in thee there is no passion so weake which mastereth not the feare of leauing it. Thou shouldst bee so farre from repining at this separation, that it should bee the chiefe of thy desires ; sith it is the passage and meanes to attaine thy perfection and happinesse. Thou art heere, but as in an infected and leprous inne, plunged in a flood of, humours, oppressed with cares, suppressed with ignorance, defiled and destained with vice, retrograd in the course of vertue ; small thinges seeme heere great vnto thee, and great thinges small ; follie appeareth wisedome, and wisedome follie. Fred of thy fleshlie care, thou shalt rightlie discerne the beautie of thy selfe, and haue perfect fruition of that all-sufficient and all-suffizing happinesse, which is God himselfe ; to whom thou owest thy beeing, to him thou owest thy well beeing ; hee and happinesse are the same. For if God had not happinesse, hee were not God, because happinesse is the highest and greatest good : if then God haue happinesse, it can not bee a thing differing from him, for if there were any thing in him differing from him, hee should bee an essence composed and not simple. More, what is differing in any thing, is either an accident or a part of it selfe : in God happinesse can not bee an accident, because hee is not subject to any accidents ; if it were a part of him, since the part is before the whole, wee should bee forced to grant that something was before God. Bedded and bathed in these earthlie ordures, thou canst not come neare this soueraigne good, nor haue any glimpse of the farre-off dawning of his vn-accessible brightnesse, no, not so much as the eyes of the birds of the night haue of the sunne. Thinke then, by death that thy shell is broken, and thou then but euen hatched; that thou art a pearle, raised from thy mother, to bee enchaced in gold, and that the death-day of thy bodie is thy birth-day to eternitie.

Why shouldst thou bee feare-stroken and discomforted for thy parting from this mortall bride, thy bodie, sith it is but for a tyme, and such a tyme as shee shall not care for, nor feele any thing in, nor thou haue much neede of her; nay, sith thou shalt receiue her againe more goodlie and beautifull, than when in her fullest perfection thou enjoyed her; beeing, by her absence, made like vnto that Indian christall, which after some reuolutions of ages, is turned into purest diamond? If the soule bee the forme of the bodie, and the forme seperated from the matter of it can not euer so continue, but is inclined and disposed to bee reunited thereinto, what can let and hinder this desire, but that some time it bee accomplished, and obtaining the expected end, rejoyne it selfe againe vnto the bodie? The soule separate hath a desire because it hath a will, and knoweth it shall by this reunion receiue perfection: too, as the matter is disposed, and inclineth to its forme when it is without it, so would it seeme that the forme should bee towards its matter in the absence of it. How is not the soule the forme of the bodie, sith by it it is, sith it is the beginning and cause of all the actions and functions of the bodie? For though in excellencie it passe euerie other forme, yet doeth not that excellencie take from it the nature of a forme. If the abiding of the soule from the bodie bee violent, then can it not bee euerlasting, but haue a regresse. How is not such an estate of beeing and abiding not violent to the soule, if it bee naturall to it to bee in its matter, and, seperate, after a strange manner, many of the powers and faculties of it, which neuer leaue

2 G

it, are not duelie exercised? This vnion seemeth not a-
boue the horizon of naturall reason, farre lesse impossible
to bee done by God; and though reason can not eui-
dentlie heere demonstrate, yet hath shee a mistie and
groping notice. If the bodie shall not arise, how can the
onelie and soueraigne good bee perfectlie and infinitlie
good? For, how shall hee be just, nay, haue so much justice as man, if he suffer the euill and vicious to haue a more
prosperous and happie life, than the followers of religion
and vertue, which ordinarlie vseth to fall forth in this life?
For, the most wicked are lords and gods of this earth,
sleeping in the lee port of honour, as if the spacious habitation of the world had beene made onelie for them,
and the vertuous and good are but forlorne cast-awayes,
floting in the surges of distresse, seeming heere either of
the eye of Prouidence not pittied or not reguarded;
beeing subject to all dishonours, wronges, wrackes; in their
best estate passing away their dayes, like the dazies in
the field, in silence and contempt. Sith then hee is most
good, most just, of necessitie there must bee appointed by
him an other time and place of retribution, in the which
there shall be a reward for liuing well, and a punishment
for doing euill, with a life where-into both shall receiue
their due, and not onelie in their soules diuested; for,
sith both the parts of man did acte a part in the right or
wrong, it carrieth great reason with it that they both,
inteire man, bee arraigned before that high iustice to
receiue their owne: man is not a soule onelie, but a soule
and bodie, to which either guerdon or punishment is
due. This seemeth to bee the voice of nature in almost
all the religions of the world; this is that generall testi-
monie charactered in the minds of the most barbarous and

saluage people ; for all haue had some rouing guesses at ages to come, and a glow-worme light of another life, all appealing to one generall iudgement throne. To what else could serue so many expiations, sacrifices, prayers, solemnities, and misticall ceremonies, to what such sumptuous temples, and care of the dead, to what all religion, if not to showe that they expected a more excellent manner of being, after the nauigation of this life did take an end? And who doeth denie it, must denie that there is a prouidence, a God, confesse that his worshippe, and all studie and reason of vertue, are vaine, and not belieue that there is a world, are creatures, and that hee himselfe is not what hee is.

But it is not of death perhaps that we complaine, but of tyme, vnder the fatall shadow of whose winges all things decay and wither. This is that tyrant, which executing against vs diamantine lawes, altereth the harmonious constitution of our bodies, benuming the organes of our knowledge, turneth our best senses sencelesse, makes vs loathsome to others, and a burthen to our selues; of which euills death relieueth vs. So that, if wee could bee transported, O happy colonie! to a place exempted from the lawes and conditiones of time, where neither change, motion, nor other affection of materiall and corruptible things were, but an immortall, vnchangeable, impassible, all-sufficient kinde of life, it were the last of things wisheable, the tearme and center of all our desires. Death maketh this transplantation; for the last instant of corruption, or leauing off of any thing to bee what it was, is the first of generation, or being of that which succeedeth. Death then beeing the end of this miserable transitory life, of necessity must bee the beginning of that other all-

excellent and eternall; and so causeleslie of a vertuous
soule it is either feared or complained on.

As those images were limned in my minde, the morning starre now almost arising in the east, I found my
thoughts in a mild and quiet calme; and not long after,
my senses, one by one forgetting their vses, began to giue
themselues ouer to rest, leauing mee in a still and peaceable
sleepe, if sleepe it may bee called, where the minde awa-
king is carried with free wings from out fleshlie bondage.
For heauy lids had not long couered their lights, when,
mee thought, nay, sure I was where I might discerne all
in this great all; the large compasse of the rolling circles, the brightnesse and continuall motion of those rubies of the night, which, by their distance, heere below
can not bee perceiued; the siluer countenance of the
wandring moone, shining by another's light; the hanging
of the earth, as enuironed with a girdle of christall;
the sunne, enthronized in the midst of the planetes, eye
of the heauens, gemme of this precious ring the world.
But whilst with wonder and amazement I gazed on those
celestiall splendors, and the beaming lampes of that glorious temple, like a poore countrie-man brought from
his solitarie mountaines and flockes, to behold the magnificence of some great citie, there was presented to my
sight a man, as in the spring of his yeares, with that
selfe same grace, comelie feature, majesticke looke, which
the late   was wont to haue; on whom I had
no sooner fixed mine eyes, when, like one planet-stro-
ken, I become amazed; but hee with a milde demea-
nour, and voyce surpassing all humane sweetnesse, appeared mee thought to say:

What is it doth thus paine and perplexe thee? Is it the

remembrance of death, the last period of wretchednesse, and entrie to these happie places ; the lanterne which lighteneth men to see the misterie of the blessednesse of spirites, and that glorie which transcendeth the courtaine of things visible ? Is thy fortune below on that darke globe, which scarce by the smalnesse of it appeareth here, so great, that thou art heart-broken and dejected to leaue it ?   What if thou wert to leaue behinde thee a so glorious in the eye of the world, yet but a mote of dust encircled with a pond, as that of mine, so louing, such great hopes ? These had beene apparant occasions of lamenting, and but apparant. Dost thou thinke thou leauest life too soone ? Death is best young ; things faire and excellent are not of long indurance vpon earth. Who liueth well, liueth long; soules most beloued of their Maker are soonest releeued from the bleeding cares of life, and with almost a sphericall swiftnesse wafted through the surges of humane miseries. Opinion, that great enchantresse and peiser of things, not as they are, but as they seeme, hath not in any thing more than in the conceit of death abused man ; who must not measure himselfe, and esteeme his estate after his earthlie being, which is but as a dreame; for, though hee bee borne on the earth, hee is not borne for the earth, more than the embryon for the mother's wombe.   It plaineth to bee releeued of its bands, and to come to the light of this world, and man waileth to bee loosed from the chaines with which hee is fettered in that valley of vanities : it nothing knoweth whither it is to goe, nor ought of the beauty of the visible works of God, neither doth man of the magnificence of the intellectuall world aboue, vnto which, as by a mid-wife, hee is directed by death. Fooles, which thinke that this faire and admirable

frame, so variouslie disposed, so rightly marshalled, so
strongly maintained, enriched with so many excellencies,
not only for necessity, but for ornament and delight, was
by that supreme wisedome brought forth, that all things
in a circulary course should bee and not bee, arise and
dissolue, and thus continue, as if they were so many shadowes careslie cast out, and caused by the encountring
of those superiour celestiall bodies, changing onelie their
fashion and shape, or fantasticall imageries, or shades of
faces into christall : but more they, which beleeue that
hee doth no other-wayes regard this his worke, than as a
theater raised for bloudy sword-playeres, wrastlers,
chasers of timorous and combatters of terrible beastes,
delighting in the daily torments, sorrowes, distresse, and
miserie of mankind. No, no, the Eternall Wisdome created man an excellent creature, though hee faine would
vnmake himselfe, and returne vnto nothing ; and though
hee seeke his felicity among the reasonlesse wights, he
hath fixed it aboue. Hee brought him into this world
as a master to a sumptuous, well-ordered, and furnished
inne, a prince to a populous and rich empirie, a pilgrime
and spectator to a stage full of delightfull wonders and
wonderfull delightes. And as some emperour or great
monarch, when hee hath raised any stately city, the
worke beeing atchieued, is wont to set his image in the
midst of it, to bee admired and gazed vpon ; no otherwise did the soueraigne of this world, the fabricke of it
perfected, place man, a great miracle, formed to his owne
paterne, in the midst of this spacious and admirable citie,
by the diuine splendor of his reason to bee an interpre-
ter and trunchman of his creation, and admired and re-
uerenced by all his other creatures. God containeth all

in him, as the beginning of all ; man containeth all in him,
as the midst of all; inferiour things bee in man more
noblie than they exist, superiour thinges more meaneley ;
celestiall thinges fauour him, earthly thinges are vassaled
vnto him, hee is the knot and band of both ; neither is
it possible but that both of them haue peace with man,
if man haue peace with him who made the couenant betweene them and him.   Hee was made that hee might in
the glasse of the world behold the infinite goodnesse,
power, magnificence, and glorie of his Maker, and beholding know, and knowing loue, and louing enioy, and
to hold the earth of him as of his lord paramount, neuer
ceasing to remember and praise him.   It exceedeth the
compasse of conceit, to thinke that that wisedome which
made euerie thing so orderlie in the partes, should make a
confusion in the whole, and the chiefe master-piece ; how
bringing forth so manie excellencies for man, it should
bring forth man for basenesse and miserie.   And no lesse
strange were it that so long life should bee giuen to trees,
beastes, and the birds of the aire, creatures inferiour to
man, which haue lesse vse of it, and which can not judge
of this goodlie fabricke, and that it should bee denyed to
man ; vnlesse there were another manner of liuing prepared for him, in a place more noble and excellent.

But, alas ! said I, had it not beene better that for the
good of his countrie A   endued with so many peerlesse giftes, had yet liued vpon earth ? How long will yee,
replyed hee, like the ants, thinke there are no fairer
palaces than their hills ; or, like to pore-blind moles, no
greater light than that little which they shunne ?   As if
the maister of a campe knew when to remoue a sentinell,
and hee who placeth man on the earth knew not how

long hee had neede of him.   Life is a gouernement and
office, wherein man is so long continued, as it pleaseth
the installer ; of the administration and charge of which,
and what hath passed during the tyme of his residence,
hee must rander an account, so soone as his tearme ex-
pyreth, and hee hath made roome for others.   As mens'
bodies differ in stature, which none can make more long
or short after their desire, so doe they varie in that length
of tyme which is appointed for them to liue vpon the
earth.   That prouidence which prescriueth causes to euerie euent, hath not onlie determined a definite and certaine
number of dayes, but of actions, to all men, which they
can-not goe beyond.

Most   then, answered I, death is not such
an euill and paine, as it is of the vulgare esteemed.   Death,
said hee, nor painefull is, nor euill, except in contemplation of the cause, beeing of it selfe as in-different as birth ;
yet can it not bee denyed, but amidst those dreames
of earthlie pleasures, the vncouthnesse of it, with the
wrong apprehension of what is vnknowne in it, are noy-
some : but the soule sustained by its Maker, resolued
and calmlie retired in it selfe, doeth find that death, sith
it is in a moment of time, is but a short, nay, sweete sigh,
and is not worthie the remembrance, compared with the
smallest dram of the infinite felicitie of this place.   Heere
is the Palace Royall of the Almightie King, in which
the vncomprehensible comprehensiblie manifesteth himselfe ; in place highest, in substance not subject to any
corruption or change, for it is aboue all motion, and so-
lide turneth not ; in quantitie greatest, for, if one starre,
one spheare bee so vast, how large, how hudge in ex-
ceeding demension, must those boundes bee, which doe

them all containe ! In qualitie most pure and orient, heauen heere is all but a sunne, or the sunne all but a heauen. If to earthlinges the foote-stoole of God, and that stage which hee raised for a small course of tyme, seemeth so glorious and magnificent, how highlie would they prize, if they could see, his eternall habitation and throne ! And if these bee so dazeling, what is the sight of Him, for whom and by whom all was created, of whose glory to behold the thousand thousand part, the most pure intelligences are fully satiate, and with wonder and delight rest amazed? For the beauty of his light and the light of his beauty are vncomprehensible. Heere doth that earnest appetite of the vnderstanding content it selfe, not seeking to know any more ; for it seeth before it, in the vision of the diuine essence, (a mirour, in the which not images or shadowes, but the true and perfect essence of euery thing created, is more cleare and conspicuous than in it selfe, all that is knowne or vnderstood ; and where as on earth our senses show vs the Creator by his creatures, heere wee see the creatures by the Creator. Heere doth the will pause it selfe, as in the center of its eternall rest, glowing with a feruent affection of that infinite and all-sufficient good ; which beeing fully knowne, cannot, for the infinite motiues and causes of loue which are in him, but bee fully and perfectly loued : as hee is onely true and essentiall bountie, so is hee onelie essentiall and true beauty, deseruing alone all loue and admiration, by which the creatures are onely in so much faire and excellent, as they participate of his beauty and excelling excellencies. Heere is a blessed company, euery one joying as much in another's felicity, as in that which is proper, because each seeth

2 H

another equallie loued of God: thus their distinct joyes
are no fewer than the co-partners of the joye; and as
the assemblie is in number answerable to the large capaci-
tie of the place, so are the ioyes answerable to the numberlesse number of the assemblie. No poore and pittifull
mortall, confined on the globe of earth, who hath neuer
seene but sorrow, or interchangablie some painted superficiall pleasures, and had but guesses of contentment, can
rightlie thinke on, or be sufficient to conceiue the tearme-
lesse delightes of this place. So manie feathers moue
not on birdes, so manie birds dint not the aire, so manie leaues tremble not on trees, so manie trees grow
not in the solitarie forestes, so manie waues turne not
in the ocean, and so manie graines of sand limit not those
waues, as this triumphant court hath varietie of delights,
and ioyes exempted from all comparison. Happinesse at
once heere is fullie knowne and fullie enjoyed, and as infinite in continuance as extent. Heere is flourishing and
neuer-fading youth without age, strength without
weaknesse, beautie neuer blasting, knowledge without learning, aboundance without lothing, peace
without disturbance, participation without enuy, rest
without labour, light without rising or setting sunne,
perpetuitie without momentes; for time, which is the
measure of motion, did neuer enter in this shining
eternitie. Ambition, disdaine, malice, difference of opi-
nions, can not approach this place, resembling those
foggie mists which couer those lists of sublunarie things.
All pleasure, paragon'd with what is heere, is paine, all
mirth mourning, beautie deformitie: here one daye's
abiding is aboue the continuing in the most fortunate
estate on the earth manie yeeres, and sufficient to con-

teruaile the extreamest tormentes of life. But, although this blisse of soules bee great, and their ioyes many, yet shall they admit addition, and bee more full and perfect, at that long-wished and generall reunion with their bodies.

Amongst all the wonders of the great Creator, not one appeareth to bee more wonderfull, nor more dazell the eye of reason, replied I, than that our bodies should arise, hauing suffered so manie changes, and nature denying a returne from priuation to a habit.

Such power, said hee, beeing aboue all that the vnderstanding of man can conceaue, may well worke such wonders ; for, if man's vnderstanding could comprehend all the secrets and counselles of that eternall maiestie, it would of necessity bee equall vnto it. The author of nature is not thralled to the lawes of nature, but worketh with them, or contrarie to them, as it pleaseth him : what hee hath a will to doe, hee hath power to performe. To that power which brought all this round all from nought, to bring againe in one instant any substance which euer was into it, vnto what it was once, should not be thought impossible ; for who can doe more, can doe lesse ; and his power is no lesse, after that which was by him brought forth is decayed and vanished, than it was before it was produced ; beeing neither restrained to certaine limits or instrumentes, or to any determinate and definite manner of working : where the power is without restraint, the work admitteth no other limits than the worker's will. This world is as a cabinet to God, in which the small things, how euer to vs hide and secret, are nothing lesse keeped than the great. For as hee was wise and powerfull to create, so doth his knowledge comprehend his own creation, yea, euery change and variety in it, of which

it is the verie source.   Not any atome of the scattered
dust of mankinde, though dayly flowing vnder new
formes, is to him vnknowne; and his knowledge doth
distinguish and discerne, what once his power shall
awake and raise vp. Why may not the arts-master of the
world, like a molder, what hee hath framed in diuers
shapes, confound in one masse, and then seuerally fashion them again out of the same? Can the spagericke
by his arte restore for a space to the dry and withered
rose, the naturall purple and blush, and cannot the
Almightie raise and refine the body of man, after neuer so many alterations in the earth? Reason her selfe
findes it more possible for infinite power to cast out from
it selfe a finite world, and restore any thing in it, though
decayed and dissolued, to what it was at first, than for man
a finit peece of reasonable miserie, to change the forme
of matter made to his hand: the power of God neuer
brought forth all that it can, for then were it bounded
and no more infinit. That time doth approach, (O haste
yee times away!) in which the dead shall liue, and the
liuing bee changed, and of all actions the guerdon is at
hand: then shall there bee an end without an end, time
shall finish, and place shall bee altered, motion yeelding
vnto rest, and another world of an age eternall and
vnchangeable shall arise. Which when hee had said, mee
thought hee vanished, and I all astonished did awake.

ON THE REPORT OF THE DEATH

OF THE AUTHOR.

IF that were true which whispered is by Fame,
That Damon's light no more on earth doth burne,
His patron Phœbus physicke would disclame,
And cloath'd in clowds as earst for Phaeton mourne.

Yea, Fame by this had got so deepe a wound,
That scarce shee could haue power to tell his death,
Her wings cutte short; who could her trumpet sound,
Whose blaze of late was nurc't but by his breath ?

That spirit of his which most with mine was free,
By mutuall trafficke enterchanging store,
If chac'd from him, it would haue com'd to mee,
Where it so oft familiare was before.

Some secret griefe distempering first my minde,
Had, though not knowing, made mee feele this losse ;
A sympathie had so our soules combin'd,
That such a parting both at once would tosse.

Though such reportes to others terrour giue,
Thy heauenly vertues who did neuer spie,
I know thou, that canst make the dead to liue,
Immortall art, and needes not feare to die.

* * * * *

SIR WILLIAM ALEXANDER.

THOUGH I haue twice beene at the doores of death,
And twice found shoote those gates which euer mourne,
This but a lightning is, truce tane to breath,
For late borne sorrowes augure fleete returne.
Amidst thy sacred cares and courtlie toyles,
Alexis, when thou shalt heare wand'ring Fame
Tell Death hath triumph'd o're my mortall spoyles,
And that on earth I am but a sad name ;
If thou e're helde mee deare, by all our loue,
By all that blisse, those ioyes heauen heere vs gaue,
I conjure thee, and by the maides of Ioue,
To graue this short remembrance on my graue :
   Heere Damon lyes, whose songes did some-time grace
   The murmuring Eske ; may roses shade the place.

TO THE MEMORIE OF THE MOST EXCELLENT LADIE, IANE COUNTESSE OF PERTH.

THIS beautie, which pale death in dust did turne,
And clos'd so soone within a coffin sad,
Did passe like lightning, like to thunder burne ;
So little life so much of worth it had !
Heauens but to show their might heere made it shine,
And when admir'd, then in the world's disdaine,
O teares, O griefe ! did call it backe againe,
Lest earth should vaunt shee kept what was diuine.
What can wee hope for more, what more enjoy,
Sith fairest thinges thus soonest haue their end ;
And, as on bodies shadowes doe attend,
Sith all our blisse is follow'd with annoy ?
   Shee is not dead, shee liues where shee did loue,
   Her memorie on earth, her soule aboue.

TO THE OBSEQUIES OF THE BLESSED PRINCE,
IAMES KING OF GREAT BRITAINE.

LET holie Dauid, Salomon the wise,
That king whose brest Ægeria did inflame,
Augustus, Helene's sonne, great in all eyes,
Doe homage low to thy mausolean frame,
And bow before thy laurell anadeame;
Let all those sacred swannes, which to the skies
By neuer-dying layes haue rais'd their name,
From north to south, where sunne doth set and rise.
Religion, orphan'd, waileth o're thine vrne,
Out Iustice weepes her eyes, now truely blind;
In Niobees the remnant vertues turne;
Fame, but to blaze thy glories, liues behind.
    The world, which late was golden by thy breath,
    Is iron turn'd, and horrid by thy death.

FINIS.

THE ENTERTAINMENT

OF KING CHARLES.

REPRINTED

FROM THE EDITION OF

M.DC.XXXIII.

THE
ENTERTAINMENT
OF THE HIGH AND
MIGHTY MONARCH
CHARLES

Kɪɴɢ of *Great Britaine,*
France, and *Ireland,*

Into his auncient and royall City of
Eᴅɪɴʙᴠʀɢʜ, the fifteenth
of *Iune,* 1 6 3 3.

Printed at Eᴅɪɴʙᴠʀɢʜ by *Iohn Wreittoun.* 1633.

THE ENTERTAINEMENT OF THE HIGH AND MIGHTY
MONARCH, PRINCE CHARLES, KING OF GREAT
BRITTAINE, FRANCE, AND IRELAND, INTO HIS
ANCIENT AND ROYALL CITIE OF EDENBOURGH,
THE 15. OF IUNE, M.DC.XXXIII.

WITHOVT the gate which is towards the west, where
the streete ascendeth to Heroite's Hospitall, did an arch
arise of height * * * of breadth * * * square with the
battlements and inmost side of the towne-wall : the face
looking to the Castle represented a citie situated on a
rock, which with pointed clifts, shrubs, trees, herbs, and
verdure, did appeare in perspectiue upon the battlements.
In great letters was written,

ΠΤΕΡΩΤΑ ΣΤΡΑ-
ΤΟΠΕΔΑ,

as Ptolomeus nameth it.   In a lesse and different character was written,

CASTRA PUELLARUM;

and under that in a different colour *M. Edenbourgh.*
The rocke was inscribed *Montagna de Diamant,* after two
Italians, which gaue that name to the greatest rocke
neere Edenborourgh, and Cardan, who in his booke
De Rerum Varietate, highly priseth the diamond of the
rocke.

In the freeze under the towne was written,

INGREDERE AC NOSTRIS SUCCEDE PENATIBUS.

Vpon one side of the towne was drawne the flood Lithus, in a mantle of sea-greene or water-colour, a crowne of sedges and reeds on his head, with long locks : his arme leaned upon an earthen pot, out of which water and fishes seemed to runne forth; in his hand hee held a bundle of flowers.   Over him was written,

PICCIOL MA FAMOSO.

On the other side of the towne appeared Neptune bestriding his Hippocampius, the Nereides about him, his trident in his hand.   The word over him was,

ADSUM DEFENSOR VBIQUE.

The theater under the arch was a mountaine, upon which appeared the Genius of the towne, represented by a nimph : shee was attired in a sea-greene velvet mantle, her sleeves and under-roabe of blew tissue, with blew buskins on her feete ; about her necke shee wore a chaine of diamonds, the dressing of her head represented a castle with turrets, her locks dangled about her shoulders. Upon her right hand stood Religion all in white taffeta, with a blew mantle seeded with starres, a crowne of starres on her head, to shew from whence she is : shee leaned her on a scutcheon, where-upon was a crosse with the word,

COELO DESCENDET AB ALTO.

Beneath her feete lay Superstition trampled, a woman blind, in old and worne garments : her scutcheon had, *Vltra Sauromatas.* On the left-hand of this nymph stood

Iustice, a woman in a red damaske mantle, her under-garments cloth of silver; on her head a crowne of gold, on a scutcheon she had ballances and a sword drawn. The word was,

FIDA REGNORUM CUSTOS.

Beneath the feet of Iustice lay Oppression trampled, a person of a fierce aspect, in armes, but broken all and scattered. The word was,

TENENTE CAROLO TERRAS.

The mountaine at the approach of the King's Majestie moved, and the nymph thus spake unto him:

SIR, if nature could suffer rockes to move, and abandon their naturall places, this towne founded on the strength of rockes, (now by all-cheering rayes of your Majestie's presence, taking not onely motion, but life,) had, with her castle, temples, and houses, moved towards you, and be-sought you to acknowledge her yours, and her indwellers your most humble and affectionate subjects, and to beleeve how many soules are within her circuits, so many lives are devoted to your sacred person and crowne. And here, Sir, she offers by me, to the altar of your glorie, whole hecatombes of most happy desires, praying all things may prove prosperous unto you, that every vertue and heroicke grace which make a prince eminent, may with a long and blissed governament attend you, your kingdomes flourishing abroad with bayes, at home with olives; pre-senting you, Sir, (who art the strong key of this litle world of Great Brittaine,) with these keyes, which cast up the gates of her affectioun, and designe you power to open all the springs of the hearts of these her most loyal citizens. Yet this almost not necessary, for as the rose at the farre appearing of the morning starre displayeth and spreadeth her purples, so at the very noyse of your happy returne to this your native country, their hearts, if they could have shined without their breasts, were with joy and faire hopes made spatious ; nor did they ever in all parts feele a more comfortable heate, than the glorie of your presence at this time darteth upon them.

The old forget their age, and looke fresh and young at the sight of so gracious a Prince, the young bear a part in your welcome, desiring many yeares of life, that they may serue you long; all have more joyes than tongues, for, as the words of other nations farre goe beyond and surpasse the affection of their hearts, so in this nation the affection of their hearts is farre above all they can expresse by words. Daigne then, Sir, from the highest of majestie, to looke downe on their lownesse, and embrace it ; accept the homage of their humble minds, accept their gratefull zeale, and for deeds accept that great good-will which they have ever carried to the high deserts of your ancestors, and shall ever to your owne, and your royall race, whilst these rocks shall bee overshadowed with buildings, these buildings inhabited by men, and while men bee endued either with counsell or courage, or enioy any peece of reason, sense, or life.

The keyes being delivered in a bason of silver, and his Majestie received by the majestrates under a pale of state, where the streete ascendeth proudest, beginning to turne towards the gate of the old towne, hee meeteth

with an arch, the height of which was * * * the breadth
* * * The frontispice of this represented, in land-skip, a
countrey wild, full of trees, bushes, bores, white kine,
along the which appeared one great mountaine to extend
it selfe, with the word upon it,

GRAMPIUS.

In some parts was seene the sea enriched with corrall,
and the mussell that conceiveth the pearle: farther off in
an iland appeared a flaming mountaine with the word,

TIBI SERVIET VLTIMA THULE.

On the chapter was a lyon rampant; the word,

IMPERAT IPSE SIBI.

On the land-skip was *Caledonia* in great letters written,
and part represented a number of men in armes flying
and retiring with S. P. Q. R. on their ensignes, which
shew them to bee Romanes ; an other part had a number
of naked persons flying and enchayned, with the figures
of the sunne, moone, and starres drawne on their skins,
and shapes of flowers, which represented the Picts, under
the Romanes, and under-written,

FRACTI BELLO, FATISQUE REPULSI.

A courten falling, the theater discovered a lady attired
in tissue ; her haire was dressed like a cornucopia, two
chaynes, one of gold another of pearle, baudricke wayes
hung downe her shoulders ; a crowne of gold hung from
the arch before her : shee represented the Genius of Caledonia. Neere unto her stood a woman with an olive-colour-
ed maske, long blacke locks waving over her backe, her

2 K

attyre was of divers coloured feathers, which shew her to
bee an American, and to represent New Scotland.   The
scutcheon in her hand bare the armes of New Scotland,
with this word,

AUSPICIIS, CAROLE MAGNE, TUIS.

His Majestie comming neere, was welcomed with these
verses by

CALEDONIA.

THE heavens have heard our vowes, our just desires
Obtained are, no higher now aspires
Our wishing thoughts, since to his native clime
The flower of Princes, honour of his time,
Encheering all our dales, hills, forrests, streames,
As Phœbus doth the summer with his beames,
Is come, and radiant to us in his traine
The golden age and vertues brings againe.
Prince so much longed for, how thou becalm'st
Minde's easelesse anguish, every care embalm'st
With the sweet odours of thy presence ! now
In swelling tydes joyes every where doe flow
By thine approach ; and that the world may see
What unthought wonders doe attend on thee,
This kingdome's angel I, who since that day
That ruthlesse fate thy parent reft away,
And made a starre, appear'd not any where
To gratulate thy comming, saving here.
    Haile Princes' phœnix, Monarch of all hearts,
Soveraigne of love and justice, who imparts
More than thou canst receive ; to thee this crowne
Is due by birth, but more it is thine owne

By just desert ; and ere another brow
Than thine should reach the same, my floods should flow
With hot vermilian gore, and every plaine
Levell the hills with carcases of slaine,
This ile become a red sea. Now how sweet
Is it to me, when love and lawes thus meet,
To girt thy temples with this diadem,
My nurselings' sacred feare, and dearest gemme !
No Roman, Saxon, Pict, by sad alarmes
Could this acquire and keepe ; the heavens in armes
From us repell'd all perills, nor by warres
Ought here was wonne but gaping wounds and scarres :
Our lion's clymacterick now is past,
And crown'd with bayes he rampants free at last.
    Heere are no Serean fleeces, Peru gold,
Aurora's gemmes, nor wares by Tyrians sold ;
Townes swell not here with Babilonian walles,
Nor Nero's sky-resembling gold-seel'd halles,
Nor Memphis' spires nor Quinzaye's arched frames,
Captiving seas, and giving lands their names :
Faith, milke-white faith, of old belov'd so well,
Yet in this corner of the world doth dwell
With her pure sisters, truth, simplicitie ;
Heere banish'd honour beares them company,
A Mars-adorning brood is heere, their wealth
Sound mindes and bodies, and of as sound a health :
Walles heere are men, who fence their cities more
Than Neptune, when he doth in mountaines roare,
Doth guard this isle, or all those forts and towres,
Amphion's harpe rais'd about Thebes' bowres ;

Heaven's arch is oft their roofe, the pleasant shed
Of oake and plaine oft serves them for a bed :
To suffer want, soft pleasure to despise,
Runne over panting mountaines crown'd with ice,
Rivers o'recome, the wastest lakes appall,
Being to themselves oares, steerers, ship and all,
Is their renowne : a brave all-daring race,
Couragious, prudent, doth this climate grace;
Yet the firme base on which their glory stands,
In peace true hearts, in warres is valiant hands,
Which heere, great King, they offer up to thee,
Thy worth respecting as thy pedegree :
Though much it be to come of princely stemme,
More is it to deserve a diadem.
    Vouchsafe, blest people, ravisht here with me,
To thinke my thoughts, and see what I doe see ;
A Prince all gracious, affable, divine,
Meeke, wise, just, valiant, whose radiant shine
Of vertues, like the starres about the pole
Guilding the night, enlightneth every soule
Your scepter swayes ; a Prince borne in this age,
To guard the innocents from tyrants' rage,
To make peace prosper, iustice to reflowre
In desert hamlet as in lordly bowre ;
A Prince, that though of none he stand in awe,
Yet first subjects himselfe to his owne law,
Who joyes in good, and still, as right directs,
His greatnesse measures by his good effects ;
His people's pedestall, who rising high
To grace this throne, makes Scotland's name to flie

On halcyon's wings, her glory which restores
Beyond the ocean to Columbus' shores.
God's sacred picture in this man adore,
Honour his valour, zeale, his piety more,
High value what ye hold, him deep ingrave
In your heart's heart, from whom all good ye have ;
For as moone's splendor from her brother springs,
The people's welfare streameth from their kings.
Since your love's object doth immortall prove,
O love this Prince with an eternall love !
   Pray that those crownes his ancestors did weare,
His temples long, more orient, may beare,
That good he reach by sweetnesse of his sway,
That even his shadow may the bad affray,
That heaven on him what he desires bestow,
That still the glory of his greatnesse grow,
That your begunne felicities may last,
That no Orion doe with stormes them blast,
That victory his brave exploits attend,
East, west, or south doe he his forces bend,
Till his great deeds all former deeds surmount,
And quaile the Nimbrot of the Hellespont ;
That when his well-spent care all care becalmes,
He may in peace sleepe in a shade of palmes ;
And rearing up faire trophees, that heavens may
Extend his life to world's extreamest day.

   The other face of the arch shew men, women, and
children, dauncing after diverse postures, with many
musicall instruments. The worde above them in great characters was,

HILARITATI PVBLICÆ
S. P. Q. E. P.

Where the great streete divideth it selfe in two, upon the old foundations, inhabited by the goldsmiths and glovers, did an arch arise of height ∗∗∗ of breadth ∗∗∗. Upon the chapter of this arch was a crowne set, with this word,

NEC PRIMAM VISA EST SIMILEM, NEC HABERE SECUNDAM.

The face of the arch had an abacke or square with this inscription,

CAROLO, MAG. BRIT. REG. JACOBI FILIO, PRINCI. OPTIMO, MAXIMO, LIBERT. VINDICI. RESTAURA-TORI LEGUM, FUNDATORI QUIETIS, CONSERVA-TORI ECCLESIÆ, REGNI VLTRA OCEANUM IN AMERICAM PROMOTORI, S. P. Q. E. P.

Amidst flourishes of armes, as helmes, lances, corslets, pikes, muskets, bowes, cannons, at the one side of the abacke stood Mars. The word by him was,

PATRIUM COGNOSCITE NUMEN.

At the other side, amongst flourishes of instruments of peace, as harpes, lutes, organs, cisseres, hauboises, stood Minerva ; her word,

QUO SINE ME.

Vpon each side was armes of the two kingdomes, and an intertexture of crownes, with a word,

NEXUS FŒLIX.

Vpon the freeze was written

***GENUS IMMORTALE MANET, MULTOSQUE PER ANNOS
STAT FORTUNA DOMUS, ET AVI NUMERANTUR AVORUM.

At the approach of the king, the theater, a courten
drawne, manifested Mercury, with his feathered hat, and
his caduceus, with an hundred and seven Scottish kings,
which hee had brought from the Elisian fields. Fergus
the first had a speech in Latine, which is here desired. * *
Vpon the crosse of the towne was a shew of panisques :
Bacchus crowned with ivie, and naked from the shoulders up, bestroad a hogshead ; by him stood Silenus, Sil-
vanus, Pomona, Venus. Ceres, in a straw coloured mantle,
embrodered with eares of corne, and a dressing of the
same on her head, should have delivered a speech to the
king, but was interrupted by the Satyres. Shee bare a
scutcheon, upon which was,

SUSTULIT EXUTIS VINCLIS AD SYDERA PALMAS;

meaning, by the king shee was free of the great abuse
of the tithes in this countrey.

In the midst of the streete there was a mountaine
dressed for Parnassus, where Apollo and the Muses appeared, and ancient worthies of Scotland for learning
was represented ; such as Sedullius, Ioannes Duns, Bishop
Elphistoun of Aberdeen, Hector Boes, Ioannes Major,
Bishop Gawen Douglasse, Sir David Lindsay, Georgius
Buchananus. The word over them was,

FAMA SUPER ÆTHERA NOTI.

The Muses were clad in varying taffetas, cloath of silver and purle; Melpomene, though her under-vesture was blacke, yet her buskines and mantle were crimson. They were distinguished by the scutcheons they bare, and more properly than by their flats. Every one had a word. The first was Clio, who bare

SI VIS OMNIA TIBI SUBJICI, SUBJICE TE RATIONI,

which was the king's simbole when hee was prince.

Melpomene had the simbole of King Iames,

PARCERE SUBIECTIS, ET DEBELLARE SUPERBOS.

Thalia had that of Queene Anna,

MIA, MA GRANDEZZA DEL EXCELSO.

Euterpe had the word of Prince Henry,

FAX GLORIA MENTIS HONESTÆ.

Terpsichore,

REGNI CLEMENTIA CUSTOS.

Erato,

PARENDO IMPERAT.

Calliope,

AUREA SORS REGUM EST, ET VELLE ET POSSE BEARE.

Vrania,

NON VINCI POTIS EST NEQUE FINGI REGIA VIRTUS.

Polyhymnia,

PATIENS SIT PRINCIPIS AURIS.

Apollo sitting in the midst of them was clad in crimson taffeta, covered with some purle of gold, with a bow-dricke like the raine-bow, a mantle of tissue knit together above his left shoulder; his head was crowned with laurell, with locks long and like gold : he presented the king with a booke.

Where the great streete contracteth it selfe, at the descent of the easterne gate of the towne, did an arch arise of height * * * * of breadth * * * *. The face of this represented a heaven, into the which appeared his Majestie's ascendant *Virgo*. Shee was beautified with sixe and twenty starres, after that order that they are in their constellatioune, one of them being of the first magnitude, the rest of third and fourth. By her was written,

HABET QUANTUM ÆTHER HABEBAT.

Beneath on the earth lay the Titanes prostrate, with mountaines over them, as when they attempted to bandy against the gods. Their word was on the freeze,

MONITI NE TEMNITE DIVOS.

The chapter shew the three Parcæ, where was written,

THY LIFE WAS KEPT TILL THESE THREE SISTERS SPUNNE
THEIR THREADS OF GOLD, AND THEN THY LIFE BEGUNNE.

The stand discovered the seven planets sitting on a throne, and Endymion. Saturne, in a sad blew mantle embrodered with golden flames, his girdle was lyke a snake byting his tayle : his scutcheon bare,

SPONDEO DIGNA TUIS INGENTIBUS OMNIA CŒPTIS.

2 L

Iupiter was in a mantle of silver, embrodered with lillies and violets.   His scutcheon bare

SAT MIHI SIT CŒLUM, POST HÆC TUA FULMINA SUNTO.

Mars, his haire and beard red, a sword at his side, had his robe of deepe crimson taffeta, embroidered with wolves and horses.   His head bare a helmet, and his scutcheon,

PER TELA, PER HOSTES.

The Sunne had a crowne of flowers on his head, as marigolds and panses, and a tissue mantle.   His scutcheon bare,

IMPERIUM SINE FINE DEDI.

Venus had the attire of her head rising like parts in a coronet, and roses; shee was in a mantle of greene damaske embroidered with doves ; instead of her cæstus, shee wore a scarfe of diverse colours ; her word,

NULLAS RECIPIT TUA GLORIA METAS.

Mercury had a dressing on his head of parti-coloured flowers, his mantle parti-coloured, his word,

FATA ASPERA RUMPES.

The Moone had the attyre of her head, like an halfe moone or cressant of pearle ; her mantle was sad damasse frenzend with silver, embrodered with chamelions and gourdes ; her word,

CONSEQUITUR QUODCUNQUE PETIT.

At a corner of the theater, from out a verdant groue came Endymion. Hee was apparelled like a shepheard in a

long coat of crimson velvet comming over his knee; hee had
a wreath of flowers upon his head, his haire was curled,
and long ; in his hand he bare a sheep-hooke, on his legs
were buskins of gilt leather. These before the King had
this actioune.

ENDYMION.

Rows'd from the Latmian cave, where many years
That empresse of the lowest of the sphæres,
Who cheeres the night, and kept me hid apart
From mortall wights, to ease her love-sicke heart,
As young as when she did me first inclose,
As fresh in beauty as the Maying rose,
Endymion, that whilome kept my flockes
Vpon Iona's flowry hills and rockes,
And warbling sweet layes to my Cynthea's beames,
Out-sang the swannets of Meander's streames ;
To whom, for guerdon, shee heaven's secret barres
Made open, taught the paths and powers of starres ;
By this deare ladie's strict commandement,
To celebrate this day I here am sent.
But whether is this heaven, which starres doe crowne,
Or are heaven's flaming splendors here come downe,
To beautify this neather world with me ?
Such state and glory did e're shepheard see ?
My wits my sense mistrust, and stay amaz'd,
No eye on fairer objects ever gaz'd :
Sure this is heaven, for every wand'ring starre,
Forsaking those great orbes where whirl'd they are,
All dismall sad aspects abandoning,
Are here assembled to greet some darling ;

Nor is it strange if they heaven's hight neglect,
Vnwonted worth produceth like effect ;
Then this it is, thy presence, royall youth,
Hath brought them here within an azymuth,
To tell by me, their herauld, comming things,
And what each Fate to her sterne distaffe sings ;
Heaven's volume to unclaspe, wast pages spread,
Mysterious golden cyphers cleere to reade.
Heare then the augur of the future dayes,
And all the starry senate of thee sayes ;
For what is firme decreed in heaven above,
In vaine on earth strive mortalls to improve.

SATURNE.

To faire hopes to give reines now is it time,
And soare as high as just desires may climbe ;
O halcyonean, cleere, and happy day !
From sorry wights let sorrow flie away,
And vexe antarticke climes, great Britaine's woes
Evanish, joy now in her zenith glowes.
The old Leucadian syth-bearing sire,
Though cold, for thee feeles flames of sweet desire,
And many lusters at a perfect height
Shall keep thy scepter's majestie, as bright
And strong in power and glory every way,
As when thy peerelesse parent did it sway ;
Ne're turning wrinkled in time's endlesse length,
But one in her first beauty, youthfull strength,
Like thy rare mind, which stedfast as the pole
Still fixed stands, however sphæres doe role.
More to inhaunce thy favours, this thy raigne
His age of gold he shall restore againe,

Love, iustice, honour, innocence renew,
Mens' spirits with white simplicity indue,
Make all to live in plentie's ceaselesse store
With equall shares, not wishing to have more.
Then shall not cold the plow-men's hopes beguile,
On earth shall skie with lovely glances smile,
Vntill'd which shall each flower and hearbe bring forth,
And with faire gardens make of equall worth:
Life long shall not be thrall'd to mortall dates,
Thus Heavens decree, so have ordain'd the Fates.

IOVE.

DELIGHT of heaven, sole honour of the earth,
Iove, courting thine ascendant, at thy birth
Proclaimed thee a king, and made it true,
That emperies should to thy worth be due;
He gave thee what was good, and what was great,
What did belong to love, and what to state,
Rare gifts whose ardors turne the hearts of all,
Like tinder when flint attomes on it fall.
The Tramontane which thy faire course directs,
Shall counsells be approv'd by their effects;
Iustice kept low by grants, and wrongs, and jarres,
Thou shalt relieve, and crowne with glistering starres;
Whom nought save law of force could keepe in awe,
Thou shalt turne clients to the force of law;
Thou armes shalt brandish for thine owne defence,
Wrongs to repell, and guard weake innocence,
Which to thy last effort thou shalt uphold,
As oake the ivy which it doth infold:
All overcome, at last thy selfe orecome,
Thou shalt make passion yield to reason's doome;

For smiles of fortune shall not raise thy mind,
Nor dismall most disasters turne declin'd,
True honour shall reside within thy court,
Sobrietie and truth there still resort,
Keepe promis'd faith thou shalt, supercheries
Detest, and beagling marmosets despise.
Thou others to make rich, shalt not make poore
Thy selfe, but give that thou mayst still give more ;
Thou shalt no paranymph raise to high place,
For frizl'd leape, quaint pace, or painted face ;
On gorgeous rayments, womanising toyes,
The workes of wormes, and what a moth destroyes,
The maze of fooles, thou shalt no treasure spend ;
Thy charge to immortality shall tend,
Raise pallaces and temples vaulted high,
Rivers ore-arch, of hospitality ;
Of sciences the ruin'd innes restore,
With walls and ports incircle Neptune's shore,
To new-found worlds thy fleets make hold their course,
And find of Canada the unknowne sourse ;
People those lands which passe Arabian fields
In fragrant wood, and muske which Zephyre yields.
Thou, fear'd of none, shalt not thy people feare,
Thy people's love thy greatnesse shall up-reare ;
Still rigour shall not shine and mercy lower,
What love can doe thou shalt not doe by power ;
New and vast taxes thou shalt not extort,
Load heavy those thy bounty should support ;
By harmlesse iustice graciously reforme,
Delighting more in calme than roaring storme,
Thou shalt governe in peace as did thy sire,
Keepe, save thine owne, and kingdomes new acquire

Beyond Alcides' pillars, and those bounds
Where Alexander's fame till now resounds,
Till thou the greatest bee among the greats :
Thus Heavens ordaine, so doe decree the Fates.

MARS.

SONNE of the lyon, thou of loathsome bands
Shalt free the earth, and what e're thee withstands
Thy noble pawes shall teare : the god of Thrace
Shall be the second, and before thy face,
To truth and iustice whilst thou trophees reares,
Armies shall fall dismay'd with pannick feares,
As when Aurora in skies' azure lists,
Makes shaddowes vanish, doth disperse the mists,
And, in a twinckling, with her opall light
Night horrours checketh, putteth starres to flight.
More to inflame thee to this noble taske,
To thee he here resignes his sworde and caske.
A wall of flying castles, armed pines
Shall bridge thy sea, like heaven with steele that shines,
To aide earth's tennants by foule yoakes opprest,
And fill with feares the great king of the west :
To thee already victory displayes
Her garlands twin'd with olive, oake, and bayes,
Thy triumphs finish shall all old debates :
Thus Heavens decree, so have ordain'd the Fates.

SUNNE.

WEALTH, wisedome, glory, pleasure, stoutest hearts,
Religion, lawes, Hyperion imparts
To thy just raigne, which shall farre farre surpasse,
Of emperours, kings, the best that ever was ;

Looke how hee dims the starres ; thy glorie's rayes
So darken shall the lustre of these dayes :
For in faire vertue's zodiacke thou shalt runne,
And in the heaven of worthies be the sunne.
No more contemn'd shall haplesse learning lie ;
The maids of Pindus shall be raysed high ;
For bay and ivie which their browes enroll'd,
Thou shalt them decke with gems and shining gold ;
Thou open shalt Parnassus' cristall gates :
Thus Heavens ordaine, so doe decree the Fates.

VENUS.

THE Acidalian queene amidst the bayes
Shall twine her mirtles, grant thee pleasant dayes ;
She did make cleare thy house, and with her light
Of cheerelesse starres put backe the dismall spight.
Thy Hymenean bed faire brood shall grace,
Which on the earth continue shall their race,
While Flora's treasure shall the meads endeare,
While sweet Pomona rose-cheek't fruits shall beare,
While Phæbe's beames her brother's emulates :
Thus Heavens decree, so have ordain'd the Fates.

MERCURY.

GREAT Atlas' nephew shall the workes of peace,
The workes of plenty, tillage, trades encrease,
And arts in time's gulfes lost againe restore
To their perfection, nay, find many more.
More perfect artists, Ciclopes in their forge,
Shall mould those brazen tiphones, which disgorge
From their hard bowels mettall, flame, and smoake,
Mufling the ayre up in a sable cloake :

The sea shrinkes at the blow, shake doth the ground,
The world's west corners doth the sound rebound,
The Stygian porter leaveth off to barke,
Black Ioue appall'd doth shrowd him in the darke.
Many a Typhis, in adventures lost,
By new found skill shall many a mayden coast
With thy sayle-winged Argoses find out,
Which like the sunne shall runne the earth about,
And farre beyond his pathes score wavie wayes,
To Cathaye's lands by Hyperborean seas.
Hee shall endue thee both in peace and warre
With wisedome, which than strength is better farre,
Wealth, honour, armes, and arts shall grace thy states :
Thus Heavens ordaine, so doe decree the Fates.

THE MOONE.

O HOW the faire Queene with the golden maids,
The sunne of night, thy happy fortunes aids !
Though turban'd princes for a badge her weare,
To whom shee wain'd, to thee would full appeare ;
Her hand-maid Thetis daily walkes the round
About the Delos that no force it wound ;
Then when thou left it and abroad did stray,
Deare pilgrim, shee did straw with flowers the way,
And turning forraine force and counsell vaine,
Thy guard and guid return'd thee home againe :
To thee she kingdomes, yeares, blisse did divine,
Quailing Medusa's grim snakes with her shine ;
Beneath thee raigne discord, (fell mischiefe's forge,
The bane of peoples, state and kingdomes' scourge,)
Pale envie, with the cockatrice's eye,
Which seeing kils, but seene doth forthwith dye :

2 M

Malice, deceit, rebellion, impudence,
Beyond the Garamants shall packe them hence,
With every monster that thy glory hates :
Thus Heavens decree, so haue ordayn'd the Fates.

ENDYMION.

THAT heretofore to thy heroicke mind
Haps, hopes not answer'd as they were design'd,
O ! doe not thinke it strange ; times were not come,
And these faire starres had not pronounc'd their doome.
The destinies did on that day attend,
When to this northren region thou should lend
Thy cheering presence, and, charg'd with renowne,
Set on thy browes the Caledonian crowne ;
Thy vertues now thy just desire shall grace,
Sterne chance shall change, and to desert give place ;
Let this be knowne to all the Fates admit
To their grave counsell, and to every witt
That spies heaven's inside ; this let Sibilles know,
And those mad Corybants which dance and glow
On Dindimus' high tops with franticke fire ;
Let this bee knowne to all Apollo's quire,
And, people, let it not be hid from you,
What mountaines' noyse and floods proclaim as true :
Where ever fame abroad his prayse shall ring,
All shall observe and serve this blessed King.

The backe face of this arch towards the east, had the
three Graces drawen upon it, which were naked, and in
others hands : they were crowned with eares of corne,
flowers, and grapes, to signifie fecunditie ; their word,

LÆTO TESTAMUR GAUDIA PLAUSU.

By them was Argus full of eyes ; his word,

VT VIDEAM.

Vnder all was written,

TALES ROMA FUIT QUONDAM ADMIRATA TRIUMPHOS.

The Emperour Iustinian appoynted that the shewes
and spectacles made to princes, should be seauen for the
east. On the battlements of the east gate, in a coat all full
of eyes and tongues, with a trumpet in her hand, as if
shee would sound, stood Fame, the wings of the bat at her
feete, a wreath of gold on her head ; and by her, Honour,
a person of a reverend countenance, in a blew mantle of
the colour of silver, his haire broydered with silver, shad-
dowing in waves his shoulders. They were aboue the
statue of King Iames, under which was written,

PLACIDA POPULOS IN PACE REGEBAT.

AT length we see those eyes
    Which cheere both over earth and skies;
Now, ancient Caledon,
    Thy beauties highten, richest robes put on,
    And let young joyes to all thy parts arise.

Here could thy Prince still stay,
    Each moneth should turne in May ;
We need not starre nor sunne,
    Save him to lengthen dayes and joyes begunne,
    Sorrow and night to farre climes hast away.

Now majestie and love
    Combin'd are from above ;
Prince never scepter sway'd
    Lov'd subjects more, of subjects more obey'd,
    Which may indure whilst heaven's great orbs do move.

Ioyes, did ye alwayes last,
    Life's sparke ye soone would wast:
Griefe followes sweet delight,
    As day is shaddowed by sable night,
    Yet shall remembrance keep you still, when past.

EPIGRAMME.

ILLUSTRIOUS top-bough of heroicke stemme,
Whose head is crown'd with glorie's anademe,
My shallow muse not daring to draw neere
Bright Phœbus burning flames in his careere,
Yet knowing surely that Appollo shines
Vpon the dung-hill, as on golden mines,
And knowing this, the bounty of best kings,
To marke the giver, not the gifted things,
Doth boldly venture in this pompous throng
To greet thy greatnesse with a welcome song,
And with the pye doth *Ave Cæsar* sing,
While graver wits doe greater offrings bring.

A PANEGYRICKE

TO THE MOST HIGH AND MIGHTY MONARCH

CHARLES,

KING OF GREAT BRITAINE, FRANCE,

AND IRELAND, &c.

BY WALTER FORBES.

ADMIRED Phœnix, springing from those syres
Whose soules the heaven, whose merit fame admires,
Whose memory is wrapped up in roles
Keept by eternity above the poles;
Thrice-blessed CHARLES, sprung from thy royall sire
Great IAMES, whose fame shall with this frame expire,
And yet beginne afresh for to be sung
By sacred quires in a celestiall tongue;
O thou, the subject of this wel-borne thought,
Immortall King! hast neither said nor wrought
Any thing yet which can detract thy praise,
Since thou'rt more old in vertues than in dayes;
Bred in the bed of honour, thou art blest
With rare perfections, farre above the rest
Of mortall kind; for as thy birth is great,
So is thy mind, too high a marke for hate:
Envie may spew her spight, yet cannot harme
The Man whom all the hoast of Heav'n doth arme.

When bright Apollo circling in his carre,
Doth drive away the day-denuncing starre,
His pow'rfull rayes diffuse in mortall minds
A sweete desire of day, which straight unbinds
Sleep-fettered senses, and his chearefull light
Doth wast all vapours closed in cloudy night :
So, my deare Phœbus, whilst thy face doth shine
Vpon this land, which by discent is thine
From hundred and eight kings, thy chearefull rayes
Doe change my nights in halcyonian dayes,
And straight dissolue those frightfull formes of woe,
Which did possesse my troubled thoughts agoe.
What sad affliction did my soule possesse,
When Iber's streames reflex'd thy glorious face !
My groanes are turn'd to greetings, and my wrongs
Are chang'd in hymnes and sweete Syrenean songs :
My spirit, then, which for thy absence groan'd,
Rejoyceth now to see thee here enthron'd.
What greater joy can I conceive than see
My native Prince his native throne supply ?
Thrice happie CHARLES, with all those gifts enricht
Which heavens allot to mortals, I'me bewitcht
In admiration of these royall parts,
Which makes thee more than monarch of men's hearts :
My heart and hands, and all submitted here,
Attest the heavens that I account thee deare,
And dearest deare of all this all : I place
My chiefest joyes in favour of thy face,
I doe not poynt my prayses, nor this land,
Although rich nature with a liberall hand
Hath bravely deckt her with all kind of things,
Which from her wombe for humane use foorth springs,

Both Pan and Pales, pleasures, gems, and ore,
Which wretched worldlings for their God adore.
   I, onely I, when all the world by warre
Was boylde in blood as red as Marses starre,
Did safely sleepe, secur'd from forraine armes,
And did disdaine Bellona's lowd alarmes :
The Gothes, the Danes, the Saxons here did feele,
And Normanes fierce, the fury of my steele ;
Here Cæsar pitcht his tent, and proudly thought
His trophees o're our tombes to Rome haue brought,
But all in vaine ; his conquering hand was stayed,
And by his troupes a wall-dividing layed
At Caron's bankes, whose ruines yet may tell
How farre in worth I did his force excell.
And as in Mars', so in Minerva's field
For armes and arts I keepe rich Pallas shield :
Did not the Germanes borrow light from me,
And France, which all posterity shall see,
Ev'n to the fatall doome, when all's in fire ?
Then shall the records of my worth expire.
Thus, gracious CHARLES, daigne with a loving eye
The sweet desires of my pure heart to spy :
Looke with what love and with what chearefull part
I consecrate to thee a loyall heart ;
My humbled knees, loe ! and my heav'd up hands,
The sacred oath of loue from thee demands.
Thrise glorious CHARLES, how amiable's thy face,
Whose loving lookes my clouds of care doe chase ;
I reape more joy from this thy comming here,
Than e're Penelope of Vlisses deare,
Who after thousand dangers did returne,
And cur'd those griefes which did her bowels burne :

O thou, more worthy than Vlisses farre,
Honour's bright ray, goodnesse and greatnesse starre,
Long did I wish to see thy sacred face,
My townes and temples with thy presence grace.
   Great Iove's vice-gerent, looke with kind aspect
On my emporium Edinbvrgh, direct
No oblique rayes, accept in love her showes,
Her verdant glory which so brauely goes,
To doe thee service, all her cost compense
With kind acceptance, with her faults dispense,
And if in her omission shall be found,
Let her endeavours braue, defects confound :
If Iove, who all the starry heavens doth guide,
Delights sometimes at Creta to abide,
As in the place where first he suck't the ayre ;
And if Apollo Delos doth repaire,
Leaving his Claros, Tenedos behind ;
Thus since th' immortall gods have such a mind
To native soyle, it is no wonder then
Though demi-gods be mov'd, and earth-borne men.
May still, great CHARLES, thy Scotland Creta be,
And Delos, where thou may delight to see
The naides and the mountaine nymphes most faire
With unaccustom'd clamours beate the ayre,
The satyres dance, the Corribantean priests
O're-joyde with joy to pulse their panting breasts.
O what great joy hath thy deare presence brought !
Let all the annals through all age be sought,
The like was never seene, the senselesse stones
Doe melt for joy, the mountaines leape at once,
The winds are calmde, and Neptune's lowdest roare,
Deavde with my shouts of joy, is heard no more ;

And when the aire with thy great name I wound,
The mountaines answere, and the rockes resound,
The woods re-echo'd, and the floods proclaime
Melodious murmures hearing of thy name;
The fishes, fowles, and beasts, are strucke with wonder,
Whilst to the clouds I tell my ioyes in thunder.
Thou art my rich palladium; while I keepe
My God and thee, I may securely sleepe,
And feare no terrour nor disturbing foe,
Whilst I have thee to ante-vert my woe.
God hath by nature wall'd me round about,
And given me Neptune sentinell and scout,
Whose tossed trident threatneth death to such
As dare in deepe disdaine my borders touch;
And if by fates I be enforc'd to warre,
And make my lyon's roare be heard afarre,
O may it be for some such sacred cause
As doth subsist with heaven and humane lawes!
O may it be to vindicate the wrong
Of thy deare sister, and her children young,
Whose matchlesse worth and vertues merit praise
From all which can set, sing, or sound sweet layes,
Till shee, deare she, be re-invest againe
With her owne rights, possest with her demaine,
Till she be safely situat on her Rhyne,
And, as the moone amongst the starres doth shine,
Till she in greatnesse doe exceed all those
Who to her glory did their rage oppose,
Till that sun-gazing eagle be forc'd to fall
Before her feete, and for her pardon call!
Let's beate alarmes, and let our trumpets sound,
Let cornets shrill the yeelding ayre now wound,

Let frightfull shouts of souldiers pierce the sky,
And reach the convexe of Olympus high
Above the thundring clouds, let noyses make
The soaring eagle for feare of CHARLES to shake ;
Let Vienn's walls, astonisht with our cry,
Like stubble before the fire fall downe and fly,
Scattred with winds of his revenging wrath,
Who in his hand hath pow'r of life and death ;
Let Rome with her seven hills be shaken too,
And at thy name, O CHARLES, obedient bow.

Heav'n grant I may victorious still returne
Drunke with the blood of foes, sleepe in the vrne
Of my ancestors, whose manes shall be glad
When it shall be to future ages said,
That I in worth did so exceed them farre,
As doth the sunne in light each little starre.

O may thy ensignes ever be displaid !
O may my heart and hand be nere dismaid
In thy defence, till all the world adore
Thy dreadfull name, from Vesper till Aurore !
Thine be the night and day, may starres bright shine,
And plannets wander o're no land but thine ;
And when by death thou shalt shut up thy dayes,
Thy memory shall still inherit praise,
And after age shall obeliskes upreare,
In which thy worth and vertues shall appeare ;
High phanes and temples shall by thy name be call'd,
And thou, among th' immortal gods install'd,
Shalt see the offrings and the yearely vowes
Posterity unto thy fame allowes :
Religious rites and games for thee erected,
Shall shew on earth how much thou wast respected.

FINIS.

COMMENDATORY VERSES.

REPRINTED

FROM THE ORIGINAL WORKS

TO WHICH THEY WERE PREFIXED.

M.DC.XIV—M.DC.XXXV.

COMMENDATORY VERSES.

SONNET,

TO SIR W. ALEXANDER.

[PREFIXED TO DOOMES-DAY, BY SIR WILLIAM ALEXANDER.

EDINBURGH, 1614, 4TO.]

LIKE Sophocles, the hearers in a trance,
With crimson cothurne on a stately stage
If thou march forth, where all with pompe doth glance,
To mone the monarches of the world's first age ;
Or if, like Phœbus, thou thy selfe advance,
All bright with sacred flames, known by heauen's badge,
To make a day, of dayes which scornes the rage,
Whilst when they end it, what should come doth scance ;
Thy Phœnix-Muse still wing'd with wonders flies,
Praise of our brookes, staine to old Pindus' springs,
And who thee follow would, scarce with their eyes
Can reach the spheare where thou most sweetlie sings.
 Though string'd with starres heauens Orpheus' harpe enrolle,
 More worthy thine to blaze about the pole.

TO THE AUTHOR, SONNET.

[PREFIXED TO THE FAMOUS HISTORIE OF PENARDO AND LAISSA, BY PATRIK GORDON.
DORT, 1615, 8vo.]

COME forth, Laissa, spred thy lockes of gold,
Show thy cheekes' roses in their virgine prime,
And though no gemmes thee decke which Indies hold,
Yeild not vnto the fairest of thy tyme.
No ceruse brought farre farre beyond the seas,
Noe poisone lyke cinabre paints thy face,
Let them have that whose natiue hues displease,
Thow gracest nakednesse, it doth thee grace.
Thy syre no pyick-purse is of other's witt,
Those jewellis be his owne which thee adorne ;
And though thow after greatter ones be borne,
Thow mayst be bold euen midst the first to sitt,
  For whilst fair Iuliett, or the Farie Queene
  Doe liue with theirs, thy beautie shall be seene.

ON THE DEATH OF GODEFRID VANDER HAGEN.

[PREFIXED TO G. VANDER HAGEN MISCELLANEA POEMATA. MIDDELBURGI, 1619, 4TO.]

SCARCE I four lusters had enjoyed breath,
When my life's threid was cut by cruel death ;
Few were my yeares, so were my sorrowes all,
Long dayes have drammes of sweet, but pounds of gall ;
And yet the fruites which my faire spring did give,
Prove some may longer breath, not longer live.
That craggie path which doth to vertue lead,
With steps of honor I did stronglie tread ;

I made sweet layes, and into notes divyne
Out-sung Apollo and the Muses nyne.
Forth's sweetest swannets did extolle my verse,
Forth's sweetest swannets now weepe o're my hearse,
    For which I pardone Fates my date of yeares ;
    Kings may have vaster tombes, not dearer teares.

OF MY LORD OF GALLOWAY HIS LEARNED COMMENTARY
ON THE REUELATION.

[PREFIXED TO PATHMOS ; OR A COMMENTARY ON THE REVELATION OF SAINT IOHN,
BY WILLIAM COWPER, BISHOP OF GALLOWAY.   LONDON, 1619, 4TO.]

To this admir'd discouerer giue place,
Yee who first tam'd the sea, the windes outranne,
And match'd the daye's bright coach-man in your race,
Americus, Columbus, Magellan.
It is most true that your ingenious care
And well-spent paines another world brought forth,
For beasts, birds, trees, for gemmes and metals rare,
Yet all being earth, was but of earthly worth.
Hee a more precious world to vs descryes,
Rich in more treasure than both Indes containe,
Faire in more beauty than man's witte can faine,
Whose sunne not sets, whose people neuer dies.
    Earth shuld your brows deck with stil-verdant bayes,
    But heauens crowne his with stars' immortall rayes.

ON THE BOOKE.

[PREFIXED TO HEPTAMERON, THE SEVEN DAYES, &c. BY A. SYMSON.

SAINCT ANDREWS, 1621, 8vo.]

God binding with hid tendons this great all,
Did make a lute which had all parts it giuen ;
This lute's round bellie was the azur'd heaven,
The rose those lights which hee did there install ;
The basses were the earth and ocean,
The treble shrill the aire ; the other strings
The vnlike bodies were of mixed things :
And then his hand to breake sweete notes began.
Those loftie concords did so farre rebound,
That floods, rocks, meadows, forrests, did them heare,
Birds, fishes, beasts, danc'd to their siluer sound ;
Onlie to them man had a deafned eare :
  Now him to rouse from sleepe so deepe and long,
  God wak'ned hath the eccho of this song.

ON THESE LOCKES.

[PREFIXED TO SAMSONS SEAVEN LOCKES OF HAIRE, BY A. SYMSON.

SAINCT ANDREWES, 1621, 8vo.]

Lockes, ornament of angels, diademes
Which the triumphing quires aboue doe crowne ;
Rich curles of bountie, pinnions of renowne,
Of that immortall sunne immortall beames ;

Lockes, sacred lockes, no, adamantine chaines,
Which doe shut vp and firme together binde
Both that contentment which in life wee finde,
And blisse which with vnbodied soules remaines ;
Faire locks, all locks compar'd to you, though gold,
Are comets' locks, portending harme and wrath,
Or bauld Occasion's locke, that none can holde,
Or Absalom's, which worke the wearer's death.
  If hencefoorth beautie e're my minde subdue,
  It shall, deare locks, be for what shines in you.

PARAINETICON.

[PREFIXED TO PALLAS ARMATA, OR MILITARIE INSTRUCTIONS FOR THE LEARNED,

BY SIR THOMAS KELLIE. EDINBURGH, 1627, 4TO.]

Poore Rhene, and canst thou see
    Thy natiues' gore thy christall curles deface,
    Thy nymphes so bright which bee,
    Halfe-blackamores embrace,
    And, dull'd with grapes, yet not resente thy case ?
Fallen are thy anadeames,
    O of such goodlie cities famous flood !
    Dimm'd bee thy beautie's beames,
    And with thy spoyles and blood
    Hell is made rich, prowd the Iberian blood.
And you, faire Europe's queen,
    Which hast with lillies deckt your purple seate,
    Can you see those haue beene
    Sterne cometes to your state,
    On neighboures' wracke to grow so hugelie great ?
                    2 o

Looke how much Iber gaines,
    By as much lessened is your flowrie throne ;
    O doe not take such paines
    On Bartholomewes alone,
    But seeke to reacquire your Pampelone.
Braue people, which endwell
    The happiest ile that Neptune's armes embrace.
    World, which doth yet excell
    In what first worlds did grace,
    Doe neuer to base seruitude giue place :
Marshalle your wits and armes,
    Your courage whett with pittie and disdaine,
    Your deeme your allies' harmes ;
    All lose or re-obtaine,
    And either palme or fatall cypresse gaine.
To this great spirit's frame
    If moulded were all mindes, all endeuoures,
    Could worth thus all inflame,
    Then not this ile were oures
    Alone, but all betweene sunne's golden boweres.

OF THE BOOKE.

[PREFIXED TO THE TRVE CRVCIFIXE FOR TRUE CATHOLICKES, BY SIR WILLLIAM MOORE.
EDINBURGH, 1629, 8vo.]

You that with awfull eyes and sad regards,
Gazing on masts of ships crost with their yards ;
Or when yee see a microcosme to swim,
At ev'ry stroake the crucifixe doe limne

In your braine's table ; or when smaller things,
As pyed butter-flyes, and birds their wings
Doe raise a crosse, streight on your knees doe fall
And worship ; you, that evrye painted wall,
Grac't with some antik face, some godling make,
And practise whoordome for the crosse's sake
With bread, stone, mettall ; read these sacred layes,
And, proselytes, proclaime the author's praise :
Such fame your transformation shall him giue,
With Homer's ever that his name shall liue.

ON THE DEATH OF LADY JANE MAITLAND.

[SUBJOINED TO A FVNERALL SERMON, PREACHED AT THE BURIALL OF THE LADY IANE MAITLANE, DAUGHTER TO IOHN EARLE OF LAUDERDAIL. EDINBURGH, 1633, 4TO.]

THE flowre of virgins in her prime of years
By ruthlesse destinies is ta'ne away,
And rap'd from earth, poore earth, before this day
Which ne're was rightly nam'd a vale of tears.

Beautie to heaven is fled, sweet modestie
No more appears ; she whose harmonious sounds
Did ravish sense, and charm minde's deepest wounds,
Embalm'd with many a tear now low doth lie.

Fair hopes evanish'd are ; she should have grac'd
A prince's marriage-bed, but, lo ! in heaven
Blest paramours to her were to be given ;
She liv'd an angel, now is with them plac'd.

Vertue was but a name abstractly trim'd,
Interpreting what she was in effect,
A shadow from her frame, which did reflect
A portrait by her excellencies lim'd.

Thou whom free-will or chance hath hither brought,
And read'st, here lies a branch of Metland's stem,
And Seaton's offspring, know that either name
Designes all worth yet reach'd by humane thought.
　　Tombs elsewhere rise, life to their guests to give,
　　Those ashes can frail monuments make live.

OF PERSON'S VARIETIES.

[PREFIXED TO VARIETIES, &c. BY DAVID PERSON OF LOGHLANDS.　LONDON, 1635, 4TO.

THE lawyer here may learne divinity,
The divine lawes, or faire astrology,
The dammaret respectively to fight,
The duellist to court a mistresse right ;
Such who their name take from the rosie-crosse,
May here by time learne to repaire their losse :
All learne may somewhat, if they be not fooles ;
Arts quicklier here are lesson'd than in schooles.

DISTICH OF THE SAME.

THIS booke a world is ; here if errours be,
The like, nay worse, in the great world we see.

A PASTORALL ELEGIE.

REPRINTED

FROM THE EDITIONS OF

M.DC.XXXVIII AND M.DC.LVI.

TO THE
EXEQUIES

OF THE HONOVRABLE,

S^r.

ANTONYE ALEXANDER,

KNIGHT, &c.

A Pastorall Elegie.

EDINBVRGH,
Printed in King *James* his College,
by *George Anderſon*, 1638.

A PASTORALL ELEGIE ON THE DEATH

OF SIR ANTONYE ALEXANDER.

In sweetest prime and blooming of his age,
Deare Alcon ravish'd from this mortall stage,
The shepheards mourn'd as they him lov'd before :
Among the rout him Idmon did deplore,
Idmon, who, whether sun in east did rise
Or dive in west, pour'd torrents from his eyes
Of liquid chrystall, under hawthorne shade ;
At last to trees and rocks this plaint he made :
Alcon, delight of heaven, desire of earth,
Off-spring of Phœbus, and the Muses' birth,
The Graces' darling, Adon of our plaines,
Flame of the fairest nymphs the earth sustaines,
What power of thee hath us bereft? what fate
By thy untimely fall would ruinate
Our hopes? O death ! what treasure in one houre
Hast thou dispersed ? how dost thou devoure
What we on earth hold dearest ? All things good,
Too envious heavens, how blast ye in the bud ?
The corne the greedy reapers cut not down
Before the fields with golden eares it crown,
Nor doth the verdant fruits the gardener pull,
But thou art cropt before thy yeares were full.

    With thee, sweet youth, the glories of our fields
Vanish away, and what contentments yields ;
The lakes their silver look, the woods their shades,
The springs their christall want, their verdure meads,

The yeares their early seasons, cheerfull dayes;
Hills gloomy stand now desolate of rayes,
Their amorous whispers zephires not us bring,
Nor do aire's quiresters salute the spring;
The freezing winds our gardens do defloure.
Ah, Destinies! and you whom skies embow'r,
To his faire spoiles his spright againe yet give,
And like another phœnix make him live.
The herbs, though cut, sprout fragrant from their stems,
And make with crimson blush our anadems;
The sun when in the west he doth decline,
Heaven's brightest tapers at his funeralls shine;
His face, when wash't in the Atlantick seas,
Revives, and cheeres the welkin with new raies:
Why should not he, since of more pure a frame,
Returne to us againe, and be the same?
But wretch, what wish I? To the winds I send
These plaints and prayers, Destines cannot lend
Thee more of time, nor heavens consent will thus
Thou leave their starry world to dwell with us;
Yet shall they not thee keep amidst their spheares
Without these lamentations and teares.
    Thou wast all vertue, courtesie, and worth,
And as sun's light is in the moon set forth,
World's supreame excellence in thee did shine;
Nor, though eclipsed now, shalt thou decline,
But in our memories live, while dolphins streames
Shall haunt, whilst eaglets stare on Titan's beames,
Whilst swans upon their christall tombes shall sing,
Whilst violets with purple paint the spring.
A gentler shepheard flocks did never feed
On Albion's hills, nor sung to oaten reed:

While what she found in thee my muse would blaze,
Griefe doth distract her, and cut short thy praise.
    How oft have we, inviron'd by the throng
Of tedious swaines, the cooler shades among,
Contemn'd earth's glow-worme greatnesse, and the chace
Of fortune scorn'd, deeming it disgrace
To court unconstancy ? How oft have we
Some Chloris' name graven in each virgin tree,
And, finding favours fading, the next day
What we had carv'd we did deface away ?
Woefull remembrance ! Nor time nor place
Of thy abodement shadows any trace,
But there to me thou shin'st : late glad desires,
And ye once roses, how are ye turned bryers ?
Contentments passed, and of pleasures chiefe,
Now are ye frightfull horrours, hells of griefe.
    When from thy native soyle love had thee driven,
Thy safe returne prefigurating, a heav̈n
Of flattering hopes did in my fancy move,
Then little dreaming it should atomes prove.
These groves preserve will I, these loved woods,
These orchards rich with fruits, with fish these flouds :
My Alcon will returne, and once againe
His chosen exiles he will entertaine ;
The populous city holds him, amongst harmes
Of some fierce Cyclops, Circe's stronger charmes.
These bankes, said I, he visit will and streames,
These silent shades ne're kist by courting beames ;
Far, far off I will meet him, and I first
Shall him approaching know, and first be blest
With his aspect ; I first shall heare his voice,
Him find the same he parted, and rejoyce

To learne his passed perills, know the sports
Of forraine shepheards, fawns, and fairy courts.
No pleasure to the fields ; an happy state
The swaines enjoy, secure from what they hate :
Free of proud cares they innocently spend
The day, nor do black thoughts their ease offend ;
Wise nature's darlings they live in the world,
Perplexing not themselves how it is hurl'd.
These hillocks Phœbus loves, Ceres these plaines,
These shades the Sylvans, and here Pales straines
Milke in the pailes, the maids which haunt the springs
Daunce on these pastures, here Amintas sings ;
Hesperian gardens, Tempe's shades are here,
Or what the easterne Inde, and west hold deare.
Come then, deare youth, the wood-nymphs twine thee boughs
With rose and lilly, to impale thy brows.
Thus ignorant, I mus'd, not conscious yet
Of what by death was done, and ruthlesse fate :
Amidst these trances fame thy losse doth sound,
And through my eares gives to my heart a wound ;
With stretched-out armes I sought thee to embrace,
But clasp'd, amaz'd, a coffin in thy place ;*
A coffin ! of our joyes which had the trust,
Which told that thou was come, but chang'd in dust.
Scarce, even when felt, could I believe this wrake,
Nor that thy tyme and glory Heavens would break.
Now since I cannot see my Alcon's face,
And finde nor vowes nor prayers to have place

---

* The preceding part of this poem has been collated with the edition of 1656, as the *unique* copy of the edition of 1638, preserved in the Library of the University of Edinburgh, is unfortunately imperfect.

With guiltie starres, this mountaine shall become
To mee a sacred altar, and a tombe
To famous Alcon: heere, as dayes, months, yeares
Do circling glide, I sacrifice will teares,
Heere spend my remnant tyme, exil'd from mirth,
Till death in end turne monarch of my earth.
   Sheepheards on Forth, and yee by Doven rockes
Which use to sing and sport, and keep your flockes,
Pay tribute heere of teares; yee never had
To aggravate your moanes a cause more sad;
And to their sorrowes hither bring your mandes
Charged with sweetest flowres, and with pure handes,
Faire nymphes, the blushing hyacinth and rose
Spred on the place his relicts doth enclose;
Weave garlands to his memorie, and put
Over his hearse a verse in cypresse cut:
" Vertue did die, goodnesse but harme did give
After the noble Alcon left to live,
Friendship an earth-quake suffer'd; loosing him,
Love's brightest constellation turned dim."

POSTHUMOUS POEMS.

REPRINTED
FROM THE EDITION OF
M.DC.LVI.

POSTHUMOUS POEMS.

SONNET.

Aye me, and I am now the man whose muse
In happier times was wont to laugh at love,
And those who suff'red that blind boy abuse
The noble gifts were given them from above?
What metamorphose strange is this I prove?
My selfe now scarce I find my selfe to be,
And thinke no fable Circe's tyrannie,
And all the tales are told of changed Jove.
Vertue hath taught with her philosophy
My mind unto a better course to move:
Reason may chide her full, and oft reprove
Affection's power, but what is that to me
   Who ever thinke, and never thinke on ought
   But that bright cherubine which thralls my thought?

MADRIGALL.

Trees happier far than I,
Which have the grace to heave your heads so high,
And over-look those plaines,
Grow till your branches kisse that lofty skie
Which her sweet selfe containes ;
There make her know mine endlesse love and paines,

And how these teares which from mine eyes do fall,
Helpt you to rise so tall :
Tell her, as once I for her sake lov'd breath,
So for her sake I now court ling'ring death.

CLORUS.

SWAN which so sweetly sings
By Aska's bankes, and pitifully plains,
That old Meander never heard such straines,
Eternall fame, thou to thy country brings :
And now our Calidon
Is by thy songs made a new Helicon ;
Her mountaines, woods, and springs,
While mountaines, woods, springs be, shall sound thy praise ;
And though fierce Boreas oft make pale her bayes,
And kill those mirtills with enraged breath,
Which should thy brows enwreath,
   Her flouds have pearles, seas amber do send forth,
   Her heaven hath golden stars to crown thy worth.

TO SLEEP.

How comes it, Sleep, that thou
Even kisses me affords
Of her, deare her, so far who's absent now ?
How did I heare those words,
Which rocks might move, and move the pines to bow ?
Aye me, before halfe day
Why didst thou steale away ?
Returne, I thine for ever will remaine,
If thou wilt bring with thee that guest againe.

AN ALMANACK

THIS strange ecclipse, one saies,
Strange wonders doth foretell;
But you whose wives excell,
And love to count their praise,
Shut all your gates, your hedges plant with thornes,
The sun did threat the world this time with hornes.

A CHAINE OF GOLD.

ARE not those locks of gold
Sufficient chaines the wildest hearts to hold?
Is not that ivory hand
A diamantine band,
Most sure to keep the most untamed mind,
But ye must others find?
O yes; why is that golden one then worne
Thus free in chaines? perhaps, love's chaines to scorne.

EPITAPH.

THE bawd of justice, he who laws controll'd,
And made them fawn and frown as he got gold,
That Proteus of our state, whose heart and mouth
Were farther distant than is north from south,
That cormorant, who made himselfe so grosse
On people's ruine, and the prince's losse,
Is gone to hell, and though he heere did evill,
He there perchance may prove an honest devill.

A TRANSLATION.

FIERCE robbers were of old
Exil'd the champian ground,

From hamlets chas'd, in cities kill'd, or bound,
And only woods, caves, mountaines, did them hold :
But now, when all is sold,
Woods, mountaines, caves, to good men be refuge,
And do the guiltlesse lodge,
And, clad in purple gowns,
The greatest theeves command within the towns.

PROTEUS OF MARBLE.

THIS is no work of stone,
Though it seems breathlesse, cold, and sense hath none,
But that false god which keeps
The monstrous people of the raging deeps ;
Now that he doth not change his shape this while,
It is thus constant more you to beguile.

THE STATUE OF VENUS SLEEPING.

PASSENGER, vexe not thy mind,
To make me mine eyes unfold ;
For if thou shouldst them behold,
Thine perhaps they will make blind.

LAURA TO PETRARCH.

I rather love a youth and childish rime,
Than thee whose verse and head are wise through time.

A LOVER'S PRAYER.

NEARE to a christall spring,
With thirst and heat opprest,
Narcissa faire doth rest :
Trees, pleasant trees, which those green plains forth bring,

Now interlace your trembling tops above,
And make a canopy unto my love;
So in heaven's highest house when sun appeares,
Aurora may you cherish with her teares.

FOR DORUS.

WHY, Nais, stand ye nice,
Like to a well-wrought stone,
When Dorus would you kisse?
Denie him not that blisse,
He's but a child, old men be children twice,
And even a toothlesse one;
And when his lips yours touch in that delight,
Ye need not feare he will those cherries bite.

LOVE VAGABONDING.

SWEET nymphs, if, as ye stray,
Ye find the froth-borne goddesse of the sea,
All blubb'red, pale, undone,
Who seeks her giddy son,
That little god of love,
Whose golden shafts your chastests bosomes prove,
Who leaving all the heavens hath run away;
If ought to him that finds him she'll impart,
Tell her he nightly lodgeth in my heart.

PHRÆNE.

AONIAN sisters, help my Phræne's praise to tell,
Phræne, heart of my heart, with whom the Graces dwell;
For I surcharged am so sore that I not know
What first to praise of her, her brest, or neck of snow,

Her cheeks with roses spred, or her two sun-like eyes,
Her teeth of brightest pearl, her lips where sweetnes lies ;
But those so praise themselves, being to all eyes set forth,
That, Muses, ye need not to say ought of their worth,
Than her white swelling paps essay for to make known,
But her white swelling paps through smallest vail are shown ;
Yet she hath something else more worthy than the rest,
Not seen ; go sing of that which lies beneath her brest,
And mounts like fair Parnasse, where Pegasse-well doth run :
Here Phræne stay'd my Muse, ere she had well begun.

DESIRED DEATH.

DEARE life, while I do touch
These corrall ports of blisse,
Which still themselves do kiss,
And sweetly me invite to do as much,
All panting in my lips
My heart my life doth leave,
No sense my senses have,
And inward powers do find a strange ecclipse :
This death so heavenly well
Doth so me please, that I
Would never longer seeke in sense to dwell,
If that even thus I only could but dye.

PHŒBE.

IF for to be alone, and all the night to wander,
Maids can prove chaste, then chaste is Phœbe without slander.

ANSWER.

FOOLE, still to be alone, all night in Heaven to wander,
Would make the wanton chaste, then she's chaste without slander.

HYMNE.

SAVIOUR of mankind, man Emanuel,
Who sinlesse died for sin, who vanquisht hell
The first fruits of the grave, whose life did give
Light to our darknes, in whose death we live,
O strengthen thou my faith, correct my will,
That mine may thine obey; protect me still,
So that the latter death may not devour
My soule seal'd with thy seale; so in the houre
When thou whose body sanctified thy tombe,
Unjustly judg'd, a glorious judge shalt come
To judge the world with justice, by that signe
I may be known, and entertain'd for thine.

A TRANSLATION OF S. JOHN SCOT HIS VERSES, BEGINNING
QUOD VITÆ SECTABOR ITER.

WHAT course of life should wretched mortals take,
In books hard questions large contention make;
Care dwels in houses, labour in the field,
Tumultuous seas affrighting dangers yield;
In forraine lands thou never canst be blest,
If rich, thou art in feare, if poore, distrest.
In wedlock frequent discontentments swell,
Unmarried persons as in deserts dwell.
How many troubles are with children borne!
Yet he that wants them, counts himselfe forlorne.
Young men are wanton, and of wisdome voyd,
Gray haires are cold, unfit to be employ'd:
Who would not one of those two offers try,
Not to be borne, or being borne to dye?

ALL good hath left this age, all tracks of shame,
Mercy is banished, and pitty dead,
Justice, from whence it came, to heaven is fled,
Religion, maim'd, is thought an idle name.
Faith to distrust and malice hath given place,
Envy with poyson'd teeth hath friendship torne,
Renowned knowledge is a despis'd scorne,
Now evill 'tis, all evill not to embrace.
There is no life save under servile bands,
To make desert a vassall to their crimes,
Ambition with avarice joyne hands,
O ever-shamefull, O most shamelesse Times !
      Save that sun's light we see, of good hear tell,
      This earth we court so much were very hell.

SONNET.

DOTH then the world go thus, doth all thus move ?
Is this the justice which on earth we find ?
Is this that firme decree which all doth bind ?
Are these your influences, Powers above ?
Those soules which vices moody mists most blind,
Blind Fortune blindly most their friend doth prove ;
And they who thee, poore idoll, Vertue, love,
Fly like a feather toss'd by storme and wind.
Ah ! if a Providence doth sway this all,
Why should best minds groane under most distresse,
Or why should pride humility make thrall,
And injuries the innocent oppresse ?
      Heavens hinder, stop this fate, or grant a time
      When good may have, as well as bad, their prime.

A REPLY.

WHO do in good delight,
That soveraigne justice ever doth reward,
And though sometime it smite,
Yet it doth them regard ;
For even amidst their griefe
They find a strong reliefe,
And death it selfe can work them no despight.
Againe, in evill who joy,
And do in it grow old,
In midst of mirth are charg'd with sin's annoy,
Which is in conscience scrol'd,
And when their life's fraile thred is cut by time,
They punishment find equall to each crime.

LOOK how in May the rose,
At sulphure's azure fumes,
In a short space her crimson blush doth lose,
And, all amaz'd, a pallid white assumes.
So time our best consumes,
Makes youth and beauty passe,
And what was pride turnes horrour in our glasse.

TO A SWALLOW, BUILDING NEARE THE STATUE OF MEDEA.

FOND Progne, chattering wretch,
That is Medea ; there
Wilt thou thy younglings hatch ?
Will she keep thine, her own who could not spare ?
Learne from her frantick face
To seek some fitter place.
What other may'st thou hope for, what desire,
Save Stygian spels, wounds, poyson, iron, fire ?

2 R

VENUS ARMED.

To practice new alarmes
In Jove's great court above,
The wanton Queen of Love,
Of sleeping Mars put on the horrid armes ;
Where gazing in a glasse
To see what thing she was,
To mocke and scoffe the blew-eyed maid did move,
Who said, sweet Queen, thus should you have been dight
When Vulcan took you napping with your knight.

THE BOARE'S HEAD.

Amidst a pleasant green
Which sun did seldome see,
Where play'd Anchises with the Cyprian queen,
The head of a wild boare hung on a tree ;
And driven by zephire's breath
Did fall, and wound the lovely youth beneath,
On whom yet scarce appeares
So much of bloud as Venus' eyes shed teares.
But ever as she wept, her antheme was,
Change, cruell change, alas !
My Adon, whilst thou liv'd, was by thee slaine,
Now dead, this lover must thou kill againe ?

TO AN OWLE.

Ascalaphus, tell me,
So may night's curtaine long time cover thee,
So ivy ever may
From irkesome light keep thy chamber and bed,
And in moon's liv'ry cled,
So may'st thou scorne the quiresters of day.
When playning thou dost stay

Neare to the sacred window of my deare,
Dost ever thou her heare
To wake, and steale swift houres from drowsie sleep ?
And when she wakes, doth ere a stollen sigh creep
Into thy list'ning eare ?
If that deafe god doth yet her carelesse keep,
In louder notes my griefe with thine expresse,
Till by thy shriekes she think on my distresse.

DAPHNIS.

Now Daphnis' armes did grow
In slender branches, and her braided haire,
Which like gold waves did flow,
In leavy twigs were stretched in the aire ;
The grace of either foot
Transform'd was to a root,
A tender barke enwraps her body faire.
He who did cause her ill
Sore-wailing stood, and from his blubbered eyne
Did show'rs of teares upon the rine distill,
Which water'd thus did bud and turne more green.
  O deep despaire ! O heart-appalling griefe !
  When that doth woe encrease should bring reliefe.

THE BEARE OF LOVE.

In woods and desart bounds
A beast abroad doth roame,
So loving sweetnesse and the honey combe,
  It doth despise the armes of bees and wounds.

I by like pleasure led,
To prove what heavens did place
Of sweet on your faire face,
Whilst therewith I am fed,
Rest carelesse, beare of love, of hellish smart,
And how those eyes afflict and wound my heart.

FIVE SONNETS FOR GALATEA.

I.

STREPHONE, in vaine thou bring thy rimes and songs,
Deckt with grave Pindar's old and withered flow'rs ;
In vaine thou count'st the faire Europa's wrongs,
And her whom Jove deceiv'd in golden show'rs.
Thou hast slept never under mirtles' shed,
Or if that passion hath thy soule opprest,
It is but for some Grecian mistris dead.
Of such old sighs thou dost discharge thy brest,
How can true love with fables hold a place ?
Thou who with fables dost set forth thy love,
Thy love a pretty fable needs must prove,
Thou suest for grace, in scorne more to disgrace :
   I cannot thinke thou wert charm'd by my looks,
   O no, thou learn'dst thy love in lovers' books.

II.

No more with candid words infect mine eares,
Tell me no more how that ye pine in anguish,
When sound ye sleep ; no more say that ye languish,
No more in sweet despite say you spend teares.

Who hath such hollow eyes as not to see
How those that are haire-brain'd boast of Apollo,
And bold give out the Muses do them follow,
Though in love's library yet no lover's he?
If we poore soules least favour but them shew,
That straight in wanton lines abroad is blazed,
Their name doth soare on our fame's overthrow,
Mark'd is our lightnesse whilst their wits are praised:
   In silent thoughts who can no secret cover,
   He may, say we, but not well, be a lover,

III.

Ye who with curious numbers, sweetest art,
Frame Dedall nets our beauty to surprize,
Telling strange castles builded in the skies,
And tales of Cupid's bow, and Cupid's dart;
Well howsoever ye act your fained smart,
Molesting quiet eares with tragick cries,
When you accuse our chastitie's best part,
Nam'd cruelty, ye seem not halfe too wise;
Yea, ye yourselves it deem most worthy praise,
Beautie's best guard, that dragon which doth keep
Hesperian fruit, the spur in you does raise
That Delian wit that otherwaies may sleep:
   To cruell nymphs your lines do fame afford,
   Of many pittifull not one poore word.

IV.

If it be love to wake out all the night,
And watchfull eyes drive out in dewie moanes,
And when the sun brings to the world his light,
To waste the day in teares and bitter groanes;

If it be love to dim weake reason's beame
With clouds of strange desire, and make the mind
In hellish agonies a heav'n to dreame,
Still seeking comforts where but griefes we find ;
If it be love to staine with wanton thought
A spotlesse chastity, and make it try
More furious flames than his whose cunning wrought
That brazen bull where he intomb'd did fry ;
     Then sure is love the causer of such woes,
     Be ye our lovers, or our mortall foes.

v.

And would you then shake off love's golden chain,
With which it is best freedome to be bound ;
And cruell do ye seek to heale the wound
Of love, which hath such sweet and pleasant paine ?
All that is subject unto nature's raigne
In skies above, or on this lower round,
When it is long and far sought, end hath found,
Doth in decadens fall and slack remaine :
Behold the moon how gay her face doth grow
Till she kisse all the sun, then doth decay ;
See how the seas tumultuously do flow
Till they embrace lov'd bankes, then post away :
     So is't with love ; unlesse you love me still,
     O do not thinke I'le yeeld unto your will.

SONNET.*

CARE's charming sleep, son of the sable night,
Brother to death, in silent darknesse borne,

---

* Drummond's friend and correspondent Daniel was the author of this sonnet, which has been generally, but erroneously attributed to the Scottish poet.

Destroy my languish e're the day be light,
With darke forgetting of my cares returne,
And let the day be long enough to mourne
The ship-wrack of my ill-adventured youth ;
Let wat'ry eyes suffice to waile their scorne
Without the troubles of the night's untruth ;
Cease dreames, fond image of my fond desires,
To modell forth the passions of to-morrow ;
Let never-rising sun approve your teares,
To add more griefe to aggravate my sorrow :
    Still let me sleep, embracing clouds in vaine,
    And never wake to feele the daie's disdaine.

AN EPITAPH OF ONE NAMED MARGARET.

In shells and gold, pearles are not kept alone,
A Margaret here lies beneath a stone ;
A Margaret that did excell in worth
All those rich gems the Indies both send forth ;
Who, had she liv'd when good was lov'd of men,
Had made the Graces foure, the Muses ten,
And forc'd those happy times her daies that claim'd,
From her to be the age of pearle still nam'd.
She was the richest jewell of her kind,
Grac'd with more lustre than she left behind,
All goodnesse, vertue, bounty, and could cheare
The saddest mind : now nature knowing here
How things but shown, then hidden, are lov'd best,
This Margaret shrin'd in this marble chest.

ON A DRUNKARD.

Nor amaranthes, nor roses do bequeath
Unto this hearse, but tamarists and wine,

For that same thirst, though dead, yet doth him pine,
Which made him so carrouse while he drew breath.

ARETINUS' EPITAPH.

HERE Aretine lies, most bitter gall,
Who whilst he lived spoke evill of all,
Only of God the arrant sot
Naught said, but that he knew him not.

COMPARISON OF HIS THOUGHTS TO PEARLS.

WITH open shells in seas, on heavenly dew
A shining oyster lusciously doth feed,
And then the birth of that æthereall seed
Shews, when conceiv'd, if skies looke dark or blew:
So do my thoughts, cœlestiall twins, of you,
At whose aspect they first begin and breed,
When they came forth to light, demonstrate true,
If ye then smil'd, or lowr'd in mourning weed.
Pearles then are orient fram'd, and faire in forme,
If heavens in their conceptions do look cleare;
But if they thunder, or do threat a storme,
They sadly darke and cloudy do appeare:
    Right so my thoughts and so my notes do change,
    Sweet if ye smile, and hoarse if ye look strange.

ALL CHANGETH.

THE angry winds not aye
Do cuff the roaring deep,
And though heavens often weep,
Yet do they smile for joy when comes dismay:
Frosts do not ever kill the pleasant flow'rs,
And love hath sweets when gone are all the soures.

This said a shepheard, closing in his armes
His deare, who blusht to feele love's new alarmes.

SILENUS TO KING MIDAS.

THE greatest gift that from their lofty thrones
The all-governing pow'rs to man can give,
Is, that he never breath, or breathing once
A suckling end his daies, and leave to live ;
For then he neither knows the woe nor joy
Of life, nor feares the Stygian lake's annoy.

TO HIS AMOROUS THOUGHT.

SWEET wanton thought, who art of beauty borne,
And who on beauty feed'st and sweet desire,
Like taper flee, still circling, and still turne
About that flame that all so much admire,
That heavenly faire which doth out-blush the morne,
Those ivory hands, those threads of golden wire,
Thou still surroundest yet dar'st not aspire.
Sure thou dost well that place not to come neare,
Nor see the majesty of that faire court ;
For if thou saw'st what wonders there resort,
The pure intelligence that moves that spheare,
Like soules ascending to those joyes above,
Back never wouldst thou turne, nor thence remove.

VERSES ON THE LATE WILLIAM EARLE OF PEMBROOK.

1.

THE doubtfull feares of change so fright my mind,
Though raised to the highest joy in love,

2 s

As in this slippery state more griefe I find,
Than they who never such a blisse did prove ;
    But fed with ling'ring hopes of future gaine,
    Dreame not what 'tis to doubt a lover's paine.

II.

DESIRE a safer harbour is than feare,
And not to rise lesse danger than to fall ;
The want of jewels we far better beare,
Than so possest at once to lose them all :
    Unsatisfied hopes time may repaire,
    When ruin'd faith must finish in despaire.

III.

ALAS ! ye look but up the hill on me,
Which shews to you a faire and smooth ascent,
The precipice behind ye cannot see,
On which high fortunes are too pronely bent :
    If there I slip, what former joy or blisse
    Can heale the bruise of such a fall as this ?

                                        E. P.

A REPLY.

I.

WHO love enjoyes, and placed hath his mind
Where fairer vertues fairest beauties grace,
Then in himselfe such store of worth doth find,
That he deserves to hold so good a place :
    To chilling feares how can he be set forth,
    Whose feares condemne his own, doubts others' worth ?

II.

Desire, as flames of zeale, feare, horrours, meets,
They rise who feare of falling never prov'd.
Who is so dainty satiate with sweets,
To murmur when the banket is remov'd ?
  The fairest hopes time in the bud destroys,
  When sweet are memories of ruin'd joyes.

III.

It is no hill but heaven where you remaine,
And whom desert advanced hath so high,
To reach the guerdon of his burning paine,
Must not repine to fall and falling dye :
  His hopes are crown'd ; what years of tedious breath
  Can them compare with such a happy death ?

W. D.

A TRANSLATION.

I.

Ah ! silly soule, what wilt thou say,
When he whom earth and heavens obey,
Comes man to judge in the last day ;

II.

When he a reason askes, why grace
And goodnesse thou wouldst not embrace,
But steps of vanity didst trace ?

III.

That day of terrour, vengeance, ire,
Now to prevent thou should'st desire,
And to thy God in haste retire.

IV.

With wat'ry eyes, and sigh-swollen heart,
O beg, beg in his love a part,
Whilst conscience with remorse doth smart.

V.

That dreaded day of wrath and shame,
In flames shall turne this world's huge frame,
As sacred prophets do proclaime.

VI.

O with what griefe shall earthlings grone,
When that great Judge, set on his throne,
Examines strictly every one !

VII.

Shrill-sounding trumpets through the aire
Shall, from dark sepulchres, each where
Force wretched mortalls to appeare.

VIII.

Nature and Death amaz'd remaine,
To find their dead arise againe,
And processe with their Judge maintaine.

IX.

Display'd then open books shall lye,
Which all those secret crimes descry,
For which the guilty world must dye.

X.

The Judge enthron'd, whom bribes not gaine,
The closest crimes appeare shall plaine,
And none unpunished remaine.

XI.

O who then pitty shall poore me,
Or who mine advocate shall be,
When scarce the justest passe shall free ?

XII.

All wholly holy dreadfull King,
Who freely life to thine dost bring,
Of mercy save me, mercies' spring.

XIII.

Then, sweet Jesu, call to mind,
How of thy paines I was the end,
And favour let me that day find.

XIV.

In search of me, thou full of paine
Did'st sweat bloud, death on crosse sustaine ;
Let not these suff'rings be in vaine.

XV.

Thou supreame Judge, most just and wise,
Purge me from guilt which on me lies,
Before that day of thine assize.

XVI.

Charg'd with remorse, loe ! here I groane,
Sin makes my face a blush take on ;
Ah ! spare me prostrate at thy throne ;

XVII.

Who Mary Magdalen didst spare,
And lend'st the thiefe on crosse thine eare,
Shewest me faire hopes, I should not feare.

XVIII.

My prayers imperfect are and weake,
But worthy of thy grace them make,
And save me from hell's burning lake.

XIX.

On that great day, at thy right hand,
Grant I amongst thy sheep may stand,
Sequestered from the goatish band.

XX.

When that the reprobates are all
To everlasting flames made thrall,
O to thy chosen, Lord, me call!

XXI.

That I one of thy company,
With those whom thou dost justifie,
May live blest in eternity.

EPITAPHS.

VPON JOHN EARLE OF LADERDALE HIS DEATH.

I.

Of those rare worthies who adorn'd our north,
And shin'd like constellations, thou alone
Remain'dst last, great Maitland, charg'd with worth,
Second in vertue's theater to none;
But finding all eccentrick in our times,
Religion into superstition turn'd,
Justice silenc'd, exiled, or inurn'd,
Truth, faith, and charity, reputed crimes;

The young man destinate by sword to fall,
And trophees of their countrie's spoiles to reare,
Strange lawes the ag'd and prudent to appale,
And forc'd sad yoakes of tyranny to beare,
    And for nor great nor vertuous minds a roome,
    Disdaining life thou shrink'st* into thy tombe.

II.

When misdevotion every where shall take place,
And lofty oratours in thundring termes
Shall move you, people, to arise in armes,
And churche's hallow'd policy deface ;
When you shall but one generall sepulchre,
As Averroes did one generall soule,
On high, on low, on good, on bad confer,
And your dull predecessors' rites controule ;
Ah ! spare this monument ; great guests it keeps,
Three grave justiciars, whom true worth did raise,
The Muses' darlings, whose losse Phœbus weeps,
Best men's delight, the glory of their daies.
    More we would say, but feare and stand in aw,
    To turne idolaters and break your law.

III.

Do not repine, blest soule, that humble wits
Do make thy worth the matter of their verse ;
No high strain'd Muse our times and sorrows fits,
And we do sigh, not sing, to crown thy hearse.
The wisest prince e're manag'd Brittaine's state,

---

* In Phillips's edition, the reading is *shouldst,* which is evidently a typographical error. In p. 327, the editor has ventured upon another conjectural emendation. The former reading of the second line is,

They rise who *fall* of falling never prov'd.

Did not disdaine in numbers cleere and brave
The vertues of thy sire to celebrate,
And fix a rich memoriall on his grave.
Thou didst deserve no lesse ; and here in jet
Gold, touch, brasse, porphyrie, or Parian stone,
That by a prince's hand no lines are set
For thee, the cause is now this land hath none :
  Such giant moods our parity forth brings,
  We all will nothing be, or all be kings.

[TO THE MEMORIE OF THE EXCELLENT LADYE ISABELL,
        COUNTESS OF LAWDERDALE.]

FOND wight, who dreamst of greatness, glory, state,
And worlds of pleasures, honours dost devise,
Awake, learne how that here thou art not great
Nor glorious, by this monument turne wise.

One it enshrineth, sprung of ancient stemm,
And, if that blood nobility can make,
From which some kings have not disdain'd to take
Their proud descent, a rare and matchlesse gemm.

A beauty here it holds by full assurance,
Than which no blooming rose was more refin'd,
Nor morning's blush more radiant ever shin'd,
Ah ! too too like to morne and rose at last.

It holds her who in wit's ascendant far
Did yeares and sex transcend, to whom the heaven
More vertue than to all this age had given,
For vertue meteor turn'd, when she a star.

Faire mirth, sweet conversation, modesty,
And what those kings of numbers did conceive
By Muses nine, and Graces moe than three,
Lye clos'd within the compasse of this grave.
   Thus death all earthly glories doth confound,
   Loe how much worth a little dust doth bound !

———————

Far from these bankes exiled be all joyes,
Contentments, pleasures, musick, care's reliefe,
Tears, sighs, plaints, horrours, frightments, sad annoies
Invest these mountaines, fill all hearts with griefe.

Here nightingals and turtles vent your moanes ;
Amphrisian shepheard here come feed thy flocks,
And read thy hyacinth amidst our groanes,
Plaine, Eccho, thy Narcissus from our rocks.

Lost have our meads their beauty, hills their gemms,
Our brooks their christall, groves their pleasant shade,
The fairest flow'r of all our anademms
Death cropped hath, the Lesbia chaste is dead.
   Thus sighed the Tyne, then shrunke beneath his urne,
   And meads, brooks, rivers, hills about did mourne.

[ON LADY JANE MAITLAND.]

LIKE to the garden's eye, the flower of flow'rs
With purple pompe that dazle doth the sight,
Or as among the lesser gems of night,
The usher of the planet of the houres,
Sweet maid, thou shinedst on this world of ours,
Of all perfections having trac'd the hight :

2 T

Thine outward frame was faire, faire inward powers,
A saphire lanthorne, and an incense light.
Hence, the enamour'd heaven, as too too good
On earth's all-thorny soyle long to abide,
Transplanted to their fields so rare a bud,
Where from thy sun no cloud thee now can hide.
    Earth moan'd her losse, and wish'd shee had the grace
    Not to have known, or known thee longer space.

    HARD laws of mortall life !
To which made thrales, we come without consent,
Like tapers lighted to be early spent :
Our griefes are alwaies rife,
When joyes but halting march, and swiftly fly
Like shadows in the eye :
The shadow doth not yeeld unto the sun,
But joyes and life do waste even when begun.

ON THE DEATH OF A NOBLEMAN IN SCOTLAND, BURIED AT AITHEN.

    AITHEN, thy pearly coronet let fall,
Clad in sad robes, upon thy temples set
The weeping cypresse, or the sable jet :
Mourne this thy nursling's losse, a losse which all
Apollo's quire bemoanes, which many yeares
Cannot repaire, nor influence of spheares.

Ah ! when shalt thou find shepheard like to him,
Who made thy bankes more famous by his worth,

Than all those gems thy rocks and streams send forth ?
His splendor others' glow-worm light did dim,
Sprung of an ancient and a vertuous race,
He vertue more than many did embrace.

He fram'd to mildnesse thy halfe-barbarous swaines,
The good man's refuge, of the bad the fright,
Unparalel'd in friendship, world's delight,
For hospitality along thy plaines
Far-fam'd, a patron and a patterne faire
Of piety, the Muses' chiefe repaire.

Most debonaire, in courtesie supreame,
Lov'd of the meane, and honour'd by the great,
Ne're dasht by fortune, nor cast down by fate,
To present and to after times a theame.
Aithen, thy teares poure on this silent grave,
And drop them in thy alabaster cave,
And Niobe's imagery become ;
And when thou hast distilled here a tombe,
Enchace in it thy pearls, and let it beare,
Aithen's best gem and honour shrin'd lies here.

FAME, register of time,
Write in thy scrowle, that I
Of wisdome lover, and sweet poesie,
Was cropped in my prime,
And ripe in worth, tho' green in yeares, did dye.

IUSTICE, truth, peace, and hospitality,
Friendship and love being resolved to dye,

In these lewd times, have chosen here to have
With just, true, pious, * * * their grave :
Them cherish'd he so much, so much did grace,
That they on earth would choose none other place.

———————

WHEN death to deck his trophees stopt thy breath,
Rare ornament and glory of these parts,
All with moist eyes might say, and ruthfull hearts,
That things immortall vassal'd were to death.

What good, in parts on many shar'd, we see
From nature, gracious heaven, or fortune flow,
To make a master-piece of worth below,
Heaven, nature, fortune gave in grosse to thee.

In honour, bounty, rich, in valour, wit,
In courtesie, borne of an ancient race,
With bayes in war, with olives crown'd in peace,
Match'd great, with off-spring for great actions fit.

No rust of times nor change thy vertue wan,
With times to change, when truth, faith, love decay'd
In this new age; like fate, thou fixed stay'd,
Of the first world an all-substantiall man.

As earst this kingdome given was to thy syre,
The prince his daughter trusted to thy care,
And well the credit of a gem so rare
Thy loyalty and merit did require.

Yeares cannot wrong thy worth, that now appeares,
By others set, as diamonds among pearles;

A queen's deare foster, father to three earles,
Enough on earth to triumph are o're yeares.

Life a sea-voyage is, death is the haven,
And fraught with honour there thou hast arriv'd,
Which thousands seeking, have on rocks been driven,
That good adornes thy grave, which with thee liv'd :
  For a fraile life which here thou didst enjoy,
  Thou now a lasting hast, freed of annoy.

WITHIN the closure of this narrow grave
Lye all those graces a good-wife could have ;
But on this marble they shall not be read,
For then the living envy would the dead.

THE daughter of a king, of princely parts,
In beauty eminent, in vertues chiefe,
Loadstar of love, and loadstone of all hearts,
Her friends' and husband's only joy, now griefe,
Is here pent up within a marble frame,
Whose paralell no times, no climates claime,

VERSES fraile records are to keep a name,
Or raise from dust men to a life of fame,
The sport and spoyle of ignorance ; but far
More fraile the frames of touch and marble are,
Which envy, avarice, time e're long confound,
Or mis-devotion equalls with the ground.
Vertue alone doth last, frees man from death,
And, though despis'd and scorned here beneath,

Stands grav'n in angels' diamantine roles,
And blazed in the courts above the poles.
Thou wast faire vertues' temple; they did dwell
And live ador'd in thee; nought did excell
But what thou either didst possesse or love,
The graces' darling, and the maids' of Jove;
Courted by fame for bounties which the heaven
Gave thee in great, which if in parcels given
To many, such we happy sure might call;
How happy then wast thou who enjoyedst them all!
A whiter soule, ne're body did invest,
And now, sequestred, cannot be but blest,
Inrob'd in glory, 'midst those hierarchies
Of that immortall people of the skies,
Bright saints and angels, there from cares made free,
Nought doth becloud thy soveraign good from thee,
Thou smil'st at earth's confusions and jars,
And how for Centaures children we wage wars:
Like honey flies, whose rage whole swarmes consumes,
Till dust thrown on them makes them vaile their plumes.
Thy friends to thee a monument would raise,
And limne thy vertues, but dull griefe thy praise
Breakes in the entrance, and our taske proves vaine;
What duty writes, that woe blots out againe:
Yet love a pyramid of sighs thee reares,
And doth embaulme thee with fare-wells and teares.

ROSE.

I.

THOUGH marble porphyry, and mourning touch,
May praise these spoiles, yet can they not too much;
For beauty last, and * * * this stone doth close,
Once earth's delight, heaven's care, a purest Rose.

And, reader, shouldst thou but let fall a teare
Upon it, other flow'rs shall here appeare,
Sad violets and hyacinths, which grow
With markes of griefe, a publike losse to show.

II.

Relenting eye, which daignest to this stone
To lend a look, behold here he laid one,
The living and the dead interr'd, for dead
The turtle in its mate is ; and she fled
From earth, her * * * choos'd this place of griefe
To bound * * * thoughts, a small and sad reliefe.
His is this monument, for her's no art
Could frame, a pyramide rais'd of his heart.

III.

Instead of epitaphs and airy praise,
This monument a lady chaste did raise
To her lord's living fame, and after death
Her body doth unto this place bequeath,
To rest with his, till God's shrill trumpet sound :
Though time her life, no time her love could bound.

POSTHUMOUS POEMS.

REPRINTED
FROM THE EDITION OF
M.DCC.XI.

POSTHUMOUS POEMS.

EPIGRAMS.

I.

THE Scottish kirk the English church do name,
The English church the Scots a kirk do call ;
Kirk, and not church, church and not kirk, O shame !
Your kappa turn in chi, or perish all,
Assemblies meet, post bishops to the court ;
If these two nations fight, 'tis strangers' sport.

II.

AGAINST the king, sir, now why would ye fight ?
Forsooth, because he dubb'd me not a knight.
And ye, my lords, why arm ye 'gainst King Charles ?
Because of lords he would not make us earls.
Earls, why do ye lead forth these warlike bands ?
Because we will not quit the church's lands.
Most holy church-men, what is your intent ?
The king our stipends largely did augment.
Commons, to tumult thus why are you driven ?
Priests us persuade it is the way to heaven.
Are these just cause of war, good people, grant ?
Hoe ! Plunder ! thou ne're swore our covenant.

Give me a thousand cov'nants, I'le subscrive
Them all, and more, if more ye can contrive
Of rage and malice ; and let every one
Black treason bear, not bare rebellion.
I'le not be mock't, hiss'd, plunder'd, banish'd hence
For more years standing for a * * * prince.
His castles all are taken, and his crown,
His sword and scepter, ensigns of renown,
With that lieutenant fame did so extol,
And captives carried to the capital ;
I'le not die martyr for a mortal thing,
'Tis enough to be confessor for a king.
Will this you give contentment, honest-men ?
I've written rebels, pox upon the pen.

III.

THE king a negative voice most justly hath,
Since the kirk hath found out a negative faith.

IV.

IN parliament one voted for the king,
The crowd did murmur he might for it smart ;
His voice again being heard, was no such thing,
For that which was mistaken was a fart.

V.

BOLD Scots, at Barnnockburn ye kill'd your king,
Then did in parliament approve the fact ;
And would ye Charles to such a non-plus bring
To authorize rebellion by an act ?
  Well, what ye crave, who knows but granted may be ?
  But if he do't, cause swadle him for a baby.

VI.

A REPLY.

SWADL'D is the baby, and almost two years,
His swadling time, did neither cry nor stir,
But star'd, smil'd, did lye still, void of all fears,
And sleep'd, tho' barked at by every cur,
 Yea, had not wak'd, if Lesly, that hoarse nurse,
 Had not him hardly rock't, old wives him curse.

VII.

THE king nor band, nor host had him to follow
Of all his subjects; they were given to thee,
Lesly. Who is the greatest? By Apollo,
The emperor thou, some palsegrave scarce seems he.
Could'st thou pull lords as we do bishops down,
Small distance were between thee and a crown.

VIII.

WHEN lately Pym descended into hell,
E're he the cups of Lethe did carouse,
What place that was, he called loud to tell;
To whom, a devil, This is the lower-house.

IX.

THE STATUE OF ALCIDES.

FLORA upon a time
Naked Alcides' statue did behold,
And with delight admir'd each amorous limb,
Only one fault she said could be of't told:
For by right simmetry
The crafts-man had him wrong'd,
To such tall joynts a taller-club belong'd,

The club hung by his thigh :
To which the statuary did reply,
Fair nymph, in ancient days your holes by far,
Were not so hugely vast as now they are.

X.

GREAT lyes they tell, preach our church cannot err,
Less lies, who say the king's not head of her ;
Great lyes, who cry we may shed others' blood,
Less lyes, who swear dumb bishops are not good ;
Great lyes they vent, say we for God do fight,
Less lyes who guess the king does nothing right ;
Great lyes and less lyes all our aims descry :
To pulpits some, to camp the rest apply.

XI.

A SPEECH AT THE KING'S ENTRY INTO THE TOWN OF LINLITHGOW,
PRONOUNCED BY MR JAMES WISEMAN, SCHOOL-MASTER THERE,
INCLOSED IN A PLAISTER MADE IN THE FIGURE OF A LYON.

THRICE royal sir, here I do you beseech,
Who art a lyon, to hear a lyon's speech ;
A miracle ; for, since the days of Æsop,
No lyon till those times his voice dar'd raise up
To such a majesty : then, king of men,
The king of beasts speaks to thee from his den ;
Who, tho' he now inclosed be in plaister,
When he was free was Lithgow's wise school-master.

XII.

A country maid Amazone like did ride,
To sit more sure, with leg on either side ;

Her mother who her spy'd said, that e're long
She should just penance suffer for that wrong ;
For when time should on her more years bestow,
That horses hair between her thighs would grow.
Scarce winter twice was come, as was her told,
When she found all to frizle there with gold,
Which first made her afraid, then turn'd her sick,
And forc'd her keep her bed almost a week.
At last her mother calls, who scarce for laughter
Could hear the pleasant story of her daughter,
But that this frenzy should no more her vex,
She swore thus bearded were their weaker sex ;
Which when deny'd, think not, said she, I scorn,
Behold the place, poor fool, where thou was born.
The girl that seeing, cry'd, now void of pain,
Ah ! mother, you have ridden on the mane.

XIII.

God's judgments seldom use to cease, unless
The sins which them procur'd men do confess.
Our cries are Baal's priests', our fasting, vain,
Our pray'rs not heard, nor answer'd us again :
Till perjury, wrong, rebellion, be confest,
Think not on peace, nor to be freed of pest.

XIV.

The king gives yearly to his senate gold,
Who can deny but justice then is sold ?

XV.

Here Rixus lies, a novice in the laws,
Who plains he came to hell without a cause.

PHYLLIS, ON THE DEATH OF HER SPARROW.

AH! if ye ask, my friends, why this salt shower
My blubber'd eyes upon this paper pour ?
Gone is my sparrow, he whom I did train,
And turn'd so toward, by a cat is slain.
No more with trembling wings shall he attend
His watchful mistress : would my life could end !
No more shall I him-hear chirp pretty lays ;
Have I not cause to loath my tedious days ?
A Dedalus he was to catch a fly,
Nor wrath nor rancour men in him could spy ;
To touch or wrong his tail if any dar'd,
He pinch'd their fingers, and against them war'd :
Then might that crest be seen shake up and down,
Which fixed was unto his little crown ;
Like Hector's, Troy's strong bulwark, when in ire
He rag'd to set the Grecian fleet on fire.
But, ah, alas ! a cat this prey espies,
Then with a leap did thus our joys surprise.
Undoubtedly this bird was kill'd by treason,
Or otherways had of that fiend had reason.
Thus was Achilles by weak Paris slain,
And stout Camilla fell by Aruns vain :
So that false horse, which Pallas rais'd 'gainst Troy,
King Priame and that city did destroy.
Thou now, whose heart is big with this frail glory,
Shalt not live long to tell thy honour's story.
If any knowledge resteth after death
In ghosts of birds, when they have left to breath,
My darling's ghost shall know in lower place,
The vengeance falling on the cattish race.

For never cat nor catling I shall find,
But mew shall they in Pluto's palace blind.
Ye who with gawdy wings and bodies light
Do dint the air, turn hitherwards your flight,
To my sad tears comply these notes of yours,
Unto his idol bring an harv'st of flowers;
Let him accept from us, as most divine,
Sabæan incense, milk, food, sweetest wine;
And on a stone let us these words engrave :
Pilgrim, the body of a sparrow brave
In a fierce gluttonous cat's womb clos'd remains,
Whose ghost now graceth the Elysian plains.

DIVINE POEMS.

PETER, AFTER THE DENIAL OF HIS MASTER.

Like to the solitary pelican,
The shady groves I haunt, and deserts wild,
Amongst woods' burgesses, from sight of man,
From earth's delight, from mine own self exil'd.
But that remorse which with my fall began,
Relenteth not, nor is by change turn'd mild,
But rents my soul, and like a famish'd child
Renews its cryes, though nurse does what she can.
Look how the shrieking bird that courts the night
In ruin'd wall doth lurk, and gloomy place:

2 x

Of sun, of moon, of stars, I shun the light,
Not knowing where to stay, what to embrace :
   How to heaven's lights should I lift these of mine,
   Sith I denyed him who made them shine ?

ON THE VIRGIN MARY.

THE woful Mary 'midst a blubber'd band
Of weeping virgins, near unto the tree
Where God death suffer'd, man from death to free,
Like to a plaintful nightingale did stand,
   Which sees her younglings reft before her eyes,
   And hath nought else to guard them save her cryes.
Love thither had her brought, and misbelief
Of these sad news, which charg'd her mind to fears,
But now her eyes more wretched than her tears,
Bear witness, ah ! too true, of feared grief :
   Her doubts made certain, did her hopes destroy,
   Abandoning her soul to black annoy.
Long fixing down-cast eyes on earth, at last
She longing did them raise, O torturing sight !
To view what they did shun, their sole delight,
Embru'd in his own blood, and naked plac't
   To sinful eyes, naked save that black vail
   Which heaven him shrouded with, that did bewail.
It was not pity, pain, grief, did possess
The mother, but an agony more strange ;
Cheek's roses in pale lillies straight did change,
Her sp'rits, as if she bled his blood, turn'd less :
   When she saw him, wo did all words deny,
   And grief her only suffer'd sigh, O my,
O my dear Lord and Son ! then she began :
Immortal birth ! tho' of a mortal born,

Eternal bounty which doth heaven adorn,
Without a mother, God ; a father, man ;
   Ah ! what hast thou deserv'd, what hast thou done !
   Thus to be treat ? Woe's me, my son, my son !
Who bruis'd thy face, the glory of this all,
Who eyes engor'd, load-stars to Paradise,
Who, as thou were a trimmed sacrifice,
Did with that cruel crown thy brows impale ?
   Who rais'd thee, whom so oft the angels serv'd,
   Between those thieves who that foul death deserv'd ?
Was it for this thou bred wast in my womb,
Mine arms a cradle serv'd thee to repose,
My milk thee fed, as morning-dew the rose ?
Did I thee keep till this sad time should come,
   That wretched men should nail thee to a tree,
   And I a witness of thy pangs must be ?
It is not long, the ways bestrow'd with flowers,
With shouts to ecchoing heavens and mountains roll'd,
Since, as in triumph, I thee did behold
In royal pomp approach proud Sion's towers :
   Lo ! what a change ! who did thee then embrace,
   Now at thee shake their heads, inconstant race.
Eternal Father, from whose piercing eye
Hid nought is found, that in this all is form'd,
Deign to vouchsafe a look unto this round,
This round, the stage of a sad tragedy :
   Look but if thy dear pledge thou here canst know,
   On an unhappy tree a shameful show.
Ah ! look if this be hee, almighty King,
Before heavens spangled were with stars of gold,
E're world a center had it to uphold,
Whom from eternity thou forth didst bring.

With virtue, form, and light, who did adorn
Skie's radiant globes, see where he hangs a scorn.
Did all my prayers tend to this? Is this
The promise that celestial herauld made
At Nazareth, when full of joy he said,
I happy was, and from thee did me bless?
How I am blest? No, most unhappy I
Of all the mothers underneath the sky.
How true and of choise oracles the choice
Was that blest Hebrew, whose dear eyes in peace
Mild death did close, e're they saw this disgrace,
When he fore-spake with more than angel's voice,
The son should, malice sign, be set a-part,
Then that a sword should pierce the mother's heart!
But whither dost thou go, life of my soul?
O stay a little till I die with thee;
And do I live thee languishing to see,
And cannot grief frail laws of life controul?
If grief prove weak, come, cruell squadrons, kill
The mother, spare the son, he knows no ill;
He knows no ill, those pangs, base men, are due
To me and all the world, save him alone;
But now he doth not hear my bitter moan;
Too late I cry, too late I plaints renew;
Pale are his lips, down doth his head decline,
Dim turn those eyes once wont so bright to shine.
The heavens, which in their mansions constant move,
That they may not seem guilty of this crime,
Benighted have the golden eye of time:
Ungrateful earth, canst thou such shame approve,
And seem unmov'd, this done upon thy face?
Earth trembled then, and she did hold her peace.

HYMN.

HIM whom the earth, the sea, and sky
Worship, adore, and magnify,
And doth this threefold engine steer,
Mary's pure closet now doth bear.
Whom sun and moon, and creatures all,
Serving at times, obey his call;
Pouring from heaven his sacred grace,
I' th' virgin's bowels hath ta'ne place.
Mother most blest by such a dower,
Whose Maker, Lord of highest power,
Who this wide world in hand contains,
In thy womb's ark himselfe restrains.
Blest by a message from heaven brought,
Fertile with Holy Ghost full fraught;
Of nations the desired king,
Within thy sacred womb doth spring.
Lord, may thy glory still endure,
Who born wast of a virgin pure;
The Father's and the sp'rit's of love,
Which endless worlds may not remove.

AN EVENING HYMN.

MAKER of all, we thee intreat,
Before the joyful light descend,
That thou with wonted mercy great
Us as our keeper would'st defend.

Let idle dreams be far away,
And vain illusions of the night;
Repress our foe, least that he may
Our bodies to foul lust incite.

Let this, O Father, granted be,
Through our dear Saviour's boundless merit,
Who doth for ever live with thee,
Together with the Holy Spirit.

COMPLAINT OF THE BLESSED VIRGIN.

THE mother stood with grief confounded,
Near the cross ; her tears abounded
　　While her dear son hanged was,
Through whose soul, her sighs forth venting,
Sadly mourning and lamenting,
　　Sharpest points of swords did pass.
O how sad and how distress'd,
Was the mother ever-bless'd,
　　Who God's only son forth-brought :
She in grief and woes did languish,
Quaking to behold what anguish
　　To her noble son was wrought.

HYMN UPON THE NATIVITY.

CHRIST, whose redemption all doth free,
Son of the Father, who alone
Before the world began to be,
Didst spring from him by means unknown ;

Thou his clear brightness, thou his light,
Thou everlasting hope of all,
Observe the prayers which in thy sight
Thy servants through the world let fall.

O dearest Saviour, bear in mind
That of our body thou a child

Didst whilom take the natural kind,
Born of the Virgin undefil'd.

This much the present day makes known,
Passing the circuit of the year,
That thou from thy high Father's throne
The world's sole safety didst appear.

The highest heaven, the earth, and seas,
And all that is within them found,
Because he sent thee us to ease,
With mirthful songs his praise resound.

We also who redeemed are
With thy pure blood from sinful state,
For this thy birth-day will prepare
New hymns this feast to celebrate.

Glory, O Lord, be given to thee
Whom the unspotted Virgin bore,
And glory to thee, Father, be,
And th' Holy Ghost, for ever more.

HYMN UPON THE INNOCENTS.

HAIL, you sweet babes, that are the flowers,
Whom, when you life begin to taste,
The enemy of Christ devours,
As whirlwinds down the roses cast.

First sacrifice to Christ you went,
Of offered lambs a tender sort;
With palms and crowns you innocent
Before the sacred altar sport.

DEDICATION OF A CHURCH.

JERUSALEM, that place divine,
The vision of sweet peace is nam'd,
In heaven her glorious turrets shine,
Her walls of living stones are fram'd,
    While angels guard her on each side,
    Fit company for such a bride.
She deckt in new attire from heaven,
Her wedding-chamber now descends,
Prepar'd in marriage to be given
To Christ, on whom her joy depends.
    Her walls wherewith she is inclos'd,
    And streets are of pure gold compos'd.
The gates adorn'd with pearls most bright
The way to hidden glory show ;
And thither by the blessed might
Of faith in Jesus' merits go
    All those who are on earth distrest,
    Because they have Christ's name profest.
These stones the work-men dress and beat,
Before they throughly polisht are,
Then each is in his proper seat
Establisht by the builder's care,
    In this fair frame to stand for ever,
    So joyn'd, them that no force can sever.
To God, who sits in highest seat,
Glory and power given be,
To Father, Son, and Paraclete,
Who reign in equal dignity ;
    Whose boundless power we still adore,
    And sing their praise for ever-more.

HYMN.

JESV, our prayers with mildness hear,
Who art the crown which virgins decks,
Whom a pure maid did breed and bear,
The sole example of her sex.

Thou feeding there where lillies spring,
While round about the virgins dance,
Thy spouse dost to glory bring,
And them with high rewards advance.

The virgins follow in thy ways
Whithersoever thou dost go,
They trace thy steps with songs of praise,
And in sweet hymns thy glory show.

Cause thy protecting grace, we pray,
In all our senses to abound,
Keeping from them all harms which may
Our souls with foul corruption wound.

Praise, honour, strength, and glory great
To God, the Father, and the Son,
And to the holy Paraclete,
While time lasts, and when time is done.

HYMN.

BENIGN Creator of the stars,
Eternal light of faithful eyes,
Christ, whose redemption none debars,
Do not our humble prayers despise :

2 Y

Who for the state of mankind griev'd,
That it by death destroy'd should be,
Hast the diseased world reliev'd,
And given the guilty remedy.

When th' evening of the world drew near,
Thou as a bridegroom deign'st to come
Out of thy wedding-chamber dear,
Thy virgin mother's purest womb.

To the strong force of whose high reign
All knees are bow'd with gesture low,
Creatures which heaven or earth contain,
With rev'rence their subjection show.

O holy Lord, we thee desire,
Whom we expect to judge all faults,
Preserve us, as the times require,
From our deceitful foes' assaults.

Praise, honour, strength, and glory great
To God, the Father, and the Son,
And to the holy Paraclete,
While time lasts, and when time is done.

HYMN FOR SUNDAY.

O BLEST Creator of the light,
Who bringing forth the light of days
With the first work of splendor bright,
The world didst to beginning raise ;

Who morn with evening joyn'd in one,
Commandedst should be call'd the day;
The foul confusion now is gone,
O hear us when with tears we pray;

Lest that the mind with fears full fraught,
Should lose best life's eternal gains,
While it hath no immortal thought,
But is inwrapt in sinful chains.

O may it beat the inmost sky,
And the reward of life possess;
May we from hurtful actions fly,
And purge away all wickedness.

Dear Father, grant what we intreat,
And only Son who like power hast,
Together with the Paraclete,
Reigning whilst times and ages last.

HYMN FOR MONDAY.

GREAT Maker of the heavens wide,
Who, least things mixt should all confound,
The floods and waters didst divide,
And didst appoint the heavens their bound;

Ordering where heavenly things shall stay,
Where streams shall run on earthly soyl,
That waters may the flames allay,
Least they the globe of earth should spoil;

Sweet Lord, into our minds infuse
The gift of everlasting grace,
That no old faults which we did use
May with new frauds our souls deface.

May our true faith obtain the light,
And such clear beams our hearts possess,
That it vain things may vanish quite,
And that no falsehood it oppress.

Dear Father, grant what we intreat,
And only Son who like power hast,
Together with the Paraclete,
Reigning whilst times and ages last.

HYMN FOR TUESDAY.

GREAT Maker of man's earthly realm,
Who didst the ground from waters take,
Which did the troubled land o'rewhelm,
And it unmoveable didst make,

That there young plants might fitly spring,
While it with golden flowers attir'd
Might forth ripe fruit in plenty bring,
And yield sweet fruit by all desir'd ;

With fragrant greenness of thy grace,
Our blasted souls of wounds release,
That tears foul sins away may chase,
And in the mind bad motions cease:

May it obey thy heavenly voice,
And never drawing near to ill,
T' abound in goodness may rejoyce,
And may no mortal sin fulfil.

Dear Father, grant what we intreat,
And only Son who like power hast,
Together with the Paraclete,
Reigning whilst times and ages last.

HYMN FOR WEDNESDAY.

O HOLY God of heavenly frame,
Who mak'st the pole's high center bright,
And paint'st the same with shining flames,
Adorning it with beauteous light;

Who framing on the fourth of days
The fiery chariot of the sun,
Appoint'st the moon her changing rays,
And orbs in which the planets run,

That thou might'st by a certain bound,
'Twixt night and day division make,
And that some sure sign might be found
To shew when months beginning take;

Mens' hearts with lightsome splendor bless,
Wipe from their minds polluting spots,
Dissolve the bond of guiltiness,
Throw down the heaps of sinful blots.

Dear Father, grant what we intreat,
And only Son who like power hast,
Together with the Paraclete,
Reigning whilst times and ages last.

HYMN FOR THURSDAY.

O GOD, whose forces far extend,
Who creatures which from waters spring
Back to the flood dost partly send,
And up to th' air dost partly bring;

Some in the waters deeply div'd,
Some playing in the heavens above,
That natures from one stock deriv'd
May thus to several dwellings move;

Upon thy servants grace bestow,
Whose souls thy bloody waters clear,
That they no sinful falls may know,
Nor heavy grief of death may bear;

That sin no soul opprest may thrall,
That none be lifted high with pride,
That minds cast downward do not fall,
Nor raised up may backward slide.

Dear Father, grant what we intreat,
And only Son who like power hast,
Together with the Paraclete,
Reigning whilst times and ages last.

HYMN FOR FRIDAY.

GOD, from whose work mankind did spring,
Who all in rule dost only keep,
Bidding the dry land forth to bring
All kind of beasts which on it creep;

Who hast made subject to man's hand
Great bodies of each mighty thing,
That taking life from thy command,
They might in order serve their king;

From us thy servants, Lord, expel
Those errors which uncleanness breeds,
Which either in our manners dwell,
Or mix themselves among our deeds.

Give the rewards of joyful life,
The plenteous gifts of grace encrease,
Dissolve the cruel bonds of strife,
Knit fast the happy league of peace.

Dear Father, grant what we intreat,
And only Son who like power hast,
Together with the Paraclete,
Reigning whilst times and ages last.

HYMN FOR SATURDAY.

O TRINITY, O blessed light,
O Unity, most principal!
The fiery sun now leaves our sight,
Cause in our hearts thy beams to fall.

Let us with songs of praise divine,
At morn and evening thee implore,
And let our glory bow'd to thine,
Thee glorify for ever-more.

To God the Father glory great,
And glory to his only Son,
And to the Holy Paraclete,
Both now and still while ages run.

UPON THE SUNDAYS IN LENT.
HYMN.

O MERCIFUL Creator, hear
Our prayers to thee devoutly bent,
Which we pour forth with many a tear
In this most holy fast of Lent.

Thou mildest searcher of each heart,
Who know'st the weakness of our strength,
To us forgiving grace impart,
Since we return to thee at length.

Much have we sinned to our shame,
But spare us who our sins confess ;
And for the glory of thy name,
To our sick souls afford redress.

Grant that the flesh may be so pin'd
By means of outward abstinence,
As that the sober watchful mind
May fast from spots of all offence.

Grant this, O blessed Trinity,
Pure Unity, to this incline,
That the effects of fasts may be
A grateful recompence for thine.

ON THE ASCENSION DAY.

O JESU, who our souls dost save,
On whom our love and hopes depend,
God, from whom all things being have,
Man, when the world drew to an end;

What clemency thee vanquisht so,
Upon thee our foul crimes to take,
And cruel death to undergo,
That thou from death us free might make?

Let thine own goodness to thee bend,
That thou our sins may'st put to flight;
Spare us, and as our wishes tend,
O satisfy us with thy sight.

May'st thou our joyful pleasures be,
Who shall be our expected gain,
And let our glory be in thee,
While any ages shall remain.

HYMN FOR WHITSUNDAY.

CREATOR, Holy Ghost, descend,
Visit our minds with thy bright flame,
And thy celestial grace extend,
To fill the hearts which thou didst frame:

2 z

Who Paraclete art said to be,
Gift which the highest God bestows,
Fountain of life, fire, charity,
Oyntment whence ghostly blessing flows.

Thy seven-fold grace thou down dost send,
Of God's right hand thou finger art,
Thou by the Father promised
Unto our mouths doth speech impart.

In our dull senses kindle light ;
Infuse thy love into our hearts,
Reforming with perpetual light
Th' infirmities of fleshly parts.

Far from our dwelling drive our foe,
And quickly peace unto us bring ;
Be thou our guide, before to go,
That we may shun each hurtful thing.

Be pleased to instruct our mind,
To know the Father and the Son,
The Spirit who them both dost bind,
Let us believe while ages run.

To God the Father glory great,
And to the Son who from the dead
Arose, and to the Paraclete,
Beyond all time imagined.

ON THE TRANSFIGURATION OF OUR LORD, THE SIXTH OF
AUGUST; A HYMN.

ALL you that seek Christ, let your sight
Up to the height directed be,
For there you may the sign most bright
Of everlasting glory see.

A radiant light we there behold,
Endless, unbounded, lofty, high;
Than heaven or that rude heap more old,
Wherein the world confus'd did lye.

The Gentiles this great prince embrace;
The Jews obey this king's command,
Promis'd to Abraham and his race
A blessing while the world shall stand.

By mouths of prophets free from lyes,
Who seal the witness which they bear,
His father bidding testifies
That we should him believe and hear.

Glory, O Lord, be given to thee,
Who hast appear'd upon this day;
And glory to the Father be,
And to the Holy Ghost for ay.

ON THE FEAST OF ST. MICHAEL THE ARCH-ANGEL.

To thee, O Christ, thy Father's light,
Life, vertue, which our heart inspires,
In presence of thine angels bright,
We sing with voice and with desires:

Our selves we mutually invite
To melody with answering quires.
With reverence we those souldiers praise,
Who near the heavenly throne abide,
And chiefly him whom God doth raise
His strong celestial host to guide,
Michael, who by his power dismays,
And beateth down the devil's pride.*

THE FIVE SENSES.

SEEING.

From such a face, whose excellence
May captivate my sovereign's sense,
And make him, Phœbus like, his throne
Resign to some young Phaeton,
Whose skilless and unstaved hand
May prove the ruin of the land,
Unless great Jove, down from the sky
Beholding earth's calamity,
Strike with his hand that cannot err,
The proud usurping charioter,
And cure, tho' Phœbus grieve, our wo:
From such a face as can work so,
Wheresoever thou hast a being,
Bless my sov'reign and his seeing.

---

* The *Elegy upon the most victorious King of Sweden, Gustavus Adolphus,* is here omitted. Although printed among Drummond's Poems in the edition of 1711, it is the undoubted production of Henry King, afterwards Bishop of Chichester, by whom it was prefixed to the third part of *The Swedish Intelligencer.*   London, 1633, 4to.

HEARING.

FROM jests prophane, and flattering tongues,
From bawdy tales and beastly songs,
From after-supper suits, that fear
A parliament or council's ear;
From Spanish treaties that may wound
The country's peace, the gospel's sound;
From Job's false friends, that would intice
My sovereign from heaven's paradise;
From prophets, such as Achab's were,
Whose flatterings sooth my sovereign's ear,
His frowns more than his Maker's fearing;
Bless my sovereign and his hearing.

TASTING.

FROM all fruit that is forbidden,
Such for which old Eve was chidden;
From bread of labours, sweat, and toyl,
From the poor widow's meal and oyl;
From blood of innocents oft wrangled
From their estates, and from that's strangled;
From the candid poyson'd baits
Of Jesuites and their deceits,
Italian sallads, Romish drugs,
The milk of Babel's proud whore's dugs;
From wine that can destroy the brain,
And from the dangerous figs of Spain;
At all bankets and all feasting,
Bless my sov'reign and his tasting.

FEELING.

FROM prick of conscience, such a sting
As slays the soul, heaven bless the king ;
From such a bribe as may withdraw
His thoughts from equity or law ;
From such a smooth and beardless chin
As may provoke or tempt to sin ;
From such a hand whose moist palm may
My sov'reign lead out of the way ;
From things polluted and unclean,
From all things beastly and obscene ;
From that may set his soul a reeling,
Bless my sov'reign and his feeling.

SMELLING.

WHERE myrrh and frankincense is thrown,
The altar's built to gods unknown,
O let my sov'raign never dwell,
Such damn'd perfumes are fit for hell.
Let not such scent his nostrils stain,
From smells that poyson can the brain,
Heavens still preserve him.   Next I crave
Thou wilt be pleased, great God, to save
My sov'reign from a Ganymede,
Whose whorish breath hath power to lead
His excellence which way it list ;
O let such lips be never kist
From a breath so far excelling ;
Bless my sov'reign and his smelling.

THE ABSTRACT.

SEEING.

AND now, just God, I humbly pray
That thou wilt take the slime away,
That keeps my sov'raign's eyes from seeing
The things that will be our undoing.

HEARING.

THEN let him hear, good God, the sounds
As well of men as of his hounds.

TASTE.

GIVE him a taste, and truly too,
Of what his subjects undergo.

FEELING AND SMELLING.

GIVE him a feeling of their woes,
And then no doubt his royal nose
Will quickly smell the rascals forth,
Whose black deeds have eclips'd his worth ;
They found and scourg'd for their offences,
Heavens bless my sovereign and his senses.

THE CHARACTER OF AN ANTI-COVENANTER,
OR MALIGNANT.

WOULD you know these royal knaves
Of free-men would turn us slaves ;
Who our union do defame
With rebellion's wicked name ?

Read these verses, and ye will spring them,
Then on gibbets straight cause hing them.
They complain of sin and folly,
In these times, so passing holy,
They their substance will not give
Libertines that we may live.
Hold those subjects too too wanton,
Under an old king dare canton.
Neglect they do our circular tables,
Scorn our acts and laws as fables,
Of our battels talk but meekly,
With four sermons pleas'd are weekly,
Swear King Charles is neither Papist,
Arminian, Lutheran, or Atheist:
But that in his chamber-prayers,
Which are pour'd 'midst sighs and tears,
To avert God's fearful wrath,
Threat'ning us with blood and death,
Persuade they would the multitude,
This king too holy is and good.
They avouch we'll weep and groan
When hundred kings we serve for one,
That each shire but blood affords,
To serve the ambition of young lords,
Whose debts e're now had been redoubled,
If the state had not been troubled.
Slow they are our oath to swear,
Slower for it arms to bear,
They do concord love and peace,
Would our enemies embrace,
Turn men proselites by the word,
Not by musket, pike, and sword.

They swear that for religion's sake
We may not massacre, burn, sack;
That the beginning of these pleas
Sprang from the ill-sped A B C's;
For servants that it is not well
Against their masters to rebel;
That that devotion is but slight
Doth force men first to swear, then fight;
That our Confession is indeed
Not the apostolick creed,
Which of negations we contrive,
Which Turk and Jew may both subscrive;
That monies should men's daughters marry,
They on frantick war miscarry,
Whilst dear the souldiers they pay,
At last who will snatch all away,
And as times turn worse and worse,
Catechise us by the purse;
That debts are paid with bold stern looks,
That merchants pray on their compt-books;
That justice dumb and sullen frowns
To see in croslets hang'd her gowns;
That preachers' ordinary theme
Is 'gainst monarchy to declaim;
That since leagues we began to swear,
Vices did ne're so black appear;
Oppression, blood-shed, ne're more rife,
Foul jars between the man and wife;
Religion so contemn'd was never
Whilst all are raging in a fever.

They tell by devils and some sad chance
That that detestable league of France,
Which cost so many thousand lives,
And two kings by religious knives,
Is amongst us, though few descry,
Though they speak truth, yet say they lye.
He who says that night is night,
That criple folk walk not upright,
That the owls into the spring
Do not nightingales out-sing;
That the seas we may not plow,
Ropes make of the rainy bow;
That the foxes keep not sheep,
That men waking do not sleep;
That all's not gold doth gold appear,
Believe him not altho' he swear.
To such syrens stop your ear,
Their societies forbear.
Ye may be tossed like a wave,
Verity may you deceive;
Just fools they may make of you,
Then hate them worse than Turk or Jew.
Were it not a dangerous thing,
Should we again obey the king,
Lords lose should sovereignty,
Souldiers haste back to Germany,
Justice should in our towns remain,
Poor men possess their own again,
Brought out of hell that word of plunder
More terrible than devil or thunder,
Should with the Covenant fly away,
And charity amongst us stay,

Peace and plenty should us nourish,
True religion 'mongst us flourish.
When you find these lying fellows,
Take and flower with them the gallows,
On others you may too lay hold,
In purse or chest if they have gold.
Who wise or rich are in this nation,
Malignants are by protestation.

A PASTORAL SONG.

PHYLLIS AND DAMON.

PH. SHEPHERD dost thou love me well?
DA. Better than weak words can tell.
PH. Like to what, good shepherd, say?
DA. Like to thee, fair cruel maye.
PH. O how strange these words I find;
Yet to satisfy my mind,
Shepherd, without mocking me,
Have I any love for thee,
Like to what, good shepherd, say?
DA. Like to thee, fair cruel maye.
PH. Better answer had it been
To say thou lov'd me as thine eyne.
DA. Wo is me, these I love not,
For by them love entrance got,
At that time they did behold
Thy sweet face and locks of gold.
PH. Like to what, dear shepherd, say?
DA. Like to thee, fair cruel maye.

PH. Once, dear shepherd, speak more plain,
And I shall not ask again ;
Say, to end this gentle strife,
Dost thou love me as thy life ?
DA. No, for it is turn'd a slave
To sad annoys, and what I have
Of life by love's stronger force
Is reft, and I'm but a dead cors.
PH. Like to what, good shepherd, say ?
DA. Like to thee, fair cruel maye.
PH. Learn I pray this, like to thee,
And say, I love as I do me.
DA. Alas, I do not love my self,
For I'm split on beauty's shelf.
PH. Like to what, good shepherd, say˙?
DA. Like to thee, fair cruel maye.

POSTHUMOUS POEMS.

REPRINTED

FROM THE TRANSACTIONS OF

THE SOCIETY OF ANTIQUARIES

OF SCOTLAND.

POSTHUMOUS POEMS.

EDINBURGH.

[TRANSLATED FROM THE LATIN OF DR ARTHUR JOHNSTON.]

INSTALL'D on hills, hir head neare starrye bowres,
Shines Edinburgh, proud of protecting powers.
Justice defendes her heart; Religion east
With temples, Mars with towres doth guard the west;
Fresh nymphes and Ceres seruing, waite upon her,
And Thetis tributarie doth her honour.
The sea doth Venice shake, Rome Tiber beates,
Whilst she bot scornes her vassall watteres' threats.
For scepters no where standes a towne more fitt,
Nor place where toune world's queene may fairer sitt.
Bot this thy praise is, aboue all, most braue,
No man did e're diffame thee bot a slave.

SONNETS.

TO THE HONORABLE AUTHOR, SIR JOHN SKENE.

ALL lawes but cob-webbes are, but none such right
Had to this title as these lawes of ours,
Ere that they were from their Cimmerian bowres
By thy ingenious labours brought to light.

Our statutes sencelesse statues did remaine,
Till thou, a new Prometheus, gaue them breath,
Or, like ag'd Æson's bodye courb'd to death,
When thou young bloud infus'd in euerye veine.
Thrice happye ghosts! which after-worlds must wow,
That first tam'd barbarisme by your swords,
Then knew to keepe it fast in nets of words,
Hind'ring what men not suffer would to doe;
     To Joue the making of the world is due,
     But that it turnes not chaos, is to you.

SONNET.

O TYMES! O heauen, that still in motion art,
And by your course confounds us mortall wights!
O flying dayes! O ouerglyding nights,
Which passe more nimble than wind, or archer's dart!
Now I my selfe accuse, excuse your part,
For hee who fixed your farr-off shining lights
You motion gaue, and did to mee impart
A mind to marke, and to preuent your slights.
Life's web yee still weaue out, still, foole, I stay,
Malgre my just resolues, on mortall things.
Ah! as the bird surprised in subtile springs,
That beates with wing but cannot flye away,
     So struggle I, and faine would change my case,
     But this is not of nature, but of grace.

SONNET.

RISE to my soule, bright Sunne of Grace, O rise!
Make mee the vigour of thy beames to proue;
Dissolue the chilling frost which on mee lies,
That makes mee lesse than looke-warm in thy loue:

Grant mee a beamling of thy light aboue
To know my footsteps, in these tymes, too-wise ;
O ! guyde my course, and let me no more moue
On wings of sense, where wandring pleasure flyes.
I haue gone wrong and erred ; but ah, alas !
What can I else doe in this dungeon dark ?
My foes strong are, and I a fragill glasse,
Howres charged with cares consume my life's small sparke ;
 Yet, of thy goodnesse, if I grace obtaine,
 My life shall be no losse, my death great gaine.

SONNET.*

FIRST in the Orient raign'd the Assyrian kings,
To those the sacred Persian prince succeeds,
Then he by whom the world sore-wounded bleeds,
Earth's crowne to Greece with bloodie blade he brings ;
Then Greece to Rome the raines of state resignes :
Thus from the mightie monarche of the Meeds,
To the west world successiuelie proceeds
That great and fatall period of all things ;
Whilst wearied now with broyles and long alarmes,
Earth's majestie her diademe layes downe
Before the feet of the vnconquer'd crowne,
And throws her selfe, great monarch, in thy armes.
 Here shall shee staye, Fates haue ordained so,
 Nor has she where nor further for to goe.

SONNET, BEFORE A POEM OF IRENE.

MOURNE not, faire Greece, the ruine of thy kings,
Thy temples raz'd, thy forts with flemes deuour'd,
Thy championes slaine, thy virgines pure deflowred,

---

* This sonnet seems to have been written in allusion to the *Monarchicke Tragedies* of the Earl of Stirling.

3 B

Nor all those greifes which sterne Bellona brings :
But mourne, fair Greece, mourne that that sacred band
Which made thee once so famous by their songs,
Forct by outrageous Fate, haue left thy land,
And left thee scarce a voice to plaine thy wrongs ;
Monrne that those climates which to thee appeare
Beyond both Phœbus and his sistere's wayes,
To saue thy deedes from death must lend thee layes,
And such as from Musæus thou didst heare ;
   For now Irene hath attain'd such fame,
   That Hero's ghost doth weepe to heare her name.

SONNET.

I FEARE to me such fortune be assign'd
As was to thee, who did so well deserue,
Braue HALKERSTONE,* even suff'red here to sterue
Amidst base-minded freinds, nor true, nor kind.
Why were the Fates and Furies thus combined,
Such worths for such disasters to reserue ?
Yet all those euills neuer made thee swerue
From what became a well-resolued mind ;
For swelling greatnesse neuer made thee smyle,
Despising greatnesse in extreames of want ;
O happy thrice whom no distresse could dant !
Yet thou exclaimed, O time ! O age ! O isle !
   Where flatterers, fooles, baudes, fidlers, are rewarded,
   Whilst vertue sterues vnpitied, vnregarded.

---

* For an account of Colonel Halkerston, see p. xiii. of Dr Irving's preface to Dempster's
Historia Ecclesiastica Gentis Scotorum.   Edinb. 1829, 2 tom. 4to.

SONETTO.

O CHIOME, parte de la treccia d'oro
Di cui fè amor il laccio, onde fui colto
Qual semplice augelletto, e da qual sciolto
Non spero esser mai piu, si pria non moro ;
Io vi bacio, io vi stringo, io vi amo e adoro,
Perche adombrasti già quel sacro volto
Che a quanti in terra sono il pregio ha tolto,
Ne lascia senza inuidia il diuin choro :
A voi dirò gli affanni, e i pensier miei,
Poi che lungi è mia donna, e parlar seco
Mi nega aspra fortuna, e gli empi diei.
Lasso ! guarda se amor mi fa ben cieco,
Quando cercar di scioglierme io dovrei,
La rete porto e le catene meco.

IN THE SAME SORT OF RIME.

O HAIRE, sweet haire, part of the tresse of gold
Of vich loue makes his nets, vher vretchet I
Like simple bird vas taine, and vhile I die
Hopelesse I hope your faire knots sal me hold ;
Yow to embrasse, kisse, and adore I'm bold,
Because ye schadow did that sacred face,
Staine to al mortals, vich from starrie place
Hath jalous made these vho in spheares ar rold :
To yow I'l tel my thochts and invard paines,
Since sche by cruel heauens now absent is,
And cursed Fortune me from her detaines.
Alas ! bear vitnesse how my reason is
Made blind be loue, vhile as his nets and chaines
I beare about vhen I should seeke my blisse.

IN FRIER SORT OF RIME.

O HAIRE, faire haire, some of the golden threeds
Of vich loue veues the nets that passion breeds
Vher me like sillie bird he doth retaine,
And onlie death can make me free againe ;
Ah, I yow loue, embrasse, kisse, and adore,
For that ye schadow did that face before ;
That face so ful of beautie, grace, and loue,
That it hath jalous made heauen's quier aboue :
To yow I'l tel my secret thochts and grief,
Since sche, deare sche, can graunt me no reliefe.
Vhile me from her foul traitour absence binds,
Vitnesse, sueet haire, vith me, how loue me blinds ;
For vhen I should seeke vhat his force restraines,
I foolish beare about his nets and chaines.

PARAPHRASTICALIE TRANSLATED.

HAIRE, suet haire, tuitchet by Midas' hand
In curling knots, of vich loue makes his nets,
Vho vhen ye loosest hang me fastest band
To her, vorld's lilie among violets,
Deare fatall present, kissing I adore yow,
Because of late ye shade gaue to these roses,
That this earth's beautie in ther red encloses ;
I saw vhile ye them hid thay did decore yow :
I'l plaine my voes to yow, I'l tel my thocht,
Alas ! since I am absent from my juel,
By vayvard fortune and the heauens more cruel.
Vitnesse be ye vhat loue in me hath vrocht,
In steed to seeke th' end of my mortall paines,
I take delyt to veare his goldin chaines.

SONETTO DEL BEMBO.

Sɪ come suol, poi che'l verno aspro e rio
Parte, e dà loco a le stagion migliori,
Vaga cervetta uscir col giorno fuori
Del suo dolce boschetto almo natio ;
Ed or su per un colle, or lungo un rio,
Di lontano e da ville e da pastori,
Gir sicura pascendo erbetta e fiori,
Ovunque più la porta il suo desio ;
Ne teme di saetta o d'altro inganno,
Se non quand' ella è colta in mezzo 'l fianco,
Da buon arcier che di nascosto scocchi :
Tal io senza temer vicino affanno
Mossi, donna, quel dì che bei vostr 'occhi
Me 'mpiagar, lasso ! tutto 'l lato manco.

IN THE SAME SORT OF RIME.

As the yong faune, vhen vinter's gone avay
Vnto a sueter saison granting place,
More vanton growne by smyles of heuen's faire face,
Leauith the silent voods at breake of day,
And now on hils, and now by brookes doth pray
On tender flowrs, secure and solitar,
Far from all cabans, and vher shephards are ;
Vher his desir him guides his foote doth stray,
He fearith not the dart nor other armes,
Til he be schoot in to the noblest part
By cuning archer, vho in dark bush lyes :
So innocent, not fearing comming harmes,
Vandering vas I that day vhen your faire eies,
Vorld-killing schafts, gaue death-vounds to my hart.

IN FRIER SORT OF RIME.

As the yong stag, vhen vinter hids his face,
Giuing vnto a better season place,
At breake of day comes furth vanton and faire,
Leauing the quiet voods, his suet repaire,
Now on the hils, now by the riuer's sides,
He leaps, he runs, and vher his foote him guides,
Both sure and solitaire, prayes on suet flowrs,
Far fra al shephards and their helmish bours ;
He doth not feare the net nor murdering dart,
Til that, pour beast, a schaft be in his hart,
Of on quho pitilesse in embush laye :
So innocent vandring that fatall daye
Vas I, alas ! vhen vith a heauenlie eie,
Ye gaue the blowe vher of I needs must die.

PARAPHRASTICALIE TRANSLATED.

As the yong hart, when sunne with goldin beames
Progressith in the first post of the skie,
Turning old vinter's snowie haire in streames,
Leauith the voods vher he vas vont to lie,
Vher his desir him leads the hills among,
He runes, he feades, the cruking brookes along ;
Emprison'd onlie with heauen's canopie,
Vanton he cares not ocht that dolour brings,
Hungry he spares not flowres vith names of kings ;
He thinkes al far, vho can him fol espie,
Til bloudie bullet part his chefest part :
In my yong spring, alas ! so vandred I,
Vhen cruel sche sent out from iettie eie
The deadlie schaft of vich I bleding smart.

MADRIGALS.

ON THE IMAGE OF LUCRECE.

WISE hand, which wiselie wroght
That dying dame, who first did banish kings
Thy light and shadow brings
In doubt the wond'ring thought,
If it a substance be, or faignet show,
That doth so liuelie smart.
The colours stroue for to have made her liue,
Wer not thy hart sayed no,
That fear'd perchance the wound so should her giue :
Yet in the fatall blow
She seemes to speake, nay speakes with Tarquin's hart ;
But death her stays, surprising her best part,
If death her stayed not, killing her best part.

NEROE'S IMAGE.

A CUNNING hand it was
Of this hard rocke did frame
That monster of all ages, mankind's shame,
Ferce Nero, hell's disgrace :
Of wit, sence, pitie void,
Did he not liuing, marble hard surpasse,
His mother, master, countrie, all destroyed ?
Not alt'ring his first case,
A stone he was when set upon a throne,
And now a stone he is, although dethroned downe.

AMPHION OF MARBLE.

THIS Amphion, Phidias' frame,
Though sencelesse it appeare,
Doth liue, and is the same
Did Thebes' towres vpreare ;
    And if his harpe he tuitche not to your eare,
No wonder, his harmonious sounds alone
Would you amaze, and change him selfe in stone.

OF A BEE.

INGENIOUS was that bee
In lip that wound which made,
And kind to others, though unkind to thee ;
For by a just exchange,
On that most liuelie red,
It giues to those reuenge,
Whom that delicious, plump, and rosie part,
All pittilesse, perhaps, now wounds the hart.

OF CHLORIS.

FORTH from greene Thetis' bowers
The morne arose ; her face
A wreath of rayes did grace,
    Her haire rain'd pearles, her hand and lap dropt flowres.
Led by the pleasant sight
Of those so rich and odoriferous showres,
    Each shepheard thither came, and nimphes bright :
Entranc'd they stood ; I did to Chloris turne,
And saw in her more grace than in the morne.

CHLORIS ENAMOURED.

AMINTAS, now at last
Thou art reuenged of all my rigour past ;
The scorning of thee, softnesse of thy hart,
Thy longings, causefull teares,
Doe double griefe each day to mee impart.
I am not what I was,
And in my miseries I thyne doe glasse ;
Ah ! now in perfect yeares,
E'r reason could my comming harmes descrie,
Made loue's fond taper flie.
I burne mee thinkes in sweet and fragrant flame.
Aske mee noe more : tongue hide thy mistres' shame.

REGRAT.

In this world's raging sea,
Where many Sillas barke,
Where many syrens are,
Saue, and not cast away,
Hee only saues his barge
With too much ware who doth it not o'recharge ;
Or, when huge stormes arise,
And waues menace the skies,
Giues what he got with no deploring show,
And doth againe in seas his burthen throw.

A SIGH.

SIGH, stollen from her sweet brest,
What doth that marble hart,
Smartes it indeed, and feels not others smart,
Grieues it, yet thinkes that others grieued jeast ?

3 c

Loue or despight, which forc't thee thence to part?
Sweet harbinger, say from what vncouth guest.
Sure thou from loue must come,
Who sigh'd to see there drest his marble tombe

STOLLEN PLEASURE.

My sweet did sweetlie sleepe,
And on her rosie face
Stood teares of pearle, which beautie's self did weepe;
I, wond'ring at her grace,
Did all amaz'd remaine,
When loue said, Foole, can lookes thy wishes crowne?
Time past comes not againe.
Then did I mee bow downe,
And kissing her faire brest, lips, cheekes, and eies,
Prou'd heere on earth the joyes of paradise.

OF A KISSE.

Lips, double port of loue,
Of joy tell all the arte,
Tell all the sweetnesse lies
In earthlie paradise,
Sith happy now yee proue
What blisse a kisse
Of sweetest Nais can bring to the hart.
Tell how your former joyes
Haue beene but sad annoyes:
This, onlye this, doth ease a long-felt smart,
This, onlye this, doth life to loue impart.
Endymion, I no more
Enuie thy happye state,
Nor his who had the fate

Rauisht to be and hugged on Ganges' shore :
Enuie nor yet doe I
Adon, nor Joue's cup-bearer in the skie.
Deare crimson folds, more sweetnesse yee doe beare
Than Hybla tops, or gardenes of Madere.
Sweet, sweet'ning Midases, your force is such,
That euerye thing turnes sweet which yee doe touch.

A LOCKE OF GOLD DESIRED.

I never long for gold ;
But since I did thy dangling haire behold,
Ah ! then, then was it first
That I prou'd Midas' thrist ;
And what both Inde and rich Pactolus hold
Can not my flames allay,
For onlye yee, faire tresseresse, this may,
Would yee but giue a lock to help my want,
Of that which prodigall to winds yee grant.

PERSUASIVE DISSUADING.

Show mee not lockes of gold,
Nor blushing roses of that virgine face,
Nor of thy well-made legge and foot the grace ;
Let me no more behold
Soule-charming smyles, nor lightnings of thyne eye,
For they, deare life, but serue to make me dye.
Yes, show them all, and more ; vnpine the brest,
Let me see liuing snow
Where strawberries doe grow ;
Show that delicious feild
Which lillies still doth yeeld,
Of Venus' babe the nest :

Smyle, blush, sigh, chide, vse thousand other charmes ;
Mee kill, so that I fall betweene thyne armes.

PROMETHEUS am I,
The heauens my ladye's eye,
From which I stealing fire,
Find since a vulture on my hart to tyre.

NON ULTRA. OF ANTHEA.

WHEN Idmon saw the eyne
Of Anthea his loue,
Who yet, said he, such blazing starres hath seene,
Saue in the heauens above ?
Shee thus to heare her praise
Blusht, and more faire became.
For nought, said he, thy cheekes that morne do raise,
For my hart can not burne with greater flame.

FRAGMENT.*

Now Phœbus whept his horse with al his might,
Thinking to take Aurora in her flight ;
But shee, who heares the trampling of his steeds,
Gins suiftlie gallop thruch heauen's rosie meeds.
The more he runs, the more he cums her neere ;
The lesse her speed, sche finds the more her feare.
At last his coursiers, angry to be torne,
Her tooke ; sche with a blush died al the morne.

----

* From the handwriting, as well as from internal evidence, these fragments appear to have been juvenile productions of Drummond.

Thetis, agast to spie her greens made red,
All drousie rose furth of her corral bed,
Thinking the night's faire queen suld thole sume harmes,
Sche saw poor Tithon's wyff in Phœbus' armes.

FRAGMENT.

IT autumne was, and cheereful chantecleare
Had warn'd the world tuise that the day drew neare :
The three parts of the night almost war spent,
When I, poore wretch, with loue and fortune rent,
Began my eies to close, and suetest sleep,
Charming my sense, al ouer me did creep,
But scars with Lethe drops and rod of gold
Had he me made a piece of breathing mold.

EPIGRAMS.

VERSES WRITTEN LONG SINCE CONCERNING THESE PRESENT
TYMES, MADE AT RANDOM, *A LA ROGUERIAS DE SES AMICOS:*
SKELTONICALL VERSES, OR DOGREL RIMES.

THE king good subjectes can not saue : then tell,
Which is the best, to obey or to rebell ?

HAPPIE to be, trulye is in some schoole-
Maistere's booke, be either king or foole.
How happie then are they, if such men bee,
Whom both great fooles and kinges the world doth see.

WHEN Charles was young, to walke straight and upright,
In bootes of lead thrall'd were his legges, though rockes;
Now old, not walking euen unto their sight,
His countrye lordes haue put him in their stockes.

THE parliament lordes haue sitten twice fiue weekes,
Yet will not leave their stooles, knit up their breekes;
Winter is come, dysenteryes prevaile:
Rise, fooles, and with this paper wype your taile.

THE parliament the first of June will sit,
Some saye, but is the yeere of God to it?
Fourtie: no, rather make it fourtie one,
And one to fourty but yee then haue none.

ZANZUMMINES they obeye the king doe sweare,
And yet against King Charles in armes appeare.
What king doe yee obeye, Zamzummines, tell,
The king of Beane, or the black prince of Walles? [of hell?]

BEHOLD, O Scots! the reueryes of your king,
Britannes, admire the extravangancyes of our king;
Those hee makes lordes who should on gibbetes hing.
S. Andrew, why does thou giue up thy schooles,
And bedleme turne, and parliament house of fooles?
                              Par.
OLD dotard Pasquill, thou mistaketh it,
Montrose confined vs here to learn some wit.

EPITAPH OF A JUDGE.

PEACE, passenger, heere sleepeth under ground
A judge in ending causes most profound ;
Thocht not long since he was laid in this place,
It's lustres ten since he corrupted was.

BISHOPES are like the turnores, most men say ;
Though now cryed down, they'll up some other day.

WHEN discord in a towne the toxan ringes,
Then all the rascalls turne unto us kinges.

A PROUERBE.

To singe as was of old, is but a scorne,
The king's chaffe is better than others' corne ;
Kelso can tell his chaffe away did fly,
Yet had no wind : Benedicite !
The corne unmoued on Duns-Law strong did shine,
Lesley, could thou haue shorne, it might beene thyne.

THE CREED.

Q. How is the Creed now stollen from us away ?
A. The ten Commandements gone, it would not stay.
Q. Then haue we no Commandements ? O wonder !
A. Yes, wee haue one for all, goe fight and plunder.

ON MARYE KING'S PEST.

TURNE, citezens, to God ; repent, repent,
And praye your bedlam frenzies may relent :

Thinke not rebellion a trifling thing,
This plague doth fight for Marie and the King.

HEERE couered lies with earth, without a tombe,
Whose onyle praise is, that he died at Rome.

A PROUERBE.

GOD neuer had a church but there, men say,
The diuell a chapell hath rais'd by some wyles.
I doubted of this saw, till on a day
I westward spied great Edinbrough's Saint Gyles.

FLYTING no reason hath, for at this tyme,
It doth not stand with reason, but in ryme.
That none saue thus should flyte, had wee a law,
What rest had wee? how would wyves stand in aw,
And learne the art of ryming! Then how well
Would this and all good flyting pamphlets sell!

ON POMPONATIUS.

TRADE softlie, passenger, upon this stone,
For heere enclosed stayes,
Debarred of mercie's rayes,
A soule, whose bodye swore it had not one.

OF THE ISLE OF RHE.

CHARLES, would yee quaile your foes, haue better luck;
Send forth some Drakes, and keep at home the ducke.*

---

* In allusion to the Duke of Buckingham, and his ill-fated expedition in the year 1627.

EPITAPH.

SANCHER, whom this earth scarce could containe,
Hauing seene Italie, France, and Spaine,
To finish his travelles, a spectacle rare,
Was bound towards heauen, but dyed in the aire.*

AN IMAGE TO THE PILGRIME.

To worship mee, why come ye, fooles, abroad ?
For artizans made me a demi-god.

RAMES ay runne backward when they would advance ;
Who knowes if Ramsay may find such a chance,
By playing the stiff Puritane, to weare
A bishope's rocket yet another yeare.†

MOMUS, with venom'd tooth, why wouldst thou teare
Our Muses, and turne Mores those virgines faire ?
Nor citizen, nor manners doe they brand,
Nor of the town ought, saue where it doth stand.
I curst, I doe confesse, some nastye mire,
And lake, deem'd poison by all Peane's quire :
Endwellares safe, I hartlie wisht the towne
Turned in one rock, and still wish 't o'rethrowne.
Elsewhere a nobler town might raised bee,
For skie, aire, sweeter, and in boundes more free ;

---

* Robert Crichton, Lord Sanquhar, was hanged at Westminster on the 29th of June 1612, for the murder of a fencing-master named Turner.

† Andrew Ramsay, professor of divinity in the university of Edinburgh, who, by his zeal for the Covenant in 1637, gave great offence to his former friends.

3 D

The noble towne might elsewhere haue been raised,
In place more faire, for skye, aire, freedom prais'd ;
Yet there to dwell no shame is, nor be borne ;
Pearles dwell in oysteres, roses grow on thorne.
His Rome when Cæsar purposed to make new,
Himselfe straight fire-brandes on their rafteres threw.
If in these wishes ought deserueth blame,
A Caledonian king first wisht the same.
My Muse, perhaps, too bold is, but farre farre
From tartnesse brest, from gall her paperes are.

ON A GLASSE SENT TO HIS BEST BELOVED.

OFT ye me aske, whome my sweet faire can be ?
Looke in this christal and ye sal her see ;
At least some schade of her it wil impart,
For sche no trew glasse hath excep my hart.
   Ah ! that my brest war made of christal faire,
   That she might see her livelie portrait there.

SEXTAIN.

WITH elegies, sad songs, and murning layes,
Quhill Craig* his Kala wald to pitie move,
Poore braine-sicke man ! he spends his dearest dayes ;
Such sillie rime can not make women love.
   Morice, quho sight of neuer saw a booke,
   With a rude stanza this faire virgine tooke.

ENCOMIASTIKE VERSES BEFORE A BOOK ENTITLED * * *†

AT ease I red your worke, and am right sorrye
It came not forth before *Encomium Moriæ,*

---

* Probably Alexander Craig of Rose-Craig, one of the minor Scottish poets of the earlier part of the seventeenth century.

† The word is partially erased in the manuscript, but it seems to have been *Follies.*

Or in the dayes when good King James the First
Carowsed the horse's spring to quench his thirst ;
I durst haue giuen my thombe and layed a wager
Thy name had grac't the Chronicles of Jhon Major.
Had thou liu'd in the dayes of great Augustus,
(Hence, vulgare dotards, hence, unlesse yee trust us,)
Thy workes, with geese, had kept the Capitole,
And thou for euer been a happy soule,
Thy statue had been raised neare Claudianus,
And thou in court liu'd equall with Sejanus.
Cornelius Tacitus is no such poet,
Nor Liuie ; I'll say more ere that I goe yet :
Let all that heere doe weare celestiall bonnetes,
Lyke thyne, they cannot write four-squared sonnets,
Which shine like to that mummye brought from Venice,
Or like the French king's relicks at Saint Denis.
It is a matter of regrate and pittye
Thou art not read into that famous citie
Of Constantine, for then the Turckes and Tartares
Had drunke with us, and like to ours worne gartares ;
And the strange muphetees and hard Mameluckes
Had cut their beardes, and got by hart thy bookes.
If any them detract, though hee were Xenaphon,
Thou shalt haue such reuenge as ere was tane of one,
From this our coast unto the wall of China,
Where maides weare narrow shoes ; thou hast been a
Man for enuie, though such forsooth was Horace,
Yet thou no lesse dost write than hee, and soare ass
As farre in this our tongue as any Latines,
Though some doe reade their verse, that ware fine satines ;
Rome's latest wonder, great Torquato Tasso,
Writing, to thee were a pecorious asse, hoe !

Now, to conclude, the nine Castalian lasses
Their maidenheades thee sell for fannes and glasses.

EPITAPHS.*

TO THE MEMORIE OF HIS MUCH LOVING AND BELOVED MAISTER, MR JOHN RAY.†

No wonder now, if mistes beclowde our day,
Sith late our earth lakes her celestiall RAY ;
And Phœbus murnes his priest, and all his quire,
In sables wrapt, weep out their sacred fire ;
Farewell, of Latin Muses greatest praise,
Whether thou read graue proses, or did raise
Delight and wonder by a numbrous straine ;
Farewell, Quintilian once more dead againe ;
With ancient Plautus, Martiall combined,
Maro and Tullie, here in one enshrined.
Bright RAY of learning, which so cleare didst streame,
Farewell, soule which so many soules did frame.
Many Olympiades about shall come,
Ere earth like thee another can entombe.

D. O. M. S.

WHAT was mortall of THOMAS DALYELL of Binnes lyeth
here.   Hee was descended of the auncient race of the Lˢ. of

---

* Of these Epitaphs, the verses upon Dalyell and Lindsay have been printed among Drummond's Poems, but the inscriptions and names are not given.

† John Ray was professor of humanity, while Drummond was a student, in the university of Edinburgh.

Dalyell, now deseruedly aduanced to be Earles of Carnewath.
His integritie and worth made him an unremoued Justice of
Peace, and . . . . . yeeres Sherife in the Countie of Linlyth-
gow.   Hee lefte, successoures of his vertues and fortunes, a
sonne renowned by the warres, and a daughter marryed to
William Drummond of Reckertown.   After 69 yeeres pilgrimage heere on earth, hee was remoued to the repose of heauen, the 10 of Februarye 1642.

JUSTICE, truth, peace, and hospitalitie,
Friendship, and loue, being resolued to dye,
In these lewid tymes, haue chosen heere to haue
With just, true, pious, kynd DALYELL their graue ;
Hee them cherish'd so long, so much did grace,
That they than this would choose no dearer place.

    T. FILIUS MANIBUS CHARISSIMI PATRIS PARENTAUIT.

EPITAPH.

If monumentes were lasting, wee would raise
A fairer frame to thy desertes and praise ;
But auarice, or misdeuotione's rage,
These tumbling down, or brought to nought by age,
Twice making man to dye, this marble beares
An embleme of affection and our teares.

To the Memorie of the vertuous Gentlewoman RACHELL
LINDSAY, Daughter of Sir Hierosme Lyndsay, Principall King

of Armes, and Wyfe to Lieutenant Colonell Barnard Lindsay, who dyed the . . day of May, the yeare 1645, after shee had liued . . . . yeeres.

THE daughter of a king, of princely partes,
In beautie eminent, in vertues cheife,
Load-starre of loue, and load-stone of all hartes,
Her freindes' and husbande's onlie joy, now griefe,
Enclosed lyes within this narrow graue,
Whose paragone no tymes, no climates haue.

MARITUS MŒRENS POSUIT.

TO THE MEMORIE OF ——

As nought for splendour can with sunne compare,
For beautie, sweetnesse, modestie, ingyne,
So shee alone unparagon'd did shyne,
And angelles did with her in graces share.

Though few heere were her dayes, a span her life,
Yet hath shee long tyme liued, performing all
Those actiones which the oldest doe befall,
Pure, fruitfull, modest, virgine, mother, wife.

For this perhaps, the fates her dayes did close,
Her deeming old ; perfection doth not last,
When coarser thinges scarce course of tyme can waste ;
Yeeres liues the worthlesse bramble, few dayes the rose.

Vnhappye autumne, spoyler of the flowres,
Discheueler of meades and fragrant plaines,

Now shall those monethes which thy date containes,
No more from hauens be nam'd, but eyes' salt showres.

TO THE MEMORIE OF THE WORTHIE LADYE, THE LADYE OF CRAIGMILLARE.

THIS marble needes no teares, let them be powr'd
For such whom earth's dull bowelles haue emboured
In child-head or in youth, and lefte to liue
By some sad chance fierce planets did contriue.
Eight lustres, twice full reckened, did make thee
All this life's happiness to know ; and wee
Who saw thee in thy winter (as men flowres
Shrunke in their stemmes, or Ilium's faire towres,
Hidde in their rubbidge), could not but admire,
The casket spoyled, the jewel so intiere ;
For, neither judgment, memorye, nor sence
In thee was blasted, till all fled from hence
To thy great Maker ; earth unto earth must,
Man in his best estate is but best dust.
Now euen though buryed, yet thou canst not dye,
But happye liuest in thy faire progenie
To out-date tyme, and neuer passe away.
Till angelles raise thee from thy bed of claye,
And blist againe with these heere lou'd thou meet,
Rest in Fame's temple and this winding sheet :
Content thou liu'd heere, happye though not great,
And dyed with the kingdome and the state.

D. O. M. S.

WHAT was mortall of W. RAMSAY lieth heere. Hee was
the sonne of John Ramsay, L. of Edington, brother to the

Right Honorable William, the first Earl of Dalhousye, a linage of all vertues in peace, and valour in warre, renowned by all tymes, and second to none ; a youth ingenuous, of faire hopes, a mild sweet disposition, pleasant aspect, countenance ; his kindred's delight and joy, now their greatest displeasure and sorrow ; hauing left this transitory stage of cares, when hee but scarce appeared vpon it, in his tender nonage.

So falles by northern blast a virgin rose,
At halfe that doth her bashfull bosome close ;
So a sweet flowrish languishing decayes,
That late did blush when kist by Phoebus' rayes.
Though vntymlie cropp'd, leaue to bemoan his fate,
Hee dyed with our monarchie and state.

His mother _{out of} ^{from} that care and loue she caryed to him, to continue heere his memorie some space, raised this Monument, Anno 1649, mense . . .

Immortale Decus Superis.

VIL. DRUMMOND'S LINES ON THE BISCHOPES:
XIV. APPRYLL M.DC.XXXVIII.

[FROM A MANUSCRIPT IN THE ADVOCATES LIBRARY, IN THE HANDWRITING OF SIR JAMES BALFOUR.]

Doe all pens slumber still, darr not one try
In tumbling lynes to lett some pasquill fly ?
Each houer a satyre creuith to display
The secretts of this tragick comick play.
If loue should lett me wrett, I think you'd see
The Perenies and Alps cum skipe to me,
And lauch themselues asunder ; if I'd trace
The hurly-burly of stait busines,

And to the vorld abused once bot tell
The legend of Ignatian Matchiuell,
That old bold smouking monster, and the pryde
Of thesse vsurping prelats that darr ryde
Vpon authority, and looke so gay
As if, goodmen, they ought forsuith to suay
Church, stait, and all: plague one that damned crew
Of such hell's black-mouth'd hounes ; it's of a new
That Roman pandars boldly dar'd to ov (woo ?)
Nay, straine a gentle king thesse things to doo,
That moue the French, Italian, and Spaine,
In a luxurious and insulting straine
To sing *Te Deum*, causse they houpe to see
The glorie of the popeish prelacie
Raissed aboue his royall throne apaice,
To droune his miner light with prouder face.
Thesse hounds they have ingaged him on the stage
Of sharpe-eyed Europe, nay, ther's not a page
Bot thinks he may laugh freily quhen he sees
Kings buffons acte, and bishopes tragedies.
Should aney dauly with the lyon's paw,
Then know a distance, serpents stand in aw.
Nay, pray you heavens, once lend me bot your thunder,
I'le crusch and teare thesse sordid slaues assunder,
And leuell with the dust ther altar's horne,
With the lasscivious organs, pietie's scorne ;
Or let me be as king, then of their skine
I'le causse dresse lether and fyne Marikin,
To couer coatches, quher they wont to ryde,
And valke in bootes and shoes made of ther hyde,
Vhipe them at neighbour princes' courts to show,
That no nouatious Scotts zeall can allow.

3 E

I sacrifisse vold such presumtious slaues
To my deir people, beat to dust the knaues,
Then of the pouder of ther bons to dray
The hare and pereuige to the pope's lackay.
I noblie should resent and take to heart
Thesse pedants' pryde that make poore Brittane smart,
Confound the church, the stait, and all the nation
With appish fooleries and abomination,
Leaues churches desolate, and stopes the mouth
Of faithful vatchmen quho dare preach bot treuth ;
Incendiary fyrebrands, whosse proud wordes
Drope blood, and sounds the clatt'ring noysse of suordis.
Had I bot half the spyte of Galloway Tom,
That Roman snakie viper, I'd fall from
Discreitter lynes, and rube their itching eare
With Spanish nouells : bot I will forbeare.
Because my foster and my amorous quill
Is not yet hard, proud pasquills to distill,
I doe intreat that droll John de Koell
To sting them with satyres hatcht in hell ;
Each doge chyde thesse tobacco-breathed deuyns,
Each pen dairt volums of acutest lynes,
And print the shame of that blacke troupe profaine
In liuid vords, with a Tartarian straine.
Since I a louer am, and know not how
To lim a satyre in halffe hyddeous hew,
Lyke to polypragmatick Macheuel,
In pleasant flame, not stryffe, I loue to dwell.
Bot nou to Paris back I goe to tell
Some neues to plotting Riceleu : fair you well.

POLEMO-MIDDINIA.

REPRINTED

FROM THE EDITION OF M.DC.LXXXIV.

COLLATED WITH THOSE OF GIBSON

AND RUDDIMAN.

Breviuſcula, & Compendiuſcula, Tellatio ;

D E

Storia memorabili Fechtæ mervelabilis

Quæ fuit

Inter *Muckreillios,* & *Horsboyos,* atque *Ladæos,* &c.

In hoc Libellulo, cujus Inſcriptio Famoſa hæc eſt,

POLEMO-MEDINIA

INTER

Vitarvam & Nebernam,

Placidè & Jocosè traĉtatur.

EDINBVRGI,

Re-printat 1684.

POLEMO-MIDDINIA INTER

VITARVAM ET NEBERNAM.

Nymphæ, quæ colitis highissima monta Fifæa,
Seu vos Pittenwema tenent, seu Crelia crofta,
Sive Anstræa domus, ubi nat haddocus in undis,
Codlineusque ingens, et fleucca et sketta pererrant
Per costam, et scopulis lobster monyfootus in udis
Creepat, et in mediis ludit whitenius undis;
Et vos skipperii, soliti qui per mare breddum
Valde procul lanchare foris, iterumque redire,
Linquite skellatas bottas shippasque picatas,
Whistlantesque simul fechtam memorate bloodæam,
Fechtam terribilem, quam marvellaverat omnis
Banda deûm, et nympharum cockelshelleatarum,
Maia ubi sheepifeda atque ubi solgoossifera Bassa
Swellant in pelago, cum sol bootatus Edenum
Postabat radiis madidis et shouribus atris.
Quo viso, ad fechtæ noisam cecidere volucres,
Ad terram cecidere grues, plish plashque dedere
Sol-goosæ in pelago prope littora Bruntiliana;
Sea-sutor obstupuit, summique in margine saxi
Scartavit prælustre caput, wingasque flapavit;
Quodque magis, alte volitans heronius ipse
Ingeminans clig clag mediis shitavit in undis.

Namque in principio, storiam tellabimus omnem,
Muckrelium ingentem turbam Vitarva per agros
Nebernæ marchare fecit, et dixit ad illos :
Ite hodie armati greppis, drivate caballos
Crofta per et agros Nebernæ, transque fenestras :
Quod si forte ipsa Neberna venerit extra,
Warrantabo omnes, et vos bene defendebo.
    Hic aderant Geordie Akinhedius, et little Johnus,
Et Jamie Richæus, et stout Michel Hendersonus,
Qui jolly tryppas ante alios dansare solebat,
Et bobbare bene, et lassas kissare bonæas ;
Duncan Oliphantus valde stalvartus, et ejus
Filius eldestus joly boyus, atque Oldomoudus,
Qui pleugham longo gaddo drivare solebat,
Et Rob Gib wantonus homo, atque Oliver Hutchin,
Et plouky fac'd Wattie Strang, atque in-kneed Alshinder Atken,
Et Willie Dick heavy-arstus homo, pigerrimus omnium,
Qui tulit in pileo magnum rubrumque favorem,
Valde lethus pugnare, sed hunc corngrevius heros
Noutheadum vocavit, et illum forcit ad arma.
Insuper hic aderant Tom Taylor et Tom Nicolsonus,
Et Tomie Gilchristus, et fool Jockie Robisonus,
Andrew Alshinderus, et Jamie Thomsonus, et unus
Norland-bornus homo, valde valde anticovenanter,
Nomine Gordonus, valde blackmoudus, et alter
(Heu pudet, ignoro nomen) slaverybeardius homo,
Qui pottas dightavit, et assam jecerat extra.
    Denique præ reliquis Geordæum affatur, et inquit,
Geordie, mi formanne, inter stoutissimus omnes,
Huc ades, et crooksaddelos, hemmasque, creilesque,
Brechemmesque simul omnes bindato jumentis ;
Amblentemque meam naggam, fattumque magistri

Cursorem, et reliquos trottantes sumito averos,
In cartis yokkato omnes, extrahito muckam
Crofta per et riggas, atque ipsas ante fenestras
Nebernæ, et aliquid sin ipsa contra loquatur,
In sidis tu pone manus, et dicito, fart, jade.
   Nec mora, formannus cunctos flankavit averos,
Workmannosque ad workam omnes vocavit, et illi
Extemplo cartas bene fillavere jigantes :
Whistlavere viri, workhorsosque ordine swieros
Drivavere foras, donec iterumque iterumque
Fartavere omnes, et sic turba horrida mustrat,
Haud aliter quam si cum multis Spinola troupis
Proudus ad Ostendam marchasset fortiter urbem.
Interea ante alios dux piperlaius heros
Præcedens, magnam gestans cum burdine pipam,
Incipit Harlai cunctis sonare Batellum.
   Tunc Neberna furens, yettam ipsa egressa vidensque
Muck-cartas transire viam, valde angria facta,
Haud tulit affrontam tantam, verum agmine facto
Convocat extemplo horsboyos atque ladæos,
Jackmannum, biremannos, pleugdrivsters atque pleughmannos,
Trimblantesque simul reekoso ex kitchine boyos,
Hunc qui gruelias scivit bene lingere plettas,
Hunc qui dirtiferas tersit cum dishcloute dishas ;
Et saltpannifumos, et widebricatos fisheros,
Hellæosque etiam salteros duxit ab antris,
Coalheughos nigri girnantes more divelli ;
Lifeguardamque sibi sævas vocat improba lassas,
Maggæam, magis doctam milkare cowæas,
Et doctam sweepare flooras, et sternere beddas,
Quæque novit spinnare, et longas ducere threedas ;
Nansæam, claves bene quæ keepaverat omnes,

3 F

Yellantemque Elpen, longoberdamque Anapellam,
Fartantemque simul Gillam, gliedamque Katæam
Egregie indutam blacko caput sooty clouto,
Mammæamque simul vetulam, quæ sciverat apte
Infantum teneras blande oscularier arsas,
Quæque lanam cardare solet olifingria Betty.
  Tum vero hungræos ventres Neberna gruelis
Farsit, et guttas rawsuinibus implet amaris,
Postea newbarmæ ingentem dedit omnibus haustum :
Staggravere omnes, grandesque ad sidera riftas
Barmifumi attollunt, et sic ad prælia marchant.
Nec mora, marchavit foras longo ordine turma,
Ipsa prior Neberna suis stout facta ribaldis,
Rustæam manibus gestans furibunda gulæam,
Tandem muckcreilios vocat ad pellmellia fleidos.
Ite, ait, uglæi felloes, si quis modo posthac
Muckifer has nostras tentet crossare fenestras,
Joru ego quod ejus longum extrahabo thropellum,
Et totam rivabo faciem, luggasque gulæo hoc
Ex capite cuttabo ferox, totumque videbo
Heartbloodum fluere in terram.   Sic verba finivit.
  Obstupuit Vitarva diu dirtfleida, sed inde
Couragium accipiens, muckcreilos ordine cunctos
Middini in medio faciem turnare coegit.
O qualem primo fleuram gustasses in ipso
Battelli onsetto ! pugnat muckcreilius heros
Fortiter, et muckam per posteriora cadentem
In creilibus shoollare ardet: sic dirta volavit.
O qualis feirie fairie fuit, si forte vidisses
Pipantes arsas, et flavo sanguine breickas
Dripantes, hominumque heartas ad prælia fantas !
O qualis hurlie burlie fuit ! namque alteri nemo

Ne vel footbreddum yerdæ yieldare volebat :
Stout erat ambo quidem, valdeque hardhearta caterva.
  Tum vero e medio mukdryvster prosilit unus,
Gallantæus homo, et greppam minatur in ipsam
Nebernam, quoniam misere scaldaverat omnes,
Dirtavitque totam peticotam gutture thicko,
Perlineasque ejus skirtas, silkamque gownæam,
Vasquineamque rubram mucksherda begariavit.
Sed tamen ille fuit valde faintheartus, et ivit
Valde procul, metuens shottam woundumque profundum ;
At non valde procul fuerat revenga, sed illum
Extemplo Gillæa ferox invasit, et ejus
In faciem girnavit atrox, et tigrida facta,
Bublentem grippans berdam, sic dixit ad illum :
Vade domum, filthæe nequam, aut te interficiabo.
Tunc cum gerculeo magnum fecit gilliwhippum,
Ingentemque manu sherdam levavit, et omnem
Gallantæi hominis gashbeardam besmeariavit.
Sume tibi hoc, inquit, sneezing valde operativum
Pro præmio, swingere, tuo. Tum denique fleido
Ingentem gilliwamphra dedit, validamque nevellam,
Ingeminatque iterum, donec bis fecerit ignem
Ambobus fugere ex oculis : sic Gilla triumphat.
Obstupuit bumbaizdus homo, backumque repente
Turnavit veluti nasus bloodasset, et O fy !
Ter quater exclamat, et O quam sæpe neezavit !
Disjuniumque omne evomuit valde hungrius homo,
Lausavitque supra et infra, miserabile visu,
Et luggas necko imponens, sic cucurrit absens,
Non audens gimpare iterum, ne worsa tulisset.
Hæc Vitarva videns, yellavit turpia verba,
Et fy, fy ! exclamat, prope nunc victoria losta est.

Nec mora, terribilem fillavit dira canonem,
Elatisque hippis magno cum murmure fartam
Barytonam emisit, veluti Monsmegga cracasset:
Tum vero quackare hostes, flightamque repente
Sumpserunt, retrospexit Jackmannus, et ipse
Sheepheadus metuit sonitumque ictumque buleti.
 Quod si King Spanius, Philippus nomine, septem
Hisce consimiles habuisset forte canones
Batterare Sluissam, Sluissam dingasset in assam ;
Aut si tot magnus Ludovicus forte dedisset
Ingentes fartas ad mœnia Montalbana,
Ipsam continuo townam dingasset in yerdam.
 Exit corngrevius, wracco omnia tendere videns,
Consiliumque meum si non accipitis, inquit,
Pulchras scartabo facies, et vos worriabo.
Sed needlo per seustram broddatus, inque privatas
Partes stobbatus, greitans, lookansque grivate,
Barlafumle clamat, et dixit, O Deus, O God !
Quid multis ? Sic fraya fuit, sic guisa peracta est,
Una nec interea spillata est droppa cruoris.

FINIS.

TABLE OF CONTENTS.